John J. Maresca

HELSINKI REVISITED

A Key U.S. Negotiator's Memoirs
on the Development of the CSCE into the OSCE

With a foreword by Hafiz Pashayev

ibidem-Verlag
Stuttgart

Bibliografische Information der Deutschen Nationalbibliothek
Die Deutsche Nationalbibliothek verzeichnet diese Publikation in der Deutschen Nationalbibliografie; detaillierte bibliografische Daten sind im Internet über http://dnb.d-nb.de abrufbar.

Bibliographic information published by the Deutsche Nationalbibliothek
Die Deutsche Nationalbibliothek lists this publication in the Deutsche Nationalbibliografie; detailed bibliographic data are available in the Internet at http://dnb.d-nb.de.

Cover pictures:

Map of Europe: Derivative work of Europe countries map en.png by San Jose, based on the Generic Mapping. Tools (http://gmt.soest.hawaii.edu/) and ETOPO2 (http://dss.ucar.edu/datasets/ds759.3/). Source: Wikimedia Commons. Licensed under CC BY-SA 3.0 (s. https://creativecommons.org/licenses/by-sa/3.0/deed.en)

Erich Honecker, General Secretary of the Socialist Unity Party, German Democratic Republic, and Chancellor Helmut Schmidt Federal Republic of Germany. © Bundesarchiv, B 145 Bild-F046227-0058 / Engelbert Reineke. Source: Wikimedia Commons. Licensed under CC-BY-SA 3.0 (s. https://creativecommons.org/licenses/by-sa/3.0/de/deed.en)

The Helsinki Final Act negotiators, the Foreign Ministers of the CSCE participating States, at the first Helsinki meeting in 1973. © OSCE. ID: 4925. 1 August 1975. Licensed under Creative Commons Attribution - No Derivative Works license.

∞

Gedruckt auf alterungsbeständigem, säurefreien Papier
Printed on acid-free paper

ISSN: 1614-3515

ISBN-13: 978-3-8382-0852-7

© *ibidem*-Verlag
Stuttgart 2016

Alle Rechte vorbehalten

Das Werk einschließlich aller seiner Teile ist urheberrechtlich geschützt. Jede Verwertung außerhalb der engen Grenzen des Urheberrechtsgesetzes ist ohne Zustimmung des Verlages unzulässig und strafbar. Dies gilt insbesondere für Vervielfältigungen, Übersetzungen, Mikroverfilmungen und elektronische Speicherformen sowie die Einspeicherung und Verarbeitung in elektronischen Systemen.

All rights reserved. No part of this publication may be reproduced, stored in or introduced into a retrieval system, or transmitted, in any form, or by any means (electronic, mechanical, photocopying, recording or otherwise) without the prior written permission of the publisher. Any person who does any unauthorized act in relation to this publication may be liable to criminal prosecution and civil claims for damages.

Printed in Germany

Soviet and Post-Soviet Politics and Society (SPPS) Vol. 150
ISSN 1614-3515

General Editor: Andreas Umland,
Institute for Euro-Atlantic Cooperation, Kyiv, umland@stanfordalumni.org

Commissioning Editor: Max Jakob Horstmann,
London, mjh@ibidem.eu

EDITORIAL COMMITTEE*

DOMESTIC & COMPARATIVE POLITICS
Prof. **Ellen Bos**, *Andrássy University of Budapest*
Dr. **Ingmar Bredies**, *FH Bund, Brühl*
Dr. **Andrey Kazantsev**, *MGIMO (U) MID RF, Moscow*
Prof. **Heiko Pleines**, *University of Bremen*
Prof. **Richard Sakwa**, *University of Kent at Canterbury*
Dr. **Sarah Whitmore**, *Oxford Brookes University*
Dr. **Harald Wydra**, *University of Cambridge*

SOCIETY, CLASS & ETHNICITY
Col. **David Glantz**, *"Journal of Slavic Military Studies"*
Dr. **Marlène Laruelle**, *George Washington University*
Dr. **Stephen Shulman**, *Southern Illinois University*
Prof. **Stefan Troebst**, *University of Leipzig*

POLITICAL ECONOMY & PUBLIC POLICY
Prof. em. **Marshall Goldman**, *Wellesley College, Mass.*
Dr. **Andreas Goldthau**, *Central European University*
Dr. **Robert Kravchuk**, *University of North Carolina*
Dr. **David Lane**, *University of Cambridge*
Dr. **Carol Leonard**, *Higher School of Economics, Moscow*
Dr. **Maria Popova**, *McGill University, Montreal*

FOREIGN POLICY & INTERNATIONAL AFFAIRS
Dr. **Peter Duncan**, *University College London*
Prof. **Andreas Heinemann-Grüder**, *University of Bonn*
Dr. **Taras Kuzio**, *Johns Hopkins University*
Prof. **Gerhard Mangott**, *University of Innsbruck*
Dr. **Diana Schmidt-Pfister**, *University of Konstanz*
Dr. **Lisbeth Tarlow**, *Harvard University, Cambridge*
Dr. **Christian Wipperfürth**, *N-Ost Network, Berlin*
Dr. **William Zimmerman**, *University of Michigan*

HISTORY, CULTURE & THOUGHT
Dr. **Catherine Andreyev**, *University of Oxford*
Prof. **Mark Bassin**, *Södertörn University*
Prof. **Karsten Brüggemann**, *Tallinn University*
Dr. **Alexander Etkind**, *University of Cambridge*
Dr. **Gasan Gusejnov**, *Moscow State University*
Prof. em. **Walter Laqueur**, *Georgetown University*
Prof. **Leonid Luks**, *Catholic University of Eichstaett*
Dr. **Olga Malinova**, *Russian Academy of Sciences*
Prof. **Andrei Rogatchevski**, *University of Tromsø*
Dr. **Mark Tauger**, *West Virginia University*

ADVISORY BOARD*

Prof. **Dominique Arel**, *University of Ottawa*
Prof. **Jörg Baberowski**, *Humboldt University of Berlin*
Prof. **Margarita Balmaceda**, *Seton Hall University*
Dr. **John Barber**, *University of Cambridge*
Prof. **Timm Beichelt**, *European University Viadrina*
Dr. **Katrin Boeckh**, *University of Munich*
Prof. em. **Archie Brown**, *University of Oxford*
Dr. **Vyacheslav Bryukhovetsky**, *Kyiv-Mohyla Academy*
Prof. **Timothy Colton**, *Harvard University, Cambridge*
Prof. **Paul D'Anieri**, *University of Florida*
Dr. **Heike Dörrenbächer**, *Friedrich Naumann Foundation*
Dr. **John Dunlop**, *Hoover Institution, Stanford, California*
Dr. **Sabine Fischer**, *SWP, Berlin*
Dr. **Geir Flikke**, *NUPI, Oslo*
Prof. **David Galbreath**, *University of Aberdeen*
Prof. **Alexander Galkin**, *Russian Academy of Sciences*
Prof. **Frank Golczewski**, *University of Hamburg*
Dr. **Nikolas Gvosdev**, *Naval War College, Newport, RI*
Prof. **Mark von Hagen**, *Arizona State University*
Dr. **Guido Hausmann**, *University of Munich*
Prof. **Dale Herspring**, *Kansas State University*
Dr. **Stefani Hoffman**, *Hebrew University of Jerusalem*
Prof. **Mikhail Ilyin**, *MGIMO (U) MID RF, Moscow*
Prof. **Vladimir Kantor**, *Higher School of Economics*
Dr. **Ivan Katchanovski**, *University of Ottawa*
Prof. em. **Andrzej Korbonski**, *University of California*
Dr. **Iris Kempe**, *"Caucasus Analytical Digest"*
Prof. **Herbert Küpper**, *Institut für Ostrecht Regensburg*
Dr. **Rainer Lindner**, *CEEER, Berlin*
Dr. **Vladimir Malakhov**, *Russian Academy of Sciences*

Dr. **Luke March**, *University of Edinburgh*
Prof. **Michael McFaul**, *Stanford University, Palo Alto*
Prof. **Birgit Menzel**, *University of Mainz-Germersheim*
Prof. **Valery Mikhailenko**, *The Urals State University*
Prof. **Emil Pain**, *Higher School of Economics, Moscow*
Dr. **Oleg Podvintsev**, *Russian Academy of Sciences*
Prof. **Olga Popova**, *St. Petersburg State University*
Dr. **Alex Pravda**, *University of Oxford*
Dr. **Erik van Ree**, *University of Amsterdam*
Dr. **Joachim Rogall**, *Robert Bosch Foundation Stuttgart*
Prof. **Peter Rutland**, *Wesleyan University, Middletown*
Prof. **Marat Salikov**, *The Urals State Law Academy*
Dr. **Gwendolyn Sasse**, *University of Oxford*
Prof. **Jutta Scherrer**, *EHESS, Paris*
Prof. **Robert Service**, *University of Oxford*
Mr. **James Sherr**, *RIIA Chatham House London*
Dr. **Oxana Shevel**, *Tufts University, Medford*
Prof. **Eberhard Schneider**, *University of Siegen*
Prof. **Olexander Shnyrkov**, *Shevchenko University, Kyiv*
Prof. **Hans-Henning Schröder**, *SWP, Berlin*
Prof. **Yuri Shapoval**, *Ukrainian Academy of Sciences*
Prof. **Viktor Shnirelman**, *Russian Academy of Sciences*
Dr. **Lisa Sundstrom**, *University of British Columbia*
Dr. **Philip Walters**, *"Religion, State and Society", Oxford*
Prof. **Zenon Wasyliw**, *Ithaca College, New York State*
Dr. **Lucan Way**, *University of Toronto*
Dr. **Markus Wehner**, *"Frankfurter Allgemeine Zeitung"*
Dr. **Andrew Wilson**, *University College London*
Prof. **Jan Zielonka**, *University of Oxford*
Prof. **Andrei Zorin**, *University of Oxford*

* While the Editorial Committee and Advisory Board support the General Editor in the choice and improvement of manuscripts for publication, responsibility for remaining errors and misinterpretations in the series' volumes lies with the books' authors.

Soviet and Post-Soviet Politics and Society (SPPS)
ISSN 1614-3515

Founded in 2004 and refereed since 2007, SPPS makes available affordable English-, German-, and Russian-language studies on the history of the countries of the former Soviet bloc from the late Tsarist period to today. It publishes between 5 and 20 volumes per year and focuses on issues in transitions to and from democracy such as economic crisis, identity formation, civil society development, and constitutional reform in CEE and the NIS. SPPS also aims to highlight so far understudied themes in East European studies such as right-wing radicalism, religious life, higher education, or human rights protection. The authors and titles of all previously published volumes are listed at the end of this book. For a full description of the series and reviews of its books, see

www.ibidem-verlag.de/red/spps.

Editorial correspondence & manuscripts should be sent to: Dr. Andreas Umland, c/o DAAD, German Embassy, vul. Bohdana Khmelnitskoho 25, UA-01901 Kyiv, Ukraine. e-mail: umland@stanfordalumni.org

Business correspondence & review copy requests should be sent to: *ibidem* Press, Leuschnerstr. 40, 30457 Hannover, Germany; tel.: +49 511 2622200; fax: +49 511 2622201; spps@ibidem.eu.

Authors, reviewers, referees, and editors for (as well as all other persons sympathetic to) SPPS are invited to join its networks at
www.facebook.com/group.php?gid=52638198614
www.linkedin.com/groups?about=&gid=103012
www.xing.com/net/spps-ibidem-verlag/

Recent Volumes

142   *Matthew Kott, David J. Smith (eds.)*
Latvia – A Work in Progress?
100 Years of State- and Nation-building
ISBN 978-3-8382-0648-6

143   *Инна Чувычкина (ред.)*
Экспортные нефте- и газопроводы на постсоветском пространстве
Анализ трубопроводной политики в свете теории международных отношений
ISBN 978-3-8382-0822-0

144   *Johann Zajaczkowski*
Russland – eine pragmatische Großmacht?
Eine rollentheoretische Untersuchung russischer Außenpolitik am Beispiel der Zusammenarbeit mit den USA nach 9/11 und des Georgienkrieges von 2008
Mit einem Vorwort von Siegfried Schieder
ISBN 978-3-8382-0837-4

145   *Boris Popivanov*
Changing Images of the Left in Bulgaria
The Challenge of Post-Communism in the Early 21st Century
ISBN 978-3-8382-0667-7

146   *Lenka Krátká*
A History of the Czechoslovak Ocean Shipping Company 1948-1989
How a Small, Landlocked Country Ran Maritime Business During the Cold War
ISBN 978-3-8382-0666-0

147   *Alexander Sergunin*
Explaining Russian Foreign Policy Behavior
Theory and Practice
ISBN 978-3-8382-0752-0

148   *Darya Malyutina*
Migrant Friendships in a Super-Diverse City
Russian-Speakers and their Social Relationships in London in the 21st Century
With a foreword by Claire Dwyer
ISBN 978-3-8382-0652-3

149   *Alexander Sergunin, Valery Konyshev*
Russia in the Arctic
Hard or Soft Power?
ISBN 978-3-8382-0753-7

*For my two only loves and my blessings—
my wife Sisi, to whom I am indebted
for her understanding and support,
and our lovely daughter Azadeh.*

Foreword

John Maresca was certainly one of the people who was most closely involved in the early development of the CSCE, from the preparations at NATO, to its early years in Helsinki and Geneva, to the key Summit meeting in Helsinki in 1975, when the historic "Final Act" was signed. He is one of the few Americans who focused on the development of the CSCE during that period. As the central US official developing the CSCE in Washington he also helped to shape policies for the follow-up to the Helsinki Conference, and his 1985 book on the Helsinki negotiations remains a unique record of those landmark events.
Later Maresca also played a key role as the Soviet Union was dissolved, the CSCE was reconvened in an effort to permit East-West dialogue and elements of restraint and cooperation as local conflicts appeared in the regions of the former Soviet Union and Yugoslavia. Uniquely, he was not only the Deputy Head of the US Delegation to the Geneva-Helsinki negotiations, but also the Head of the US Delegation to the negotiation of the "Charter of Paris for a New Europe," the first attempt to chart new relations in Europe following the end of the Cold War. The Charter became the basis for the organization now known as the Organization for Security and Cooperation in Europe (the "OSCE"). Maresca was a pioneer in seeking to promote dialogue and negotiation on the first local conflict to appear at that time in the post-Soviet space, the conflict between Armenia and Azerbaijan, which remains unsettled more than twenty years later. This conflict was the precursor of a number of conflicts that have developed in the former Soviet space, and continue to fester today.
I met Maresca in March 1993 during my first appearance as a physicist-turned- diplomat at a Congressional hearing on the conflict in the very early stage of my Ambassadorial tenure in Washington, D.C. His insights and analyses regarding the negotiating process during the key years of transition from the height of the Cold War to its conclusion

with the Charter of Paris and the Joint Declaration of Twenty-Two States are very relevant today, as the world faces new challenges in the European region, many of which relate to the commitments contained in the Helsinki Final Act and the Charter of Paris. They are especially relevant to the situation in Ukraine and Crimea, and to Russia's approach to these problems.

The Organization for Security and Cooperation in Europe—the OSCE—which grew out of the negotiation of the Helsinki and Paris agreements, has become a significant element in the European equation, one which has unique capacities for entering and influencing potential conflicts in the region. The OSCE's Observers in Ukraine, for example, have played a positive role in maintaining a watchful outside presence. And the potential of this organization goes well beyond what it has been used for up to now.

Maresca has a broad and sophisticated understanding of these complex elements, including the important relationship between Europe and the states of the Caucasus and Central Asia, which have an essential role to play as Europe's relations with its neighbors to the East become increasingly important. His insights are particularly relevant at this key period of history, when the West is confronted with a newly-active Russia, and an evolving strategic equation in Europe and its neighboring regions.

This book is written as a memoir, and contains new information and many fascinating insights about the development of the CSCE and its evolution into the OSCE. But it also contains some very astute analyses of current events, based on the history of the issues, which surround them. It is, in fact, a commentary on the current situations in these regions, based on the way these situations developed.

It is a book, which should be of great interest to anyone who is interested in the recent history and the current and future state of affairs in Europe, including the Caucasus, Central Asia, and what Russians call their "Near Abroad."

Hafiz Pashayev
Rector
ADA University
Baku, Azerbaijan

Table of Contents

Foreword VII
Stresa, 1940 1
Introduction 3

Part I 9
Brussels, 1970-73 11
The Finnish Invitation 19
Geneva, 1973-75 29
Negotiations and Realities 38
A Second Year 45
Pressing Ahead, for History 51
1975—Ford and Brezhnev Go To Helsinki 59

Part II 69
Washington, 1975 71
The President Changes, and Policies Change 80
Career Planning 85
Belgrade, 1977 87
Human Rights Activists and the CSCE 92
Leaving the CSCE 96
Europe and the Communists, 1977-85 103
Washington and the Pentagon 106
Vienna, 1989 110
Preparing the Paris Summit of 1990 122
1990—Bush and Gorbachev Go To Paris 129

Part III	137
Dissolution of the USSR—1991	139
Ambassador to the "Near Abroad"	146
Albania	152
Nagorno Karabakh	155
"Full Metal Jack"	158
The Caucasus and A First Peace Proposal	166
A Washington Farewell	173
Reflecting on Russia and the Near Abroad	183
Prague	187
Epilogue	189
Annex	191

Stresa, 1940

International events, and war, marked my life from the very beginning. I was born in the Villa degli Azalees, in the gardens of the Grand Hotel et des Iles Borromees, a huge luxury hotel which is a national historical monument in Stresa, on the shores of Lago Maggiore in the alpine northern reaches of Italy. Italy was ruled by Benito Mussolini.

My father was the long-time Director of the hotel, and my mother was an award-winning American painter, cartoonist and designer who met and married my father while on a travelling fellowship. My older sister and I spent our early years at my father's villa on the grounds of the hotel, or at the Maresca family home in Sorrento, in the South. Marescas have been citizens of Sorrento since the 12th century.

It was a glamorous life. My parents spent their social hours with the many European aristocrats and other prominent figures of the time, who came to the hotel for their holidays. And of course Ernest Hemingway had left his mark—it is the hotel which features in "A Farewell to Arms," where the two lovers start rowing north, to Switzerland, to escape from the First World War in Italy. That imaginary overnight rowing effort, from my father's hotel to the Swiss shore, was their "farewell to arms."

But developments in Europe once again were ominous. Italy invaded and annexed Albania in April of 1939, and when the Germans invaded Poland in September, my parents decided that my mother should take the two children to America for the duration of the war, which they thought would last about six months. Under Italian wartime laws, my father could not leave the country, so my mother, my sister and I left Genoa on the *Conte di Savoia*, the iconic flagship of the Italian Line, in the spring of 1940, when I was two years old. We never saw my father again.

The trans-Atlantic passage was already perilous; ships were being sunk. The Conte di Savoia had been guaranteed safe passage to Gibraltar, where British citizens disembarked, and onward to New York—lit up at night so that it would not be torpedoed. The *Conte di Savoia* was indeed torpedoed, later in the war.

When we arrived in New York we had some difficulty getting off the ship. The Italian customs official said my sister and I were Italian, and under the wartime regulations would have to return to Italy. But the Italian Line was part-owned by my father's hotel company, the influential CIGA chain of luxury hotels, and the Captain of the ship knew who we were. He pressed the Italian official, who shrugged and let us disembark.

We presented ourselves to the American Immigration Officer on the pier, and my mother handed over her US passport, issued by the Consulate in Milan, which included her two small children, aged 2 and 4. She had been living in Europe for ten years. After some nervous hesitation, she asked: "Can you please tell me: what is the nationality of my two children?"

The Immigration Officer took a few moments to reply as he looked over our documents. Then he said, in a classic Brooklyn accent: "Lady, . . . as of now (and he stamped our papers), they're American citizens." It was our farewell to arms.

Introduction

"Frontiers can be changed, in accordance with international law, by peaceful means and by agreement."

Final Act, Helsinki, 1975

The historic evolution of events which has taken place in Europe since the early 1970's is on-going, and we cannot yet see how it will stabilize, whether it will settle out peacefully or will continue to be filled with bloody local conflicts.

The division of Europe, as originally conceived at Yalta in 1945, was validated in Helsinki in 1975. But in that same supreme moment of détente the key notion of peaceful change was also accepted and agreed, along with many openings for peaceful movement of people and ideas, to permit the historic evolution of Europe. And it was this acceptance of peaceful change which made possible the development of Europe we have seen since that time.

Aspects of the European situation which were simply no longer relevant were put aside in response to the popular will. As a consequence, we have seen the peaceful reunification of Germany, the gradual cementing of the European Union, the release of the countries of Eastern Europe from their domination by the USSR and Communism, the withdrawal of Soviet and most American military forces, and the break-up of the Soviet Union itself into the Russian homeland and a range of "newly independent States" stretching from Eastern Europe to Central Asia.

And there have been other changes, or attempted changes, which were not so peaceful—principally the break-up of Yugoslavia after a prolonged and vicious civil war, the current conflict in Ukraine, and other conflicts which continue and are unresolved. Forty years after it was agreed at Helsinki, the central guideline that any changes in frontiers must take place "by peaceful means and by agreement," remains the key to enduring peace in the European region. When this rule breaks down, or is ignored, the consequences can be disastrous for the people concerned.

The transformation of the former USSR is one of the central historical factors in the situation which exists in Europe today. In several parts of this vast area ethnic tensions continue, and some of these situations have become on-going military confrontations, with no easy solutions in sight.

The area which formed the Russian Empire and its successor, the USSR, is peopled by many national and ethnic groupings, some of which—not all—now have their own statehood. But during the period when Moscow dominated these regions, Russians migrated, intermarried and gradually settled in many parts of the vast national territory. History cannot be re-written, and the gradual migration of ethnic Russians into the areas which Russians call their "near abroad" was and is a historical reality. Millions of Russians transferred their homes to these areas during the two centuries, and more in some areas, of Russian and Soviet domination. The long existence of the Russian Empire, and of the Soviet Union, is a central reality in the history of these regions, even in areas with quite different cultural heritages, resulting in numerous tensions and inter-ethnic disputes over the years, and some of these disputes have become military confrontations in the aftermath of the breakup of the USSR.

The situation in Ukraine is the principal current focus of this ongoing evolution, and Russia's annexation of Crimea is the severest infringement of Helsinki's key language on changes of frontiers which we have witnessed—a textbook violation of the concept of changes taking place "by peaceful means and by agreement." The violent breakup of former Yugoslavia was another violation of this notion of "peaceful change," but the Crimean episode was more shocking—and ironic—because it was carried out so deliberately, smoothly, and with such cold disregard for the fundamental conditionality insisted upon by Moscow itself, in its effort to ensure that European borders would be maintained as they were in 1975.

The history of Crimea is special, and this must also be taken into account—its transfer from Russian to Ukrainian rule as an anniversary "gift" at a time when both countries were part of a single sovereign state, and when no one expected that the USSR would ever break apart. This history is perhaps an extenuating factor, giving the Crimean seizure a special character and, hopefully, making it unique.

But Russian support for military action in the Donbass is more clearly objectionable, and finds no justification in international law or practice. Russian willingness, even deliberate determination, to support separatist efforts in that region is directly contrary to the basic concepts of the Final Act, and requires re-evaluation of the entire European balance, as well as the specific conflict situations which continue to exist within the vast former Russian and Soviet space. Russia's actions in this region call into question its commitment to adhere to the basic lines of behavior which made it possible to conclude the Cold War and restore normal relations among the countries of Europe and North America, and may open a new period of confrontation between East and West.

The Russian Empire was not the same as other European empires in that the lands colonized by Russia were contiguous to the Russian homeland. This was fundamentally different from the British, French, Spanish or Portuguese colonial empires, which were formed during the same long period of history. This difference has, perhaps, made separation and withdrawal from colonized territories more difficult and complicated in the case of Russia. In some cases conflicts arose, rooted in disputes over territory and historical rights to certain regions.

There have been many attempts to resolve the conflicts in the area during this period, but those conflicts continue or are dormant, and some new ones have developed. The heavy-handed role of Russia in relation to Europe and its other neighboring regions continues to be a key element of regional stability, sometimes stimulating unrest. This can be particularly worrisome in a time when there is growing turbulence in the nearby Muslim world. Parts of southern Russia include large, restive, Muslim populations and some separatist activism.

Russia traditionally views the so-called "near abroad" areas of the former USSR as regions of special interest to Moscow—regions where Russia has a natural prerogative to take initiatives and to undertake, or continue, policies and activities that are designed to maintain stability and to protect the interests of Russia or the ethnic Russian populations of those countries. At the same time the outside world, particularly Russia's neighbors in Europe, have sought to improve the situation through stabilizing agreements, as well as unilateral policies designed to establish the limits of what is acceptable by Russia in its behavior toward its neighboring states. There has been considerable caution regarding any possible outside interventions in the former Soviet space, as Russians remain sensitive to the spread of European influence and allegiance into the regions it has traditionally dominated.

Russia's relationship with its "Near Abroad" emerged over time as an unspoken, but very important, underlying challenge for the CSCE/OSCE, as the USSR dissolved and the rules for international behavior established by the CSCE became applicable also to the relations among these newly-independent states. It was only then that the relationship between the concept of statehood, as applied to these new states, and the concept of Russian identity, came into contradiction and became an emotional issue among Russians in and around Russia itself. The sensitivity of this broad subject has grown as the issues and problems have emerged and evolved, especially in relation to events in Ukraine, and the probability is that it will continue to grow, in unforeseeable ways.

The OSCE, which was created as a consequence of the signing of the "Final Act" at the Summit-level meeting in Helsinki in August of 1975, as developed, expanded and concretized by the "Charter of Paris for a New Europe," also signed at the summit level, in Paris in 1990, and through a number of later agreements, has an important role to play in building mutual understanding and avoiding confrontations so that these regions can develop peacefully and with mutually beneficial cooperation across national frontiers and throughout the vast European-Central Asian space.

This book is an informal memoir of my personal involvement in some of the efforts, during this long period of change and evolution, to harmonize the many elements of the process of up-dating the relations among states in the European region, through the development of the CSCE/OSCE. This on-going conference and international context was originally a broad attempt to recognize and incorporate the historical facts that have emerged in Europe, and Central Asia, before and during this period of history, while at the same time establishing some recognized standards of international behavior and respect for basic human rights, and opening possibilities for historical evolution, freer movement of people and ideas, and more open, normal relationships among the peoples of the region.

With the evolution of history the OSCE has become a broad organizational framework for examining multiple issues that relate to Europe and Europeans, and a soft-edged instrument for seeking or supporting peaceful and balanced solutions where possible. The use of OSCE Observers in the Ukraine-Russia crisis has been the latest instance in which the OSCE has been involved in such a role. But this type of role is marginal in real confrontation and conflict situations, and questions remain about what the OSCE can actually do to enhance security and cooperation in Europe.

This book does not attempt to present a broad analytical overview of such issues. It is a very personal view, from the inside, of the complex multilateral negotiating process which has been evolving within the framework of the CSCE/OSCE, especially during its early, formative years. It is focused on my personal activities during that period, from 1970 to the 1990s, and the impressions I had as the European situation moved forward, and as my own activities evolved from watching over the general development of the institution to the application of its concepts in an attempt to resolve one specific conflict within its region.

I became the Deputy Head of the United States Delegation which negotiated the Helsinki Final Act of 1975, and, by an extraordinary turn of fate, was also the Ambassador and Head of the United States

Delegation which negotiated the Charter of Paris for a New Europe, signed in 1990. My account of this period is written in the first person as an informal history, reflecting my personal involvement and my continuing interest in this European evolution, because of my own life story, which began in Europe and returned there when I became a United States diplomat at the center of this very European negotiating process.

This book does not draw conclusions, which would not in any case be possible because the evolution it observes is broad and complex, involving many countries and inter-related issues, and is also ongoing. It simply adds to the material which is available to scholars, and to others who are interested, about how this expansive negotiating process moved forward, sporadically and unevenly, thru this very active period of history, from what was certainly détente's supreme moment, in Helsinki in 1975, through the complex years which followed and what was universally perceived as the "End of the Cold War," to the present day. It reflects the candid personal impressions and analyses of the author, an Italian-American diplomat who was at the center of this negotiating process during key periods over three decades, from 1970 until the final years of the 20th century.

***

Part I

Part I

Brussels, 1970-73

In 1970, in Washington, I was interviewed by the Secretary General of NATO for the position of Deputy Director of his Office, in the International Staff of the North Atlantic Treaty Organization, in Brussels. It was a unique position and was reserved for a professional American diplomat. But the Secretary General, Manlio Brosio, was Italian, and wanted someone who could speak Italian in addition to French, which, with English, constituted the two official NATO languages. Much of Brosio's correspondence, as well as some of his meetings and discussions, took place in Italian, so he naturally wanted someone who could deal with that aspect of the job. The office of personnel in the State Department had done its homework and had discovered that I was born in Italy and was half Italian. My file showed that I spoke French and Italian. I was, in fact, the French Desk Officer in the Bureau of European Affairs at the time. It was a very brief interview. Brosio selected me for the job, and my transfer to Brussels was arranged shortly afterward.

NATO at that time was consulting intensively on how to open discussions and eventually negotiations with the Soviet Union, to ease tensions, to lower the level of military confrontation in Europe while ensuring Western Europe's security, and to begin to move toward more normal relations between the two military blocs—NATO and the Warsaw Pact—which had been confronting each other with huge military forces since the end of the Second World War. I was plunged into the principal Western forum for discussion of these matters—the North Atlantic Council, which was comprised of Ambassadors from all the member states and which met at least weekly to consider the latest developments between East and West, and to formulate a strategy for approaching and engaging with the Soviet Union and its allies to advance the Western agenda.

My immediate boss was an Italian diplomat, Fausto Bachetti, the Director of the Secretary General's Office, but he was as senior as the Ambassadors accredited to the Council, so he maintained his own role. I went wherever the Secretary General went, to assist him, and since he chaired the North Atlantic Council, I was in on even the most restricted discussions.

The North Atlantic Council's agenda during that period was principally focused on the political aspects of NATO's defense responsibilities—not only maintaining the overall political unity which ensured the general harmony among the member states, but also looking for ways to reduce the military confrontation, which was costly, risky, and was seen as a major obstacle to the restoration of normal ties among European countries, without putting at risk West European security. The Soviet Union at that time had about 100,000 tanks in Eastern Europe, pointing West, and the countries which were members of the Warsaw Pact were counted as probable enemies in any military confrontation. It was an accepted principle at NATO that the military forces which faced each other in Europe should be reduced, but that this should happen in a way which took account of and hopefully would correct the existing imbalance. In other words, the forces on the Eastern side, which were significantly bigger, should be reduced more than those on the Western side, so that the balance would be stabilized and the danger of a military confrontation reduced. This was the origin of the terminology which emerged on the Western side, of "Mutual and Balanced Force Reductions," or "MBFR," as the overall Western objective in a negotiating process with the East. Engaging the USSR in discussion and eventually in negotiations on "MBFR" became a principal objective of the Alliance and its member states.

As a parallel matter it was generally thought that there should also be some sort of talks or negotiations on what went under the commonly-used heading of "Freer Movement of People and Ideas." This was the nascent concept of opening more normal relations between East and West—to increase contacts, interaction, travel and exchange of ideas. The two halves of Europe had been cut off from each other since the end of the Second World War, and the two Germanies, in particular, were divided by the Wall. The emerging idea, set forth i.a. in a study on the "Future Tasks of the Alliance," conducted by Belgian Foreign Minister Pierre Harmel and adopted by the NATO Allies in 1967, was that a strong defense should be balanced by diplomatic efforts to improve relations with the East. The Harmel Report suggested that the NATO member states should begin to normalize relations between the two parts of Europe—East and West—through increased contacts and greater openness among peoples—"freer movement of people and ideas," which became the commonly-used phrase for this objective, or just "freer movement." So this was generally agreed to be a parallel Western objective, along with reductions in the military confrontation.

NATO at that time was the principal locus for such discussions among the Western countries. The European Union of course did not yet exist, though there were some informal discussions going on among some of the European States, and these gradually became more formalized. But the main reason why NATO was the center of these discussions and, later, for the preparations for negotiation, was that NATO included the US and Canada, without which the Europeans, at that time, felt they would be at a disadvantage in any negotiating process with Moscow. The NATO relationship gave the Europeans confidence that they could negotiate with the USSR on an equal basis.

At the time I arrived in Brussels NATO was very actively considering ideas, strategies and proposals for pursuing the by then anticipated, discussion and—possibly, or potentially—a negotiating process with the USSR. The format, timing and agenda for such a process were not yet known, but the Allies wanted to be ready with ideas which had been agreed among them. The spirit at NATO headquarters took much from its military side—strategies and tactics, and full agreement among the member states, were considered essential, and it was a very serious preparatory process. The basis for agreement on anything at NATO was consensus, and it took time to develop a consensus among such diverse countries on questions of military and negotiating strategy, even more to develop concrete proposals for negotiation on such new subjects as the ones on the "Freer Movement" agenda. It was assumed that East-West negotiations would take place—it was only a question of time and the format in which they would be organized. So the preparation process was steaming ahead.

I had a privileged position of observation in my post as Deputy Director of the Secretary General's Office. The NATO International Staff has expanded since those days, but at that time there was only one Director of the Secretary General's Office, and only one Deputy Director, and we had considerable influence because we spoke in the name of the Secretary General, and were welcome observers in any meeting because it was essential that the Secretary General eventually support and approve agreed Alliance positions. I went to all the meetings—even the most sensitive ones—reviewed all the documents, and could influence some aspects of the agenda through my advice to the Secretary General, by talking to people at all levels in the organization and even by approaching diplomats in the national delegations which had their offices in the NATO headquarters building. I was considered something of a shadowy but key player, and was sought-after by Ambassadors and their senior staff members.

During my lunch hours—which were very long because Brosio took a traditional Italian attitude toward lunch (which means that "lunch" also includes a period for rest)—I would walk through the corridors of the vast, rambling NATO Headquarters building to the offices of the United States Mission to NATO, where I had an arrangement with the Deputy Chief of the US Mission, George Vest, under which I had access to his file of communications with Washington. I would sit in his office and quietly read through this file every day during my lunch hour, which gave me full information and intelligence on what was happening in the world, through the many reports from US embassies, and also on Washington's perspectives—and instructions—on the main issues of the day. The US Representative to NATO during that period was Donald Rumsfeld, who was close to the White House and the Republican leadership at the time, while Vest was an experienced career official. As the Deputy, and sometimes Acting US Representative to NATO, Vest received even the most sensitive communications, and I was able to read virtually all of them, in order to fully understand the US position on the issues before the Alliance.

Sometimes Vest would be in his office when I visited to read his communications file. He was a relaxed and philosophical presence, with a great sense of the real importance of things, who gained the respect and loyalty of all who knew him. He was from rural Virginia, and his folksy sense of humor was famous. He also brought a canny wisdom to his work, and we gradually became friends, which later ensured my transfer to the Helsinki and Geneva negotiations, when they opened.

Brosio was nearing the end of his term as Secretary General, and at one of the bi-annual meetings of the NATO Council of Foreign Ministers the Dutch Foreign Minister, Joseph Luns, announced his interest in replacing the Italian. Brosio took this announcement as an indication that he no longer had the full support of the NATO Council, and announced that he intended to step down at the end of his term of appointment. The succession was thus clear, and Luns was elected to be the next Secretary General. Brosio was philosophical about the matter, citing the case of the human cannonball in the circus, who had to have "just the right caliber" for the job: "not too small, and not too big."

But Brosio was highly respected by everyone in the NATO circle, and he quickly became the favorite figure to lead the anticipated negotiations with the USSR and the other Warsaw Pact member states. When Luns took office Brosio was designated as the prospective leader of the coming NATO negotiations with the USSR and its allies. NATO set up a special office for him in Brussels, and I spent much of my time bringing him the latest reports and keeping him informed of developments. A communication was sent by NATO to Moscow, announcing that the former Secretary General would be NATO's special envoy to "explore" negotiating possibilities with the Soviets and their allies. Brosio had a detailed mandate on what the Allies were interested in pursuing in a formal negotiating format. It was anticipated that his contacts with the Soviets, and possibly with other Warsaw Pact member states, would help to shape the negotiating process which would follow, and that it would help to maintain the implicit linkage which was emerging, between a negotiation on "balanced" reductions in the military forces of the two alliances in Europe, and a more political negotiation on reducing tensions and creating more normal ties among the European states. The linkage between the MBFR negotiations on force reductions, and the CSCE negotiations on political issues was maintained from this period. Washington was especially pleased with the format for Brosio's proposed exploration of negotiating possibilities, and Brosio made it clear that he wanted me to go with him on this mission. Time passed, but there was no response from the Soviets, and many people in the NATO group began to conclude that this concept was not going to work after all.

After quite a long lapse of time without any communication, a communiqué was issued in Moscow saying that the USSR would not negotiate with a representative of a military bloc. I took the text to Brosio, and he immediately concluded that he would not be able to negotiate on behalf of the Western allies. He told me about his meeting with Palmiro Togliatti, the iconic leader of the Italian Communist Party, the most powerful in Europe. Brosio, a Liberal who was clearly on the right side of the political spectrum but who was widely respected in his country for having rebuilt Italy's armed forces as the first post-war Minister of Defense, was about to depart for Moscow to be the Italian Ambassador there, and paid a courtesy call on Togliatti. They had a friendly discussion about what Brosio might expect in Moscow and the Soviet Union. At the end of the meeting, Togliatti walked with Brosio to the door of his apartment. At the door he said: "Brosio, let me give you a little friendly advice about how to understand Communists: always read our statements and declarations very carefully. If you do, you will understand exactly what we are thinking." Brosio thanked Togliatti, and left for Moscow.

Brosio, the tall and elegant Italian gentleman, with his exceptionally sharp mind and clear ideas, who never went out without gloves, a hat and a cane, looked me in the eye. "I have always followed Togliatti's advice," he said, "and it has never failed me." He concluded that the negotiating mission he had been named to carry out was a non-starter, and withdrew from Brussels to his home in Torino, where he was elected as Senator and resumed his political activities.

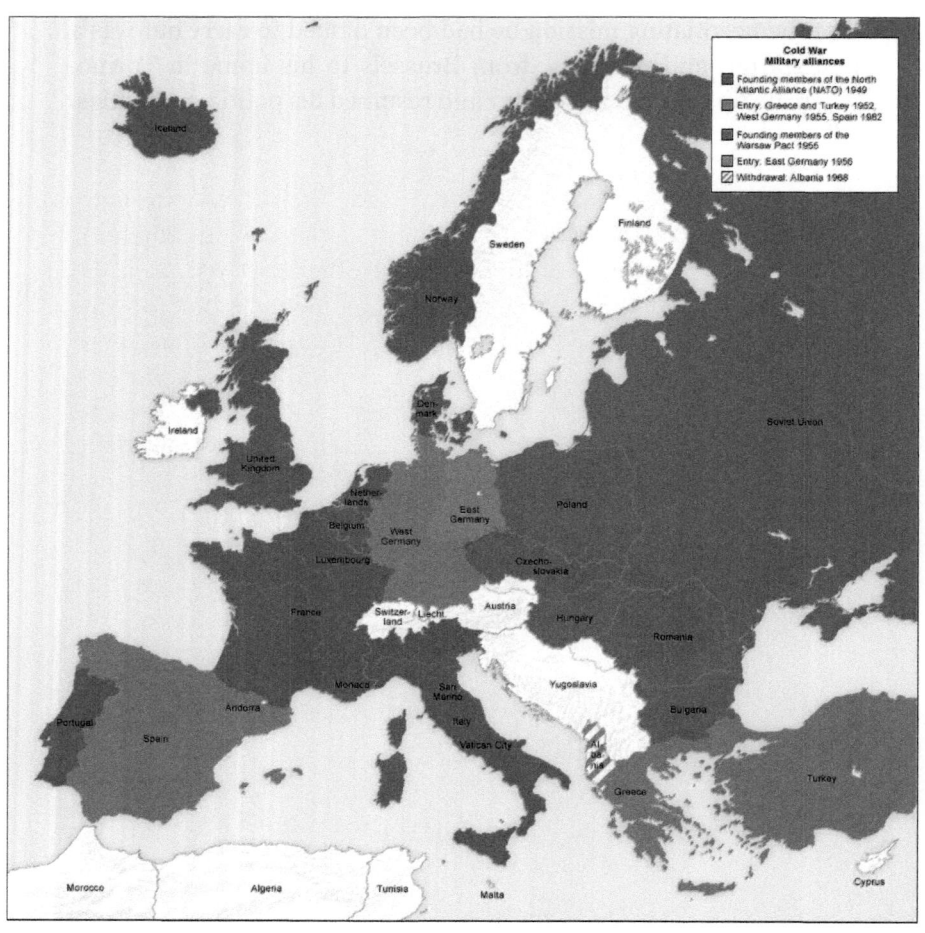

Europe during the Cold War.
© San Jose. Source: Wikimedia Commons.
Licensed under CC BY-SA 3.0 (s. https://creativecommons.org/licenses/by-sa/3.0/deed.en)

The Finnish Invitation

The signal from Moscow about not negotiating with a representative of a military bloc was only one part of the Soviets' emerging strategy for engaging with the West; the other part was their encouragement of the Finnish Government to invite all the European countries, plus the United States and Canada, to a sort of "tea party" in Helsinki, to discuss the format, arrangements and agenda for discussions/negotiations among all the European states, and the USA and Canada. The Soviets knew that they could exercise discipline over the East European countries in such a negotiating process, and they calculated that the Western countries would split and follow their own national inclinations. So direct discussions and negotiations with the full range of European governments, all on an equal footing in one broad conference, looked like a negotiating environment which would be favorable for Moscow. This approach also meant that the Soviets could aim to reach a political understanding about the division of Europe before actually committing to reductions in military force levels, which was their preference. The West European governments were also interested in such a political approach, for their own reasons. West Europeans yearned to have normal relations with their neighbors to the East.

The Finnish government's invitation convened all these participants—NATO and Warsaw Pact members and the neutral European states, big and small (even the European "mini-states"—Monaco, San Marino, Liechtenstein, and The Vatican were included)—all except Albania, which simply did not respond to the Finnish invitation—at the "Dipoli" conference hall, in Helsinki, on November 22, 1972. These became the "Multilateral Preparatory Talks," sometimes referred to as the "MPT." In this way, the long-anticipated East-West discussions on Europe's future, opened. Exempted from this format were discussions and eventually negotiations on "Mutual and Balanced Force Reductions (MBFR)," which were to be the negotiations on military force levels in Europe and would only include the member countries of NATO and the Warsaw Pact. While this was to be a parallel negotiation, agreement to which was considered essential for the opening of the CSCE, it was separate, included only the members of the two military alliances, and proceeded on its own course when it began.

I was still at NATO, still the Deputy Director of the Office of the Secretary General, who was now Joseph Luns, and whose Office Director was Paul van Campen, also Dutch, when the US delegation to the MPT at Dipoli, led by George Vest, left for Helsinki. The US Ambassador resident in Helsinki was nominally the head of the US delegation for this opening round, as often happens in diplomatic practice, but there was no doubt anywhere that it was Vest who led the US participation in the conference, and this became clearer as the Western Allies pursued the discussions about the format and agenda for the coming negotiations. Vest was a canny and amicable negotiator, who in my experience always got what he wanted. But he did it in such a folksy way that his negotiating partners and opponents often never realized that he was reaching his objectives; they usually thought, on the contrary, that they were convincing him to agree with their positions! The beginnings of the caricature of the "low profile" of the US delegation in the CSCE came from this situation—Vest did not even have the title of Ambassador, and he usually did not present a formal US proposal. He let other national representatives present the NATO-agreed proposals, which he knew very well, and which were usually based on papers drafted in the NATO office in the State Department, and presented as proposals by the US delegation to NATO in Brussels. Most of the Western proposals presented derived from this process. But Vest's approach was to obtain agreement on US and NATO objectives through his informal personal diplomacy. The "low profile" concept suited his personal style extremely well. He once told me that just sitting in the large vestibule outside the negotiating hall was useful—delegates from other delegations would approach him with their issues, and seek his advice. "If you just sit there," he said, "people will come and explain their problems." And this worked well for him—he became widely respected among all the delegations to the negotiations, for helping them to resolve their problems and to agree to NATO-based texts.

Everyone at Dipoli understood that a vast negotiating panorama was opening when the discussions started there, but the background of the careful preparations which had been carried out in the NATO context was not well known. Many western positions and proposals had, in fact, been prepared in advance during very thorough discussions in Brussels, in the NATO Political Committee and the NATO Council. Vest, without detailed formal instructions (I will come back to this peculiarity later), mustered the disparate Western group through the NATO caucus, and, without making himself into a visible leader, promoted these Western (e.g. NATO-agreed) positions and proposals. This was more formal in the military part of the process—which focused on military "confidence-building measures" (CBMs), and where the NATO positions were supported in a more disciplined way by all the NATO members. But it was also the case in the negotiation of the basic principles of interstate relations in Europe, which would later be the vital vehicle for retaining the possibility of the future reunification of Germany, and the "Basket 3" agenda, which was based on the broad concept of "freer movement of people and ideas." This was the basic Western approach, which had been developed in the NATO political committee, both in its overall strategic dimensions, and in the very specific concrete elements of several proposals.

Many of the participants in the conference, at Dipoli and later in Geneva, did not know that the Western proposals that lay behind, and explained, the conceptual division into three "baskets" in Dipoli and later in Geneva, derived largely from papers and concepts developed in the NATO office in the European Bureau of the State Department ("EUR/RPM"), tabled by the US delegation in the political committee at NATO, which had then evolved into NATO papers tabled by specific national delegations in the CSCE. This was deliberate, to avoid the appearance of a "bloc-to-bloc" negotiation and to ensure that the neutral and non-aligned states in Europe would support a broad Western position.

This was a key element of the US strategy—and the broader strategy of the NATO allies—in Helsinki and later in Geneva. The Western concepts were represented in these papers, tabled by individual European delegations as their national proposals, and supported by the full NATO group. The US stayed in the background in order to support the West Europeans and to avoid making the conference into a US-Soviet negotiation. Roles were taken by different NATO allies, who became the floor leaders in the negotiating process for the several western proposals, each of which reflected US contributions in the earlier discussions at NATO.

The US side, led by Vest with his extraordinary instinct for low-key maneuvering in a multilateral context, reasoned that it would not be useful to make the Helsinki discussions into a US-Soviet negotiation, which it could easily have become. Such a negotiating format would have been counter-productive; it would have put the Soviets on the defensive at the very beginning, and would have alienated the NATO Allies as well as the neutrals. So it was better—much better, as it turned out—to let individual European states take the lead on each of the "freer movement" concepts—this was less threatening for the USSR, because the USA seemed to be disinterested. At the same time these concepts genuinely had a greater impact for the Europeans themselves, who sought freer cross-border flows of people and ideas, the iconic motto of Basket Three. The Europeans had a much more direct interest in such issues. While there were a few exceptions in which the US delegation, for one reason or another, might take the lead (there was even one token US proposal in the exchanges part of Basket III, which was developed later to avoid the potentially embarrassing accusation that the US had made no formal proposals at all), the general rule was for other Western delegations to table the proposals and to become the floor leaders for the Western side.

There was another element which led the US side to the so-called "low profile," which the US delegation maintained for much of the CSCE negotiating process. It can be described here as the "Kissinger factor." The "Kissinger factor" was the tendency, real or imagined, of Henry Kissinger to personally take up key East-West issues and find solutions for them himself. Certainly Kissinger was very effective and successful in doing this, and later, as I have recorded in my book, "To Helsinki," he entered the scene, and the CSCE negotiations, to personally resolve one of the most difficult issues—indeed the central issue—in the CSCE's broad agenda. This was the challenge of retaining the possibility of peaceful changes of frontiers in order to keep open, or at least not to exclude, the possibility of eventual reunification of Germany. Recognizing the possibility for peaceful changes in national frontiers was a sine qua non for the Germans, while for the Russians the central objective of the CSCE negotiation was to confirm, at the highest and broadest level, the permanent division of Europe, and therefor of Germany, and to enshrine that division thru signature by the European Chiefs of State or Government, in a historic all-European summit document, at Helsinki. The fact that the Helsinki Final Act specifically kept the door open for peaceful changes in frontiers became an essential basis for the reunification of Germany in 1990, and an ironic counterpoint when, almost 40 years after Helsinki, Vladimir Putin ignored the Final Act's requirement for "peaceful means" and "agreement" to unilaterally annex the Crimea.

But in the context of the 1970's it would not have been a true all-European conference if the negotiations were simply conducted by the US and the USSR, over the heads of the European states, and a negotiation of that kind would have created resentment rather than satisfaction. So a considerable effort was expended by US diplomats to prevent the conference from becoming a US-Soviet negotiation, at least at the public level, even while the Soviets were constantly attempting to pursue such bilateral negotiations. The US delegation, and the US government, affected key issues behind the scenes, in particular the agreement on the language preserving the possibility of peaceful changes in frontiers, which was agreed secretly by Kissinger and Gromyko outside the conference, with the full knowledge and discreet participation of the West German government. That agreed language was then introduced anonymously into the CSCE negotiation on the Principles of Relations among States, and accepted without objection from any participant because it already had the support of the key players—the USSR, the Federal Republic of Germany, and the USA, which had also obtained the concurrence of the two other "occupying powers" in Germany—the UK and France.

There has been much criticism and even derision of the US strategy of maintaining a "low profile" throughout the original CSCE negotiations—at Dipoli and in Geneva—but I believe that the success of those Geneva negotiations, as well as the ability of the CSCE to then hold a summit signing ceremony in Helsinki, was largely due to this deliberately self-effacing strategy, perhaps unique in history for such a dominant power as was the USA in Europe in 1975.

Vest recruited me to be his deputy while he was negotiating in Dipoli. The key US officials who had led the preparatory discussions in the NATO political committee could not, for various professional reasons, be transferred to the negotiating effort which now looked like it would take place in Geneva. Meanwhile, with Brosio's retirement and replacement by Joseph Luns, who was a very different personality from Brosio, my role at NATO had changed. While Brosio was super-attentive to the details of every NATO issue or position, Luns had a different approach. He told me once, after a meeting with some regional officials visiting NATO headquarters, that "the only thing that matters is that they go away with a good feeling about NATO." Of course he was right, in that particular context, but for negotiations with the East we needed to focus on the details as well as the big picture. My own role at NATO became more important with this change in the Secretary General's focus—the Director of the Office and I had to watch carefully over all the details, because the Secretary General was only personally concerned with the broad issues and trends.

Over the years, and particularly as a result of the change of Secretary General and the fact that I was the only holdover from one Secretary General's Private Office to that of his successor, I had developed into quite an authoritative official at NATO—despite the fact that my rank in the US Foreign Service was still very low. In the NATO structure it was clear that I was a responsible senior official.

To illustrate: at one point, while Brosio was still the Secretary General, the unpredictable political leader Dom Mintoff was elected Prime Minister of Malta. At that time NATO had a headquarters on the island, dating from the British era. Malta was not a member of NATO, and as soon as he was elected Mintoff sent a telegram to the Secretary General in Brussels, stating that the NATO headquarters in Malta had to be closed, and all NATO personnel removed from the country, within 24 hours.

I received this telegram, as the one person available from the Secretary General's office, in the middle of the night. Brosio was away on vacation in the mountains without a telephone number—he did not like to be disturbed while on vacation. The Deputy Secretary General, Osman Olcay, had just left Brussels to become the Foreign Minister of Turkey, and his replacement had not yet been elected. So the Acting Secretary General was a senior career German diplomat, Jorg Kastl, who was the Assistant Secretary General for Political Affairs. Kastl later headed the German delegation at the CSCE Review Meeting in Madrid. I called Kastl at his home, and explained what had happened. He asked me what we should do, and I replied that we really had no choice; we had to comply with Mintoff's demand. Malta was a sovereign state, Mintoff was the legitimate head of government, they were not members of NATO, so the case was clear. Mintoff had asked (actually it was more of an order) that NATO leave, so we had to conform, and leave. In addition, it was worth noting that the headquarters in Malta, which had been left to NATO by the British, had little unique value. It was not a base for NATO forces, and its functions had been reduced to a symbolic level. Residual NATO functions could easily be transferred to nearby alternative installations, like the major base facility we had in Naples.

Kastl agreed with my analysis, and I crafted a response to Mintoff, saying essentially that NATO would close its headquarters, as he had requested, and that we would evacuate as soon as possible, but that it would of course take longer than 24 hours, and requesting a point of contact with whom we could discuss the details. This course of action, and the response to Mintoff, were approved the next day at an emergency meeting of the North Atlantic Council, and from that day we organized to close the NATO establishment in Malta.

This experience turned out to be very useful when Mintoff later held up the final negotiations in Stage 2 of the CSCE with his over-blown insistence that all foreign fleets should be withdrawn from the Mediterranean.

So I was used to taking responsibility, to being creative even without guidance, I knew the issues, maintained my self-control in demanding circumstances, and I was a proven negotiator. I was ideal to be Vest's deputy, especially since we knew each other well and he trusted me. And within a few days I left for Helsinki to join the US Delegation for Phase I, the Ministerial session to approve the agenda for what was, by then, called the Conference on Security and Cooperation in Europe. Our delegation to Phase I was headed by Secretary of State William Rogers, and Vest insisted that I take a visible place in the meeting hall, in order to ensure that I would be recognized by the other negotiators as someone they would have to deal with when Phase II of the Conference, the actual negotiation of what became the Final Act, began in Geneva.

The author at the time of the Helsinki negotiations.
© John J. Maresca, 1975.

The US Delegation to Stage 1 of the CSCE, with Secretary of State William Rogers in the foreground to the right. The author is shown seated, at the top of the photo.
© John J. Maresca, 1975.

Geneva, 1973-75

I had a young family, and we up-rooted ourselves from our very comfortable life in Brussels to move to the hotel that the US delegation had reserved in Geneva. Our delegation members all had bachelor quarters, since they were there on temporary assignments, without their families—I was the only exception, since I was transferred with my family to Geneva for the duration of the negotiations. In fact, I was one of the very few people in the conference who was transferred to Geneva—most delegations assumed that the negotiations would take just a few months, at most, so they sent their delegates there on short-term assignments, without their families. In addition, it is worth noting that there were almost no women in the conference—1973 was still a period when women diplomats were very few in number.

I simply drove from Brussels to Geneva, with my family, in our Volvo van. But my family was not happy with the hotel, so we immediately looked for alternatives, and found an extraordinary lakefront apartment which had been the home of a European aristocrat—a Spanish Baron if memory serves. In what I later learned was a common Geneva story, he had fled the country in the middle of the night, leaving behind a broad range of debts. All his material possessions, including the apartment, were tied up in complex litigation, and so (consistent with local practice) the apartment was rented at low cost, without a lease, on the understanding that the tenants (me and my family) would have to leave immediately when the court reached its decision on the disposal of the aristocrat's personal property to pay off his debts. But that did not happen while we were there, and so we stayed in that apartment throughout the two years of the "Phase II" negotiations.

The CSCE negotiating process began lazily in Geneva in late September of 1973, following the traditional European vacation habits. We had an excellent delegation, all chosen by Vest—people who were serious and knowledgeable but also unpretentious and good team-players. They all understood the overall approach, and were responsible for negotiating their part of the overall conference agenda. In many ways this phase of the CSCE was a set of related but separate negotiations, which had to be conducted by specialized negotiators, in parallel with each other. For the Principles of Relations between states we had Hal Russell, who was an experienced lawyer from the legal section of the State Department, who was relieved periodically by David Small; for the military issues there was Ed Smith, a State Department Foreign Service Officer on loan to the Defense Department, and Col. Frank Wilson. Basket two was covered by Bob Drexler, the Counselor for Economic Issues at the US Mission in Geneva, and later also Jean Tartter, Bob Brungart and Terry Healy. Scientific issues were covered mainly by Walter Jenkins, from the Bureau for Scientific and Environmental Affairs in the State Department, and Basket three responsibilities were divided between Guy Coriden for the sensitive "freer movement" subjects and Charles Stefan on educational and cultural exchanges, which was an established field that everyone wished to expand. All were low-key experts in their specialties, and were prepared to work as a team. And all respected George Vest as the team leader. Most of these people were relieved or replaced as the negotiations dragged on.

On September 23, just a few days after we opened the negotiations in Geneva, Henry Kissinger became the Secretary of State, replacing Rogers, who had resigned on September 3. We all knew that this might mean some significant changes for the US delegation, but it was still a shock when Vest called me into his office and told me that Kissinger had asked him to return to Washington to be the Press Spokesman for the State Department. Apparently Kissinger had liked the way Vest had dealt with the press at NATO and at Dipoli, during the first phase of the CSCE. I asked Vest when he would be leaving, and he shocked me by saying "Tomorrow morning."

I could hardly believe my ears; Vest WAS the US delegation to the CSCE. But the next morning I drove with him to the airport. He told me not to accompany him on that short ride, but I replied that there was no way I would not go with him to the airport, so we rode together. He told me then what my instructions were—the same State Department instructions that he had been following since the beginning of the CSCE process in Dipoli: "Consult closely with the Allies and support allied positions; avoid confrontations with the Soviets but do not concede any important points; and if you have a problem, call."

And so Vest confirmed what I already knew: the US delegation to the CSCE had no written instructions. In fact, it really had no instructions at all. All we had was the general guidance to consult closely with, and support, our NATO allies on the basis of the agreed approach which had been worked out in Brussels, to avoid overt confrontations with the Soviets, and, of course, "If you have a problem, call."

Needless to say, this situation was very unusual. Normally a national delegation to an international negotiation—especially a US delegation—has very specific and detailed instructions—for clarity and to ensure that everyone in the chain knows what the objectives are, as well as what may be unacceptable as a conclusion of the negotiating process. This was the consistent practice in the US Government as well—it was standard diplomatic practice. I asked Vest how I could manage it, and he said I was in charge "in every way except officially," and that I would have to manage things. I was too junior to be named officially as the Deputy Head of Delegation—much less as its head—but Vest was confident that I was the right person to do this, and that I could manage it. He had made it clear to everyone—colleagues in other delegations as well as the members of the US delegation itself, who were all senior to me, as well as to our partners and our "home office" in Washington, that I was the person who was responsible for the overall management of the delegation. I had to do this by advising the other members of the delegation, not instructing them, which is what I did, and the other US delegates always respected this arrangement. They knew that I was connected to our home office—the Office of NATO Affairs in the European Bureau of the State Department in Washington, and they all understood the general approach we were supposed to take, so there were never any problems. I had learned a lot about negotiation while I was at NATO, and I was a skillful back-room operator. So I knew I could do this. But I hated to see Vest go, because he made the whole operation an adventure and a pleasure.

And so, the morning he left Geneva, Vest left the overall coordination of the US participation in the CSCE in my hands. And this had to be handled discreetly because otherwise the whole idiosyncratic structure for the management of the US participation in this negotiation—the lack of written instructions, the low-profile tactical strategy, the stress on coordinating with our allies and quietly supporting them, and the need to avoid confrontation with the Soviets—all of it—could easily have come tumbling down in the face of some negative press report, political criticism or many other un-anticipated developments. That was what I was left with that morning, and what I carried for the next two years—a discreet arrangement known only to a handful of people, to maintain a carefully balanced US role in one of the key negotiations of the last half of the twentieth century, one which, arguably, affected the future shape and history of the continent.

But this arrangement was not as flimsy and risky as it might appear in such a basic description. Washington had for about two years been contributing to the NATO consultation process well-considered analyses of Soviet concepts, and their ambitions for the Conference, and more recently the State Department had tabled at NATO a range of draft proposals on issues which would be discussed during the CSCE. Many of the NATO-agreed proposals were based on, or drew heavily from, Washington's ideas. All the US delegation needed to do, in most cases, was to support the position of the Allies, who designated one NATO country delegation as "floor leader" for each subject to be discussed at the CSCE. In some cases there were additional concepts and ideas which entered the negotiating process as time passed, but the main issues were covered in this manner. It was entirely possible for the US delegation to fulfill its support for a Western proposal simply by quietly backing the NATO-agreed text. So the idea of "if there is a problem, call," was pretty reasonable in the circumstances, even if it was not exactly the kind of forthright, public leadership which is usually expected from a US delegation in a major international conference.

I recently read an interview which Guy Coriden, our delegation member who handled the sensitive "freer movement" issues of Basket Three, had some years ago, in which he explained that the instructions to the US Delegation to the CSCE negotiations were to "Support the Allies, but don't confront the Soviets." This was a practical version of the very general guidance we were working with, and covers it pretty well. All of our delegation members knew that this was the general guidance we were instructed to follow.

The negotiations were getting started slowly and smoothly, with different allies taking the "chef de file" role for different subjects in the many committees which started discussion and negotiation of bits and pieces of text. Without any advance notification a new Head of Delegation, Gene Boster, arrived to join us in Geneva and to take up Vest's role. Boster had no prior knowledge of the CSCE, nor the skills and experience needed for this type of negotiation, and he had no awareness of our special arrangements and the fact that we had no written instructions. He was a very nice, competent and accomplished, career US diplomat who had most recently been the Deputy Ambassador in Poland. He was on his way back to Washington from that assignment when he was literally detoured to Geneva to take up the position which had been vacated by Vest. Someone in the personnel department had concluded that his assignment in Warsaw, and his career focus on Eastern Europe, qualified him for this role in the CSCE.

Boster was not at all happy about getting these orders, and, more importantly, he was not really qualified for this special challenge. He was a very decent, intelligent and experienced person, but he had two problems, which he admitted to me privately somewhat later. First, he had no experience of multilateral diplomacy—the maneuvering, the coordination, and the compromising on texts which it entails. These comprise a very special set of skills; experience is essential, and in this particular case also depended on understanding the background of preparation for the negotiations which had gone on for at least two years at NATO.

In addition, and perhaps even more importantly, he had a deep-seated anxiety about public speaking, a necessary aspect of leading a key national delegation in a multilateral setting. He could not bring himself to turn on the microphone and address the Conference. He confessed this to me after an episode when, as the US representative, he should have taken the floor to support a key NATO position, but did not. I had given him a written text which he could easily have taken the floor to read. But he did not, despite my urging from my seat just behind him in the negotiating hall. Later he apologized, saying he had broken out in a cold sweat, and simply could not do it. In fact, he was at the time pulling as many strings as he could to be relieved of this temporary assignment and to go on to something else more in line with his genuine skills and experience. The other problem was just as bad in such a context. Of course, we had to maneuver, to support allies, to lobby for our favored texts, and all the many other "corridor" activities that are routine aspects of multilateral negotiations. This was expected of the US Delegation. But he would not do any of this; it was as difficult for him as public speaking. As he became accustomed to the peculiarities of the situation, he did gain confidence and became more active, but as soon as he could he applied for and got another assignment—within months after he had arrived—and very happily departed Geneva for his new assignment, with me again left holding the bag.

A further word about the so-called "low profile" strategy, for it was indeed a strategy. The Washington team which managed the US delegation in these negotiations was based in the NATO office of the European Bureau of the State Department. The Director was a very canny foreign service officer named Ed Streator, who later became the US Ambassador to the OECD in Paris, and his deputy was Arva Floyd, who came to Geneva briefly as the Deputy Head of the US Delegation when the negotiations became very active. Together they developed the US approach in coordination with Vest, who was at NATO in Brussels, and who was to carry it out—the approach was tailored perfectly to his style and his ability to get people to agree, with his folksy warmth and good humor. And once it had been agreed among the NATO Allies it had strong support across the bureaucracies and at top levels in Washington.

The fear was always that Henry Kissinger, both when he was the National Security Advisor in the White House, and later when he also became Secretary of State, might simply co-opt the process and reach agreements bilaterally with the Soviets over the heads of the Europeans. This would have been a disaster for US relations with our allies, who considered this to be "their" negotiation, a European negotiation, and who badly wanted to play the leading roles in reaching positive results. This was a political imperative for them and the governments they represented—it was a European negotiation, about European issues. But to capture such an approach in writing would have been very difficult, if not impossible, since it would have had to be approved by the National Security Council in Washington, and would have appeared very strange if it was written down in a formal document. It would have appeared as a sort of cop-out, leaving the outcome of the negotiations to the Europeans. And so it was deemed wiser to just arrange things informally, without developing written instructions which would reflect this unique approach.

This was fine for Vest, who had the experience, the confidence and the universal respect to make it work, and who was not so focused on honors and titles, but when he left it posed some problems. Fortunately, there were only a couple of episodes when I actually had to call for guidance, and each time I was given some flexible and very general instructions over an encrypted phone line which permitted us to advance on course.

The "low profile" approach was intended to permit the Europeans to take the lead in a negotiation which was, after all, about their relations with their neighbors. And we all knew that it would be easier to get Soviet agreement to Western proposals if they did NOT appear to come from the USA. In this sense the approach was a subtle and future-oriented concept. It was not at all what some people might have expected from Washington at that time, but in this case I believe we found the right approach.

The consultation process among the countries which later formed the core of the European Union was just beginning, and in fact the CSCE negotiation was the first real test of the ability of the European countries to negotiate important issues as a group, to get over their tendencies to follow their own traditional individual national policies, and to adhere to a common line. Usually, the US position became a catalyst for the Europeans, and they would either rally around the US position or use it to unify their own ideas, and then react against the US view. For the US to stand aside and permit the development of a European position, and to support it in the actual negotiating process without seeking to dominate it, was entirely new. But it was timely, and appropriate to this particular negotiation, because it was so predominantly European in its context, substance and projected outcomes. And it was foresighted, permitting the Europeans to play a key, coordinated role in the negotiating process, which then became a reinforcing element for the emerging European Union and its ability to develop coordinated policies among its members. It was indeed a first joint negotiating effort involving the European countries as a group, alongside and in step with the USA and Canada.

Our second delegation head was soon replaced by Ambassador Albert "Bud" Sherer, a distinguished career diplomat who was actually the US Ambassador in Prague at the time—so he did the CSCE negotiating as a part-time duty, and traveled back-and-forth between Geneva and Prague to fit the requirements of the two jobs. Having the title of Ambassador—even though it was related to his post in Prague, not at the CSCE—made Sherer the first US delegation head in the CSCE negotiations who actually had such a title (in the Dipoli phase the US Ambassador to Finland was the nominal head of the US delegation, but did not participate in the actual negotiations). Sherer was a great leader and was universally admired and liked, but by the time he arrived the issues had become so entangled and complicated that he never was really able to master them all. As the negotiations intensified and became more complicated and time-consuming, the Deputy Director of our home office in Washington, Arva Floyd, came to Geneva as Deputy Head of the delegation and to handle some of the negotiating work-load. He was very effective but left after a few months—I think he lost patience with the complexity and the slow pace of the process—once again leaving me with the responsibility of guiding the US delegation.

Negotiations and Realities

The Conference faced the first real test of its political stability when, on February 12, 1974, the Soviet government arrested Alexandr Solzhenitsyn, for publishing parts of his monumental work, "The Gulag Archipeligo," a detailed description of the huge network of very harsh prison camps to which the USSR sent its political dissidents and problem-makers of all kinds. Solzhenitsyn was widely known in the West as the dissident author of "One Day in the Life of Ivan Denisovich," and "Cancer Ward." He had become a symbol of the efforts to liberalize the Communist system, and this symbolism was of course directly connected to the objectives of the CSCE. So Solzhenitsyn's fate would inevitably have an important impact on the future of the negotiations we were conducting. The Conference held its breath while Solzhenitsyn was interrogated in Moscow, well aware of his symbolic status, and that the future of the negotiations depended on how the Soviets would decide to treat him. If Solzhenitsyn had been sent back to the Gulag, or worse, it would probably have meant the end of the CSCE; it would likely have simply adjourned, "sine die," in very negative circumstances, and there was some quiet discussion of this possibility in the corridors of the conference.

But instead, within a day the Soviets, well aware of the implications in the West if they were to punish Solzhenitsyn in some drastic way, chose another path; he was deported to West Germany. As soon as he was out of the USSR he was charged with treason in Moscow, and his Soviet citizenship was revoked. This of course was harsh treatment, but at the time, and in the circumstances, it was generally seen as letting Solzhenitsyn go. The author was free, but he had been expelled from his country, where he felt he had an important mission. Much later, in 1989, Solzhenitzyn's Russian citizenship was restored and he returned to Moscow. (See also Soviet Delegation Head Anatoly Kovalev's brief account of this episode in the portion of his memoirs included as Annex 1. to this book).

Within the CSCE, the episode passed, and the conference resumed its work. People could breathe again. But everyone understood that this showed how fragile the Conference was, and how close it was to the actual day-to-day existence of many people in the Eastern half of Europe. Incidents could occur at any time which could impact, and possibly derail, the negotiations in the CSCE.

And then, on August 8, 1974, one year after we had begun the substantive negotiations in Geneva, another event occurred which, while not directly related to the CSCE, reminded us all of how fragile our negotiating effort was. Richard Nixon resigned from the Presidency of the United States, because of his personal involvement in the Watergate phone-tapping episode. His departure put many US policies in question, including the overall movement toward detente with the Soviet Union and, related to this, the entire CSCE effort. Everyone who was associated with the Conference wondered whether the US would continue to be interested in this complicated negotiating venture, and whether we would pursue our broad effort to build more positive relations, and to negotiate for military force reductions with the Soviet Union. The whole strategy of negotiations with the Russians, as well as the tactical approach I have described, was open to revision under a new President.

The continuing presence of Kissinger as Secretary of State seemed to ensure continuity, but we all knew that there was likely to be some sort of pause in the momentum of the negotiating process, if only because of the assumption, and the clear commitment of the USSR, that the Conference should be concluded at the summit level. It was assumed that the Soviets would want to assure themselves that the new US President was prepared to join in a summit-level conclusion for the CSCE, before committing themselves to an all-out effort to make that happen. Everyone waited and watched while there were changes in the White House staff and the US Administration, and while the Soviets also assessed whether the previous US commitment to the CSCE project was still sufficient to lead to the summit-level conclusion which Brezhnev was now clearly seeking to pin down. Gerald Ford was a different sort of person from Richard Nixon—a hero of the football field and the war in the Pacific, and a traditional conservative from the American middle-west. For Moscow, the key question was whether the new President, who was not well known to them, would ultimately be willing to go to Helsinki and to personally sign up to the results of this conference, with all their potential implications.

There would certainly be a pause in the progress of the negotiations while judgments were made, and Kissinger's role now became even more essential. He was central for ensuring foreign policy continuity from one Presidency to the next. For the Soviets the US willingness to participate in a summit-level conclusion for the Conference was the key test of US commitment to continuity between the Nixon and Ford administrations. From the Soviet perspective, the US President had to agree to participate in a summit-level conclusion to the CSCE, or the whole enterprise would be a huge and embarrassing Soviet failure.

In the US delegation in Geneva I was the only permanent element, and also the only person with an ongoing, broad perspective of the negotiations. The other members of the delegation, who were all very competent, responsible officials in their designated fields, with significant experience and negotiating ability, were assigned for temporary periods, including the Head of the Delegation, Ambassador Sherer, whose "day job" was as Ambassador in Prague. In addition, most of my colleagues in the delegation were responsible for a single subject, a sub-heading of the full three-basket conference agenda, whereas my responsibility was to assemble these very different subjects and to see them as a whole, related to the overall policies from Washington and to our relations with our European Allies as well as the USSR. Some members of the delegation were assigned for temporary periods, but became interested and committed to the negotiations. They kept coming back, so that in the end they were at the conference from start to finish, and were responsible for specific sections of the Final Act, but even they had a limited perspective.

The negotiating process included legal and military issues, economic subjects, and Basket 3, which was, itself, divided into two distinct parts—the "freer movement" issues, and the more traditional (because they were government controlled) areas of educational and cultural exchanges. So we had legal, military, economic, freer movement and cultural exchanges experts as our representatives in the various committees, and some of them changed periodically. Each committee's negotiations advanced at a different pace, but they had to be linked because the overall issue was whether we could find agreement on all these subjects, in a single, unified document, and in a way which would be politically balanced and acceptable to all.

My role was to keep all our negotiators and their subjects within a single conceptual context, to explain it to Washington in these terms, to capture and understand the development of the conference as a whole, and to keep it moving in a positive direction, consistent with our overall approach. At the same time, and based on my experience at NATO, I was expected to ensure that the US position on the main issues was consistent with the general views of our allies, based on our earlier preparations at NATO, and the position papers which resulted from those preparations.

As time moved forward, it also became my responsibility to judge the emerging results of this vast negotiation, and to somehow convey to Washington whether it looked like the results of the negotiations would make it apparent to all concerned that it would be in the overall US interest to sign it—or not. Of course it would be Bud Sherer, the head of our delegation, who would speak directly to the leadership in Washington to state our views on the conference results. But our weekly written reports were the official record, indicating successes and failures and constantly evaluating the progress made and the degree to which it was consistent with US interests. Everyone involved in this enterprise—in Washington and in Geneva, and including Sherer himself—knew that I was the only one who understood all the details of these negotiations, their history and the sometimes hidden implications or connections, and their relationships both with each other and with the central issues before us. And so I was in a unique position to provide an overall judgment of progress, at any moment, and of course, at the end of the negotiation. So Sherer looked to me to provide him with this judgment, as time, and the negotiating process, advanced.

Two additional negotiating groups were added to the three CSCE "Baskets" as the negotiations developed, and I became the US representative in both of these subsidiary negotiations. They covered the issue of "follow-up to the CSCE," which meant what—if anything—would happen in terms of on-going contacts and negotiations after the formal CSCE had reached its results and Stage III of the planned conference had been concluded, and the question of the Mediterranean—how it would be addressed, specifically, in the final document to be signed at the Phase III meeting in Helsinki, and as a broader issue.

On both of these subjects I was the best-qualified person in the US delegation. During my military service as a naval officer I had been on the staff of the Admiral who commanded the Sixth Fleet, which comprised the US naval presence in the Mediterranean, and of course I had also served in a key position at NATO. And as the overall coordinator of the activities of the US Delegation at the Conference, I was also well placed to judge how the follow-up to the Conference should be shaped.

Following the invited contributions by a certain number of non-participating Mediterranean countries there was an effort by the European Mediterranean countries—especially Spain, Italy and France—to develop some sort of on-going role or relationship for the non-participating Mediterranean states with the CSCE, insofar as those countries were interested. And some of them clearly were interested, particularly the North African Mediterranean riverain states. So a Working Group was established to formulate some language and possible future activity on this subject, to be included in the Final Act. My main effort in this group was to limit the way in which this future participation would take place.

Washington's view was that the CSCE was complicated enough as it was, and that opening the door to these non-European countries would make it too complicated to accomplish anything. The focus of the North African countries was not on the East-West confrontation in Europe, but rather on the dispute with Israel, and their priorities would shift the focus of the Conference. For the US this was not very attractive as a prospect, so we wanted simply to limit the Mediterranean aspect of the discussions to hearing the views and ideas of those Mediterranean countries which decided to come to the Conference to make contributions.

The CSCE participating countries which were also Mediterranean riverain states included countries which were close allies of the US—particularly Spain, France and Italy—and they wanted a more expansive treatment of the Mediterranean as a subject in the CSCE, while the US wanted this treatment to be very limited. Of the Europeans who focused on this issue, Jacques Andreani, the French delegation leader, and Javier Ruperez, the number two in the Spanish delegation, became the most active, and both became long-time friends. Ruperez was married while the Geneva phase of the CSCE was going on—a scene which I described in my book on those negotiations, "To Helsinki," and both later served as the Ambassadors of their countries in Washington.

Over time, and especially in the final days of the CSCE Geneva phase, when Maltese Prime Minister Dom Mintoff demanded the inclusion of some language on the overall aim of "reducing armed forces" in the Mediterranean, some language of this kind had to be accepted in the text of the Final Act, but for the year leading up to the conclusion of the negotiations in Geneva my role was simply to maintain a very negative position, and to quietly refuse any more ambitious ideas about expanded language on Mediterranean-related issues. It is worth noting here that the Mediterranean area has certainly been recognized since that time as a region with its own enormous challenges, and probably deserving of a CSCE of its own. But during this original CSCE conference there was a real need to maintain a focus on the East-West agenda.

My role in the working group on the Follow-up to the Conference was similar. Washington did not foresee any on-going follow-up to the CSCE at all. An on-going institution, even an agreement for on-going meetings of this forum, were seen with great suspicion in Washington—any such format was seen as a potential competitor with NATO, which was Washington's principal, and well-trusted institutional arrangement for dealing with Europe and European issues. Since Washington dominated the NATO forum, it did not want to see another forum emerge from the CSCE where its domination would inevitably be weaker. As a former central official at the heart of the NATO system, I was well placed to defend this line, which I did.

There were many ideas for follow-up to the Conference, but in the end the only element which was agreed was a single follow-up meeting, to take place in Belgrade two years after the conclusion of the CSCE, with the sole purpose of evaluating how the commitments of the Final Act had been implemented. So my role in the committee which considered the question of Follow-up to the conference was also very negative—to refuse anything but the most minimal follow-up activity. This was to the great dismay of a number of conference delegations, such as the Romanian delegation, which were hoping to see the establishment of an on-going CSCE body.

Of course years later, at the Paris Summit meeting of 1990, such an on-going CSCE body was created, and as the leader of the US delegation I was a key participant in that effort. The Conference was, shortly thereafter, even re-named the Organization for Security and Cooperation in Europe (OSCE as opposed to CSCE) to signal that it was to be an on-going institutional organization, but that was much later, in a context which had changed entirely. The Europe of 1990 was very different from the Europe of 1975.

A Second Year

The Conference had started its negotiating existence in Geneva, in 1973, in the newly-built Geneva Conference Center, which was well suited for this sort of event. But the Swiss had assumed that the negotiations would not take more than a year, and this judgement turned out to be wrong. Political events, including the unexpected change in the US President, had complicated this scenario, and as a result the conference had continued much longer than anyone could have anticipated. The Conference Center had been reserved for other conferences and after a year in the Center, the CSCE had to move. The Swiss proposed the use of the former headquarters of the International Labor Organization (ILO), a venerable institution which was established in the 1930's, before the UN. The handsome lakeside building had recently been vacated when the ILO had moved to its new headquarters. This old ILO building has, since that time, become the headquarters of the World Trade Organization and has been subjected to substantial modernization and expansion.

To see whether this building would be suitable for the CSCE negotiations I went to visit it one day, accompanied by Robert Frasure, who had joined our delegation. Frasure, a bright and promising young Foreign Service Officer who later became a key Washington official, died in a tragic automobile accident in Bosnia in 1995, during the conflict there, along with one of my successors in the position I held later in the Pentagon.

But on that day Frasure brought a welcome sense of humor to our quiet visit to the 1930's art-deco halls of the old ILO headquarters. When we entered the unused main meeting hall, designed as though it was the parliament of a small and very art-conscious European republic in the 1930's, Frasure said in a low tourist-guide voice, "The Ukrainian parliament has not met in many years . . . ." But the old ILO building, though something of an antique, was well suited for our negotiations. It had many meeting rooms, and labyrinthine corridors where delegates could meet, exchange ideas and gossip, and where the many issues could be resolved as the conference ground forward. And so the Conference moved to this lakeshore location, and remained there until "Phase II" was completed and the delegates moved to Helsinki for the Phase III conclusion.

By the time of the move to the old ILO Building, the negotiations had become very intense and complicated. Following a period for evaluation of the position of the new US Administration (the Soviets obviously wanted to reassure themselves that the US Administration under President Gerry Ford was still committed to the conference, its anticipated results, and the concept of a summit-level conclusion), the negotiations picked up and moved ahead at the same deliberate pace we had seen previously. The implication was that the Soviets had come to a judgement that US policies would not be changed in major ways, and that Moscow was again confident that the conference would reach acceptable results.

I went to Washington during a break in the negotiations in the early months of 1975, and met with the Deputy Assistant Secretary of State for European Affairs, Jim Lowenstein. I told him how the work of the delegation was actually being carried out, with me as the behind-the-scenes manager, and our various operations, including the rotating personnel assigned for periods of time to represent us in the different negotiating committees. I told Lowenstein that Arva Floyd had been a real plus for us, during his period in Geneva, but that without that type of senior person with direct experience of this idiosyncratic negotiating process, I was the de facto deputy head of the delegation, and was discreetly managing that role. I pleaded with him not to send us a new deputy head of delegation who had no experience of these negotiations. Things were moving rapidly and had become very complex, and bringing in someone new in this situation could be a disaster for the delegation, or at least make things needlessly complicated.

Lowenstein listened carefully, and then arranged for me to be officially designated as the Deputy Head of the Delegation. I was still a junior diplomat, and this was a very unusual appointment. But this title gave me all I needed in terms of influencing other delegations and moving the negotiations ahead toward an acceptable conclusion.

Back in Geneva I carried out this role as the negotiations intensified and we advanced toward agreement on the full text of what by now—after long discussions—had taken the name of the Final Act. By this time, as a result of Kissinger's broader discussions with the Soviets, and the agreement on the language concerning possible peaceful changes in frontiers, we were instructed to cooperate closely (but privately and consistent with our NATO-agreed objectives) with the Soviet delegation, in order to facilitate movement toward what looked like it would be a complex set of concluding negotiations before the Conference could be successfully completed.

We began to have discreet periodic lunches or dinners to coordinate with the Soviets, and got to know them well. The senior members of the Soviet delegation were quite high-ranking—these officials held far more important positions in their country than those of any other delegation at the Conference. Anatoly Kovalev, the Head of the Soviet Delegation, was a Vice Minister in the Foreign Ministry in Moscow; his deputy, Yuri Dubinin, was head of the First European Department (and was later the Soviet Ambassador to the United Nations in New York, and to Washington), and the third-ranking official, Lev Mendelevich—the cleverist and most creative of the Soviet negotiators but too individualistic to become a major Soviet Ambassador—held Ambassadorial rank and had broad negotiating experience and legal expertise. So the Soviets had several "Ambassadors."

An additional senior official joined the Soviet delegation some months after work had begun in Geneva. He was Sergei Kondrashov, and he was known to be a Lieutenant General in the KGB, an expert in disinformation. Kondrashov, a polished and sophisticated person and an accomplished linguist, mixed easily with the other conference participants. He was well-respected and became known among the Western delegates as one of the easier people to deal with among the Soviet hierarchy. Also, he often seemed to have a moderating effect on Soviet positions. The Western group welcomed this addition; the Soviet experts within the Western group asserted that it would be essential for the KGB to concur in anything which was agreed, so it was useful—essential, really—to have a senior KGB official present as things were finalized. This would help to ensure that the results of the Conference would not be opposed by the KGB in Moscow. (See also Kovalev's memoire, included as Annex 1 to this book.)

My personal opposite number was Vladimir Petrovsky, the (quite senior) Secretary of the Soviet Delegation, and we became life-long friends. He later became an Under Secretary General of the United Nations, responsible for oversight of all UN institutions in Geneva, and I saw him often there after I moved to that city. When I became President of the Open Media Research Institute (OMRI) in Prague, the successor to the Radio Free Europe/Radio Liberty Research Institute, following my retirement from the US Foreign Service, Petrovsky sent me Kovalev's memoirs of the negotiation, asking if I would publish them. They arrived in my office in Prague in the form of a very long fax scroll, in Russian. I had them translated into English, which was easy to do since we had a permanent staff of translators. I read thru Kovalev's entire memoirs, and found most of them quite bureaucratic and uninteresting. But I did indeed publish part of them, in English, in the June 30, 1995 edition of the magazine "Transition," OMRI's slick monthly on developments in the post-Cold War East, and some of Kovalev's descriptions of what was happening on the Soviet side during the CSCE negotiations have been included as Annex 1 to this book.

I arranged for a normal honorarium to be sent to Kovalev, who was retired in Moscow, and Petrovsky reported back to me that he was very grateful. The full irony of this episode struck me at the time: the young hardliner in the US delegation, much later in life, publishes the memoirs of the hard-line communist head of the Soviet delegation, about how he obtained Moscow's approval of concessions to the West designed to conclude the overall CSCE negotiations and permit Brezhnev to reach the goal of his dreams—the Helsinki Summit to celebrate the permanent division of Europe, with the USSR in control of the Eastern half—forever. Who could have foreseen such a thing? And who could appreciate the ironies in the way history actually evolved over the following years? But in the context of the CSCE it was somehow normal, just as unforeseen as the historical events which surrounded us.

These ironies continued; Kovalev, who we viewed as a hard-liner, opened the way to a conclusion of the negotiations in Geneva by proposing that Moscow accept some very modest concessions. According to his memoire, he proposed these concessions to Moscow personally, despite the opposition of Dubinin, Mendelevich and Kondrashev, and they were immediately approved, opening the way to agreement on the Final Act. But Gromyko apparently never forgave him, and although he retained his position as the Deputy Foreign Minister responsible for Europe, he never received another Ambassadorial posting.

And then, to cap the story, he was selected by Mikhail Gorbachev to receive the Nobel Peace Prize and to give his acceptance speech on his behalf, after the Paris Summit Meeting of the CSCE in 1990. I was recently in touch with Kovalev's son, Andrei, and told him that in my view this was almost like receiving the Prize himself. But Kovalev, toward the end of his life, apparently remained embittered about all this.

Anatoly Kovalev, Head of the USSR Delegation to the CSCE, receiving the Nobel Peace Prize on behalf of Mikhail Gorbachev, Oslo, 1991.
© Andrei Kovalev, 1991.

Pressing Ahead, for History

Another very specific aspect of the CSCE negotiations in Geneva was the role of the neutral and non-aligned states—particularly the respected neutral delegations—Switzerland, Austria, Finland, Sweden and—Spain (yes, Spain played the role of a non-aligned country during these negotiations, which took place before they joined NATO. In private they would explain with just a touch of irony that they were not neutral, but they were non-aligned). These delegations played a unique role in bridging gaps between the positions of East and West, and without them it would have been difficult, perhaps impossible, to reach a conclusion to the Conference. The most active of the neutral and non-aligned diplomats was surely Edouard Brunner, the Deputy Head of the Swiss Delegation. Brunner was more like a Head of Delegation, because the Head of his Delegation did not participate actively in the daily activities of the Conference. And Brunner was everywhere—convening small meetings, floating ideas, prodding delegations to be more reasonable, etc. He was so active in trying to move these negotiations that he at times aroused suspicions and even resentment, but it is a fact that several of the bits and pieces of language which formed the essential bridges of compromise were his unique inventions. Of course there were also issues on which Switzerland had its own positions, and in such cases Brunner would fade into the background and let others take the lead, but in general he played a unique and positive role, and went on to be Switzerland's Ambassador in Washington.

But the other neutrals were also active—the Swedish delegation, the Austrian delegate Helmut Liedermann, and of course Finnish Ambassador Iloniemi, who was broadly influential in many important ways.

I was something of an anomaly in the Geneva negotiations, and I had no obvious counterparts in the other delegations, except for Petrovsky. Most delegations had Ambassadors as the head of delegation, and senior professional experts for each of the CSCE "Baskets."

Sometimes they also had military experts or officers for the negotiations on military Confidence-Building Measures (CBMs, which later came to be called Confidence and Security-Building Measures, or CSBMs). But very few delegations had an overall Deputy Head of Delegation or an active Secretary of Delegation.

So my contacts were based more on logic and personal rapport than on the others being my direct opposite numbers. I was friendly and close to several Ambassadors, including especially Jacques Andreani, the active and canny Frenchman, Jaako Iloniemi, the intelligent head of the Finnish delegation, and Valentin Lipatti, the head of the Romanian delegation (he gravitated toward me because he spoke fluent French but no English, and I was the only French-speaking American). Lipatti, (whose brother was a world-famous pianist and who was married to a well-known Romanian actress), liked to play a maverick, theatrical role, to underscore Romania's independence. These contacts, and many others, were very useful, and helped me to maintain a broad understanding of where the Conference as a whole was heading. And I maintained contacts with many other diplomats, across the conference spectrum.

As the negotiations progressed, however, I started dealing with more subjects personally, such as the Mediterranean issue, which required a lot of time and patience because of the various political sensitivities, (especially after the non-participating Mediterranean states were invited to come to present their views to the Conference), the question of follow-up to the conference, and the range of issues relating to the Helsinki summit event, when that emerged as a reality and a Working Group was established to pin down a detailed scenario which everyone could accept. I was generally considered a hard-liner, inflexible and unwilling to move from my positions. But toward the end of the negotiations, when we needed to complete the full text of the Final Act and move on to the Summit in Helsinki, I quietly introduced, or arranged behind the scenes, a number of compromise solutions to resolve pending issues.

Throughout the negotiations I kept track of what was going on in the different committees through the device of a weekly delegation reporting telegram to Washington, which summarized events in each of the negotiating "Baskets." We did not normally send specific reporting cables unless there was some problem on which we needed specific guidance or expertise. At the end of each week I received reports from our representatives in each of the negotiating committees, which I assembled into a single weekly report and edited carefully in order to ensure that they were always bland and undramatic. This was deliberate, so that Washington would not think there were any major issues or confrontations developing, and would more-or-less just ignore us, which was what we, and our partners in Washington, wanted. The only issues which really required Washington guidance were related to the military confidence-building measures, since this was a new area and was watched carefully by the defense community in Washington to ensure that there would be no undesirable limitations on US defense capabilities. Later, the form of the follow-up to the Conference, which would represent an onward commitment for the US, something on which Washington was, shall we say, "less than enthusiastic," also became an issue on which we had to be very prudent. The key language on peaceful changes in frontiers, as mentioned earlier, was being handled separately and privately.

My role in the Geneva CSCE negotiations was just as essential with Bud Sherer as it had been previously, and I brought together a number of the final negotiating points which were still outstanding as the Geneva negotiations drew to a close. These were not the central issues for Washington, but were sometimes subject to rigid national positions, and finding appropriate compromise language was always challenging. This was a period of growing excitement, and there were some stubborn last-minute attempts to get approval of pet national ideas, etc. by not joining consensus and thereby holding up progress. In the end there were many linked and inter-related reservations, by a whole range of delegations, which had to be lifted from a tangled web of language, one by one, so that there could be final agreement on the full text of the Final Act. This was when I became more active, and encouraged our delegation members to pin down a number of final language "fixes" to complete the agreement on texts.

In the spring of 1975 the Soviets made a strong effort to guarantee that all delegations would be convinced that the negotiations were coming to a successful conclusion, in order to gain political commitments and ensure the summit-level signature ceremony which they wanted for the Final Act. Kovalev explains this in his memoires (see annex), and I have described in my book, "To Helsinki," the dinner which the US and Soviet Delegations were having together when Kovalev received Moscow's positive responses to his recommendations for some specific concessions to move the process forward.

With hind-sight the specific elements on which the Soviets gave some ground at that time seem relatively unimportant to the outsider, but they were all key unresolved issues, so as a whole the Soviet "package" of minor concessions seemed important to all the other negotiators, particularly because getting any concessions at all from Moscow was so difficult. The really important elements of the overall East-West "deal" which permitted the Conference to conclude were more general and had broader implications. Basically, the West obtained some general commitments on freer movement of people and ideas, while the Soviets got a broad, high-level recognition of the status quo in Europe. As it turned out, the effects of freer movement soon began to undercut the status quo, which started to evolve rapidly after Helsinki. This is why the Final Act, in retrospect, looks like it was very favorable for the objectives of the West.

In the final weeks of the Geneva negotiations Maltese Prime Minister Dom Mintoff finally made his move, and sent a special delegate to Geneva to propose entirely new language which would have required foreign fleets to leave the Mediterranean. This occurred, certainly deliberately, while Kissinger and Gromyko were having one of their periodic meetings in Geneva, and so news of the Maltese announcement was immediately brought before them, by members of the Soviet delegation, while the two foreign ministers were dining together at the Soviet Mission.

Everyone at the dinner was taken aback, and it was a momentary embarrassment for Bud Sherer, who was at the dinner table and had to admit to Kissinger that he had not yet received this latest news.

One of the Soviet delegates had simply jumped into a car and raced to the Soviet Mission to be the first to deliver this dismal news.

Mintoff's proposal—to insert language in the Final Act which would require foreign fleets to withdraw from the Mediterranean—seemed so outlandish that it could hardly be taken seriously, but it threw the whole conference into confusion because no one knew how seriously Mintoff would insist on his precise phraseology. He had the reputation of being a maverick who loved to put himself forward and stick to an extreme position, just for the publicity. So there was a general scene of perplexity throughout the halls of the Conference when the Maltese representative announced this new position.

But at the Kissinger-Gromyko dinner the issue was quickly seen as a common problem, and neither side really saw it as a major threat to the conclusion of the Conference. There were some strong words expressing the common feeling of frustration over this last minute problem. But it was taken as an annoyance and a distraction, to be resolved in some generalized fashion so that it would not derail the CSCE Stage III denouement, which both Moscow and Washington were now expecting. Both the US and Soviet sides quickly indicated that they could accept a general formulation on the long range objective of reducing armed forces in the region, and this swept the brief "Mintoff Problem" off the dinner table.

If nothing else, the CSCE boasted a veritable army of accomplished experts in re-phrasing and rendering sentences innocuous, or even meaningless, by adding tricky grammatical caveats which were so obscure as to be hardly noticeable. And so, within about a day, some general language about the desirability of reducing military forces in the region had been found which met the requirements of the moment. Mintoff, sitting on his distant island, was satisfied, and the conference resumed its steady steaming ahead, on course toward its anticipated summit-level conclusion.

Bud Sherer left for Washington to report on the results of Stage II of the conference, and to participate in briefings for the White House staff, and the President, about the Summit-level conclusion. Preparations had now swung into high gear for having the President sign the Final Act, and Washington was feverishly preparing for the event. Last minute negotiations were still proceeding in Geneva, to complete the text of the Final Act, and to pin down all the details of the planned Helsinki scenario. I was left as the Acting Head of the US Delegation in this situation, to complete this work and to close the Geneva phase of the CSCE. There were some days of very hectic efforts to close off the details of the remaining issues, including some delicate points of phraseology, as well as to get the many national reservations lifted and to pin down the complicated scenario and arrangements for the Helsinki Summit.

The final day in Geneva was quite strange, with its late-night denouement, described in very different ways in my book "To Helsinki," and in Yuri Dubinin's "oral history," published many years later by the OSCE documents office in Prague. The feature of that final session which struck me most vividly was the nasty public bickering between Dubinin and Mendelevich, two very different characters from the same national delegation, who visibly hated each other and traded exaggerated procedural proposals before the whole Conference. I suspect Dubinin wanted to prolong the discussions beyond midnight, so that he, as Acting Head of the Soviet Delegation, could personally bring the Stage II negotiations to a close (and receive the souvenir gavel awarded to every rotating chairman). And indeed at midnight he assumed the final rotating chairmanship of the two-year negotiation. Even then the exchanges continued for some time, until the Vatican representative asked for the floor to deliver an oral message of good wishes and blessings from the Pope, and the meeting tapered away to the final closure of Stage II, reported to the world that night only by the one Soviet journalist who was still waiting outside the meeting hall for the news. In the end it was Dubinin who closed the meeting with his Chairman's gavel. It was July 21, 1975.

I walked back to the US Delegation office alone that night, needing to breath, and to think. And in the early hours of the morning, as described in my book, "To Helsinki," and in my role as Acting Head of the US Delegation, I sent our final reporting telegram to the State Department, announcing that Stage II of the CSCE had been successfully completed, and the way was open to the summit signing in

Helsinki in August. By that time everyone in Washington was asleep. In any case, the officials there who were waiting for news that the negotiations had been completed and plans for Helsinki could go ahead, knew I would finish the job reliably, and that if there was a problem, I would call.

President Gerald Ford greeting General Secretary Leonid Brezhnev in Helsinki in 1975.
© picture alliance / Lehtikuva. Foto: Vesa Klemetti.

1975—Ford and Brezhnev Go To Helsinki

President Gerald Ford signed the Final Act on behalf of the United States one year after he had been sworn in as President, following Richard Nixon's resignation on August 8, 1974. In doing this Ford followed the script developed by Kissinger and Nixon, agreed with the NATO allies during a long consultation process, and intended to open more dialogue and cooperation with the Soviet Union, as well as permitting the opening of arms reductions talks.

But probably Ford did not have in mind the full scope and complexity of the relationship with Moscow which Nixon and Kissinger had imagined, which included also planned agreements on nuclear and conventional military forces. These elements together formed a strategic agenda, which had to be seen and understood as a whole. Ford's later stumble in responding to a reporter's question on Soviet domination of Eastern Europe, in a televised debate with Jimmy Carter during their race for the Presidency, may have cost him the Presidential election in 1976. Ford was gaining ground in the polls, and might have won, had he not asserted that Eastern Europe was not dominated by the Soviet Union. Even the moderator of this nationally-televised debate was visibly surprised by this statement.

I recently reviewed that episode of the Ford-Carter debate, on the web, and even now, years later, it looks deeply embarrassing. Ironically, it may have been Ford's participation in the Helsinki Summit which led him to argue so boldly (and of course wrongly at that time) that Russia did not dominate Eastern Europe. Ford later explained that he meant the Poles did not <u>accept</u> Russian domination, but the damage was done. It was a close election, and certainly this episode cost Ford some votes. The American negotiating agenda with the USSR could be justified in terms of its overall balance, but it could not be said that the East European countries were free of Soviet control, nor that the Helsinki Final Act had somehow liberated them.

The Soviet grip on Eastern Europe remained, and it would take the slow evolution of time, as well as much internal effort by the dissidents and opposition groups in each of these countries, for them to break loose of that grip. Polish Americans, and other Americans with origins in the countries of Eastern Europe, strongly resented Soviet dominance of their homelands, and did not forgive Ford for his statements on this matter, which were transmitted by black-and-white TV, live, across America.

Surely the Final Act, and the process it set in motion, the uses made of it by dissidents, human rights activists and governments over time, and the growing pressures on the Communist governments in the East, played an important role in the ultimate demise of Communist, and Soviet, domination in the East. But this was a slow process and was dependent more than anything else on the steady pressures of many elements on the decaying Communist systems which were still in control, but were outmoded and unresponsive to the needs of modern societies. These complex factors made it difficult to over-simplify this process in any analysis or conclusion about the role of the Helsinki Final Act.

It was only years later, looking back at the evolution begun by Helsinki, that it was possible to understand fully the role played by the Final Act. Many people have concluded that this role was key, even essential, and that it set in motion the extraordinary changes which took place in the years that followed. There have been a wide range of wise and moving comments to this effect. I cite here just one, by Natan Sharansky, one of the founders of the Helsinki Group in Moscow, a central figure in the dissident activities which grew rapidly following Helsinki:

"His (Ford's) administration's signing of the Helsinki accords, which established a clear link between international relations and human rights, was the most important step in the struggle to win the Cold War—even though, when they were signing it, both sides didn't necessarily realize this."[1]

---

[1] Ben Harris: "Ford's term was pivotal for Soviet Jews". Jewish Telegraphic Agency, January 2, 2007. (http://www.jta.org/2007/01/02/life-religion/features/fords-term-was-pivotal-for-soviet-jews)

Far from freezing the situation as it was, Helsinki set in motion a period of evolutionary change in Europe, which we are able to see and understand now, looking back, forty years later.

The US Delegation went to Helsinki a few weeks after the closure of Stage II in Geneva for the summit-level conference and signing ceremony, and once again I was included as the junior member along with the Head of our Delegation, Bud Sherer, this time in support of President Gerald Ford. Arthur Hartman, the gracious and intelligent Assistant Secretary of State for European Affairs, presented me to Ford and Kissinger in the Conference hall, saying that I was "the only American who understood all the issues, and all their linkages, throughout this negotiation." This might sound exaggerated to the layman, but as Hartman knew at the time, it was true. Kissinger's humorous but somewhat disparaging response was that "it's a good thing somebody did." But I think he meant it as a complement, and he referred to that moment on several occasions when I met him in later years, in very different contexts.

In any case the key issue, and the agreement which made the summit-level signing of the Helsinki Final Act possible, had been resolved privately between Kissinger himself, who was essentially negotiating on behalf of the Federal Republic of Germany, and Gromyko. That slow, secret negotiating process had been the <u>sine qua non</u> of the negotiations, and we all knew it. So for Kissinger that key language was what the conference was all about. He even famously spoke disparagingly on one occasion about a negotiation which depended entirely on "the placement of commas." This was of course a reference to the language in the Final Act which preserved the possibility for peaceful changes in frontiers in Europe, thereby keeping the door open for eventual German reunification. Kissinger's personal negotiating role had focused, very precisely, on the placement of the commas in this key sentence:

"Frontiers can be changed, in accordance with international law, by peaceful means and by agreement."

Erich Honecker, General Secretary of the Socialist Unity Party, German Democratic Republic, and Chancellor Helmut Schmidt, Federal Republic of Germany at the CSCE meeting in Helsinki in 1975.
© Bundesarchiv, B 145 Bild-F046227-0058 / Engelbert Reineke.
Source: Wikimedia Commons. Licensed under CC-BY-SA 3.0
(s. https://creativecommons.org/licenses/by-sa/3.0/de/deed.en)

The FRG would not have been able to agree to the Final Act without preserving the possibility of peaceful changes in frontiers—and the reunification of Germany—while the key Soviet objective in the conference was exactly the opposite: to fix forever the existing division of Germany—and Europe—so that it could never be changed. These were the stakes in this landmark negotiation, and they were very high: would Europe evolve and change over time, or would it remain divided, with Germany split into two sovereign countries, forever? The language agreed between Kissinger and Gromyko finessed this issue, left the door open for peaceful change, and made agreement on the Final Act possible. The peaceful reunification of Germany did indeed take place, many years later—very specifically permitted by this key language—and thus changed the course of modern history.

Of course, as I noted in the opening sentences of my 1985 book on the CSCE negotiations, "To Helsinki," all things do change, and nothing ever remains the same. So Brezhnev's life objective—to fix forever the permanent division of Germany and Europe—was ultimately a futile illusion, which showed just how illusory it was when the Berlin wall came down, when the Communist governments of Eastern Europe collapsed and were removed from office, and when even the Soviet Union itself was dissolved, in the early 1990's. By then Europe had, indeed, completely changed.

Did the Helsinki Final Act play a role in the evolution which led to that dramatic denouement, years later? Yes, unquestionably it did, if only by encouraging the dissidents and human rights activists in the USSR, and what was then called Eastern Europe, to agitate and demand the freedoms which were so visibly available in the West. The process took some time, but it was a steady movement toward peaceful change, and in the end it was very decisive, in fact unstoppable.

So the preservation of the possibility of peaceful changes in frontiers in Europe, as well as the modest openings offered for freer movement of people and ideas, and the guiding principles contained in the Final Act, became important beacons, beyond what any of us in the conference could possibly have imagined as we were immersed in that tedious, complicated and many-faceted negotiating process. These features have given the Final Act its historic importance, and its place among the guiding documents for Europe at the close of the twentieth century. It permitted peaceful change.

My impressions of the ceremonies which accompanied the signing of the Final Act by all the Heads of State or Government of Europe and North America, in Helsinki in the summer of 1975, are reflected to some extent in my 1985 book, "To Helsinki". Attitudes at the time toward that signing ceremony were very much a mix of support and opposition, suspicion and perplexity, based on incomplete or oversimplified information on the significance of the Final Act, what it was about, what it contained, and why it was important. How could it be explained in simple terms, and how could anyone anticipate its future influence? We who were a part of those negotiations speculated and wondered about the future significance of the Final Act, just as much as anyone else. And the truth is that we did not know. It was the dissidents and activists in the USSR and Eastern Europe who picked it up, and made it into their instrument, their rallying cry, their lever for opening up the closed systems in the East. The word "Helsinki" became synonymous with "human rights," and "freedom." Very simply, it became a symbol for what Europe could become—a free and open space, with all its many national identities, stretching from the Atlantic to the Urals, and beyond.

In the United States there was at first considerable hostility toward the Final Act—the negotiations had not attracted much attention, because they were held at a low level and were overshadowed by other events. Also, the public had not been prepared, as usually happens before such high-level signature events, through a process of governmental explanation of why the issue was so important. So when it was announced that President Ford would travel to Helsinki to sign something called a "Final Act" there was a considerable amount of questioning and cynicism, even ridicule. The Wall Street Journal, in particular, urged in a front-page headline "Gerry, Don't Go," based on its quick reading of the matter as a give-away to the Soviet Union of official recognition of its dominance over Eastern Europe, as well as the permanent division of Europe, and many other negative implications.

Years later the Journal retracted and apologized for this headline. It recognized then that the Final Act was positive for the West, and for the eventual unraveling of Soviet domination in Eastern Europe. This was one of the few times in its history that the Wall Street Journal has publicly retracted a position it has taken. And in this case it was on a fundamental historical turning point, which many people misunderstood and got wrong. Helsinki opened the doors, and the dissidents and activists on all sides picked it up and ran with it, with the effects over time which we can now plainly see.

But at the time there were mixed feelings all around, and many intellectuals and commentators, both in Europe and in the United

States, did not agree that the bargain which had been struck between the West and the Soviets was a good one which would be positive for Eastern Europe. As a result, the mood at the summit-level conference, which should have been celebratory, impressed me as one of muted disappointment and caution. No one was really overjoyed by the results, and even the speeches of the heads of state were reserved. The notable exception was that of Brezhnev, who spoke as though the Final Act was a Soviet triumph, and thus fed the doubts of observers in the West. The mood in the streets of Helsinki was particularly cool—the crowds along the sidewalks simply stood there and watched—no cheering, no flag waving, no smiles. Significantly, they did not know whether to understand this unique high-level meeting as a positive step for them, for the West, and for Europe, or a negative one. Only time would tell.

Watching again the black-and-white films of these events is a reminder of how long ago it all was—perhaps not in chronological terms, but surely in terms of the changes which have taken place since those events. These blurry newsreels, showing quaint 1970s vehicles arriving, with scratchy recordings of speeches made in an out-moded style, even the clothes these world leaders wore, and the striking absence of women—all these elements—remind us of how long ago it was, how different that world was from the one we live in today.

And the speeches were reserved—everything depended on whether commitments were carried out, and that would only become known much later. So there was a sense—at best—of suspension of judgment, to see what would actually happen. As President Ford wisely said, in concluding his speech, "History will judge this Conference not by what we say here today, but by what we do tomorrow—not by the promises we make, but by the promises we keep."

The working delegates, who had carried out these negotiations, were invited to a dinner at an estate deep in the Finnish forest, and, as I described in "To Helsinki," they speculated about what would happen now. But most of them were off to other assignments, and were happy to be out of this long and tedious negotiating process. They were, after all, professional diplomats.

Looking back now, and re-reading Brezhnev's Helsinki speech, with its ringing: "the hour has struck for the inevitable collective conclusions to be drawn from the experience of history," one can only think: How wrong he was.

The leaders of the four Western powers — Prime Minister Harold Wilson, President Gerald Ford, President Valerie Giscard d'Estaing, and Chancellor Helmut Schmidt — in Helsinki, August, 1975.

© picture alliance / dpa. Foto: Esa Pyysalo.

President Ford awaiting his turn to sign the Helsinki Final Act, as Erich Honecker, General Secretary of the Socialist Unity Party, German Democratic Republic signs, August 01, 1975.

© Attribution: Bundesarchiv, Bild 183-P0801-026. Foto: Horst Sturm.
Licensed under CC-BY-SA 3.0
(s. https://creativecommons.org/licenses/by-sa/3.0/de/deed.en)

Part II

Part II

Washington, 1975

I was transferred back to Washington at the end of the summer of 1975 to take charge of the office which was responsible, among other things, for following up on the commitments contained in the Helsinki Final Act, and I hit the ground running, with no time for reflection. President Gerry Ford was already campaigning for re-election, and his opponent, Jimmy Carter, was challenging him on many foreign policy issues. The incident in one of the debates between the two candidates, when Ford was questioned about Eastern Europe and gave a lame response, certainly lost Ford the support of numerous Americans of Polish and other East European origin. He appeared to think that the Helsinki Final Act, which he had signed, had guaranteed the independence of the East European countries, which it certainly had not.
And it was true that many Americans were not happy with the results of the CSCE negotiations as they were announced in Helsinki. Brezhnev's triumphal remarks, and the low-key way in which the US government responded, led many Americans to assume that the Conference had been a give-away, traded for Soviet concessions in other domains. These other areas related at the time to Jewish emigration from the USSR, on which Kissinger had obtained a Soviet commitment, and a future agreement on mutual and balanced force reductions ("MBFR") in Europe. Negotiations on these reductions were for the moment stalled, and the whole area of freer movement of people and ideas and a greater respect for human rights in the USSR and Eastern Europe was still a disputed area, which would have to be pursued with patience and resolve to bring any improvement.
But, ironically, and regardless of the debate in the US, the Eastern European and Soviet dissidents generally welcomed the Final Act, and began to use its language to justify and support their activities. This effect gradually improved the image of the Final Act in the USA and Western Europe. And there were also specific cases in which

the provisions of the Final Act could be used for the benefit of ordinary citizens in the East. For example, in the State Department we used the "family reunification" provisions of the Final Act as leverage, to help to obtain the release of children who had been separated from their parents when the parents fled their Eastern European homelands. It took a little time for diplomatic colleagues around the world to understand and start to use the Final Act commitments in their daily demarches to government officials to improve the conditions of dissidents. But the dissidents themselves were actively citing the Final Act, not at all bothered by the nuances or ambiguities of the text, in Moscow and the capitals of Eastern Europe, immediately after it had been signed.

I was invited to speak at the Harvard Faculty Club in the autumn of 1975. This was arranged by Professor William ("Bill") Griffith, the head of the political science department at MIT, who was one of the few American academics who had followed the CSCE negotiations from the beginning. He had visited the negotiations in Geneva several times, along with our mutual friend from Paris, Dimitri ("Dimi") Panitza, who at that time was the Foreign Editor of the Reader's Digest. Dimi was a heartily anti-Communist Bulgarian whose family had fled the post-war Communist takeover in Sofia, and who helped to establish the American University of Bulgaria after the end of the Cold War and the restoration of democracy in Eastern Europe. I had briefed the two of them on developments in the negotiations in Geneva, and Griffith later not only arranged for my book on the CSCE to be published by the Duke University Press, but also wrote the introduction.

At Harvard I spoke to a packed room of professors and researchers, and explained the way the CSCE negotiations had taken form and evolved. Some in the audience were indignant, and one professor asked why American academics had not been better informed on what was going on. I replied that we had been entirely open, that our work had not even been classified, that we had held regular press conferences, etc. It was the academics themselves, with a few exceptions, who had not looked into what we were doing, and I cited Bill Griffith as an exception—an academic who had come to visit the negotiations and had followed their development. And it was true that American academics tended to be more interested in negotiations on reductions of strategic weapons than they were in the prospects for improving the human rights situation in the East.

Another question was, very simply, "Was it worth it? With all the time and negotiating effort you put into it, was the Helsinki Final Act really worth all this effort?" In response, I cited a case which we had handled just the previous week in the State Department, in which three small children were reunited with their parents. They were Czech, and had been separated from their parents during the popular revolution in Prague, when the parents had abruptly fled the country. We had successfully requested release of these children, to be reunited with their parents on the basis of the "family reunification" provisions of the Final Act. The children had indeed been released to join their parents in the US.

And then I added: " If even one child can be reunited with his or her parents as a result of this negotiation, then it was worth it." After that, no one challenged me at this meeting. Gradually, US academics began to look at the Final Act on its merits, and to evaluate it on the basis of the on-going evolution in Europe, and most came to favorable judgments about its value for the West. This value became clearer as time moved forward and the human rights activists and dissidents in the East made use of the Final Act.

My office was a part of the NATO office in the Bureau of European Affairs of the State Department, so we were used to using the relationship with the NATO Allies to advance US positions, as well as the basis for establishing US policies—this was often done in the form of instructions to our delegation to NATO, which would then communicate US positions to the Allies in one of the NATO bodies, either the NATO Council, which met at the level of Ambassadors of the member states, or in the NATO Political Committee, which met at the level of First Secretary of Delegation, or, occasionally, with experts from capitals.

There was great interest in the US Congress in the Final Act and how it was being implemented, so my small office in the State Department undertook a vast monitoring effort, trying to measure the possible results and impact of the Final Act. These results were often ephemeral or at least difficult to measure. Meanwhile, US Embassies in the USSR and Eastern Europe were sometimes strangely reluctant to use the provisions of the Final Act in their dealings with the local authorities, and had to be encouraged to do so. They were not used to it, and were not confident of its usefulness as a lever in dealing with the communist regimes of Eastern Europe. We pressed them both to use the Final Act provisions, and to report on cases and situations which were related to these provisions. Each case was different, and needed to be recorded and approached differently. Some could easily be resolved by citing "Helsinki" provisions, while others were more complicated. Simply tracking all these individual cases was a challenge.

I learned that there were some new machines, called "computers," which could be used to track large amounts of statistical information, and so I ordered one for our office. It arrived looking like a large filing cabinet, and a couple of my colleagues learned how to use it to file and retrieve information, to categorize and summarize related items, and to measure trends. We were told at the time that this was the first use of computers in the State Department (this was 1975), and it did indeed help us to track the broad trends, and to see whether the signing of the Final Act had led to statistical improvements.

But the traditional tracking of individual cases was also necessary, since each one was different. In some cases an intervention by a Western government might be useful, but sometimes it could be counter-productive; and in some cases such an intervention might be more useful if it was on behalf of a government other than the US. All this required judgment regarding the individual case, and there were thousands of such cases. Some of them related to the US, but others were related to one West European country or another, and all we could do was to monitor these cases, as statistics, and in some well-known and well-documented cases as prominent examples.

There were also some examples of efforts by the Soviets and the East European governments, after the signing of the Final Act, to show they were complying with its intent, but statistically there was not a huge immediate change. Reporting from US posts in these countries, and the judgment of experts regarding each case, was indispensable, and gradually the skeptics were convinced that the Helsinki commitments were indeed a new element, a reference which could be cited to argue that the governments concerned had taken up new obligations to deal with individual cases more fairly and openly. In some cases this had a positive effect, but, once again, each case was different and subject to a variety of different factors, both practical and political.

In Washington the approach was focused on individual cases, and on judgments in each case as to whether and when it might be useful to cite the commitments of the Final Act, either in general approaches or in relation to the individual case. Such cases included people who wanted to emigrate, or in some cases activists who had been arrested. Tracking of individual cases, and compiling of statistics for each East European country, and the USSR itself, became important. We also needed to be able to measure overall trends, and to make "before" and "after" comparisons, in order to judge the degree to which the Helsinki commitments were having some effect. The computers were useful for this purpose. Ironically, it was President Ford's comment, in his speech in Helsinki, which came closest to the mark: "The success of détente," he said, "depends on new behavior patterns that give life to all our solemn declarations. The goals we are stating today are the yardsticks by which our performance will be measured." We needed statistics in order to judge whether, and to what degree, the performance matched the promises.

Over the reluctance of some State Department experts, I sent instructions to our embassies in Eastern Europe and the Soviet Union, to report regularly on a number of indicators, in order to be able to measure the performance of these countries in following up on their "Helsinki" commitments. We needed this information in order to prepare for the first CSCE review meeting, which was planned for Belgrade, just two years later, and also to be able to support the broad monitoring effort we were developing in cooperation with our NATO Allies, in Brussels.

But getting information was not easy, since habits are hard to change, and embassies in the East European countries had their habits, developed over many years of fruitless demarches to the local regimes, as well as a cautious approach to sharing information, even with Washington. Cases involving individuals are always sensitive, and foreign pressures, or public pressures, can backfire in some circumstances. But gradually we started to build a base of information, and to be able to see some results, both statistically and in some individual cases.

In this internal State Department effort I was the key official pushing for more activism on human rights issues, against the entrenched bureaucracy of Soviet and Eastern European specialists, who were more focused on the traditional Cold War issues, were very reluctant to "go public," and were not keen to rock the boat. They had been numbed by years of fruitless efforts of raising individual human rights issues with the governments in Eastern Europe, and had little faith in the commitments given by East European regimes in a large multilateral negotiating situation. Sometimes raising a case could even make the situation worse. Colleagues focused on the Communist countries also saw us (the people pursuing CSCE commitments) somehow as outsiders; there was a "fraternity within the fraternity" of the State Department Foreign Service, which was focused on dealing with the USSR and Eastern Europe, and which felt it was a special skill, learned over time and through long, usually unpleasant, experience.

In Washington there were a few people who were interested in what we were doing, but not many. Bill Griffith, on a visit from Boston, introduced me one day to a colleague of his, a professor named Madeleine Albright, who was interested in the evolution in Eastern Europe. I also met Max Kampelman for the first time, a senior Washington lawyer who followed Jewish emigration and other human rights issues closely, and who later headed the US delegation in the complex series of Helsinki Follow-up meetings which continued, and grew, as the years went by. Kampelman was already a respected figure in Washington, and became an authoritative voice on CSCE matters.

And in Congress there was growing interest, especially from members who had significant numbers of constituents from Eastern Europe and the Soviet Union, or who had an interest in the issue of Jewish emigration from the USSR. This political interest in the CSCE and its results developed rapidly and very broadly, despite the original puzzlement over President Ford's trip to Helsinki. The interested activists and political leaders wanted to use any possible leverage to support the dissidents in the USSR and Eastern Europe, and they very quickly understood the potential of the Helsinki Final Act in this effort. This included people who were simply interested in the principle of helping the dissidents living under the Communist regimes, but it also included people of East European or Russian origin who wanted to support compatriots in their native countries. Many were Jewish constituents, and so these issues resonated with a broad range of politicians in both houses of Congress. These people all saw Helsinki as offering new leverage for human rights. Attitudes toward "Helsinki," and especially its potential, were beginning to change.

The Members of Congress who emerged initially as leaders of this broad effort included especially Representative Millicent Fenwick, Republican of New Jersey, who enlisted Senator Clifford Case, a Democrat, also from New Jersey. Together they co-sponsored a bill to establish a "Commission on Security and Cooperation in Europe," which would include members of both parties and from both houses of Congress, as well as representatives of the Administration. This was an important and innovative initiative because it would bring both the Administration and the Congress together to pursue the matter. And it was supported by members of both houses of Congress and from both parties. The bill creating this Commission was signed into law by President Ford, at a White House ceremony including Senator Case and Representative Fenwick.

Representative Dante Fascell, a Democrat from Miami, and Senator Claiborne Pell, Democrat of Rhode Island, were designated as the first Co-Chairmen of this new "CSCE Commission" which included members from both houses of Congress and also from the Administration. The new body began its work by establishing its own monitoring effort, and soon became known as the "Helsinki Commission." This Commission developed into a broad-ranging, bi-partisan group representing both Congress and the Administration, with a mandate to monitor, and inquire into the results of the Helsinki Final Act, and how the US Administration was doing in its post-Helsinki efforts. And of course the members of this new Commission were quite critical of the way the Administration was carrying forward the implementation of the provisions of the Final Act. They wanted much tougher public criticism of the Soviet Union and its allies, as well as more concrete action based on the Final Act. My small—and low-level—office of four people began to have difficulty keeping up with what was going on—even in Washington—especially since the Commission had a substantial budget and staff, and could carry out activities which were not possible for a small office in the State Department.

It should also be understood that my office was a pretty humble, working-level operation, that we were not policy-makers, and that we also had a range of other responsibilities. I considered that we had a very specific task to carry out, and that we also had the responsibility to activate our Western European allies to pursue the same sort of human rights monitoring which we were doing, in order to give some reality, especially to the commitments in the Basket Three section of the Helsinki Final Act. Most of the Allies were not very keen to do this—there was a kind of CSCE fatigue after the long negotiations in Helsinki and Geneva. I felt we had a mandate to do this, since the President had signed the Final Act, and we also had a natural leadership role among the Western Allies to encourage them to do the same sort of monitoring we were doing. So we pressed for a monitoring and reporting effort by all the NATO Allies, in which we could compare experience and statistics on human rights cases, and which would enable us to draw conclusions and press for better implementation of the provisions of the Final Act when we would go to the planned follow-up meeting scheduled for

Belgrade in just two years. The objective was also to ensure unity among the NATO Allies as we approached the Belgrade meeting.

But this was an up-hill battle; the allies were not keen to pursue such a broad and detailed effort. Sometimes the relationship of a Soviet or East European dissident (family relationship or simply close contact) was with a West European country, and so it was easier and more relevant for that country to follow that particular case. And there were many, many individual cases, each of which was different. These cases cried out for monitoring, and the individuals involved needed some sort of support. The Final Act, as imperfect as it was, did give a basis for discussing these cases, and even some minimal leverage for seeking information and for pressing for improvements. In NATO we pushed the Allies to carry out national monitoring efforts which were similar to ours, as well as an overall NATO tracking effort on the general trends.

But no Western country went so far as establishing a special commission for tracking the results of the Helsinki Final Act, as was done by the US Congress. This was a unique development, which resonated throughout the CSCE countries.

The President Changes, and Policies Change

The background of US politics unavoidably affected our work, because "Helsinki" became politicized in the US as soon as the President had signed the Final Act. In general terms and with some exceptions, the Democrats seized on the Final Act both to blame the Republican Administration of Gerry Ford for naively accepting Soviet claims to legitimacy and domination in Eastern Europe, while simultaneously seeking to exploit the Final Act by creating pressures in favor of the East European dissidents, as well as family reunification and greater possibilities for emigration from the Soviet Union and the East European states, especially for Jewish persons hoping to emigrate to Israel. On these matters they were aggressively pulled and pushed by the broad spectrum of NGOs and human rights groups in the US, as well as Americans of Eastern European or Russian heritage, and the very influential Jewish groups who were seeking greater possibilities for Russian Jews to leave the USSR and emigrate to Israel. The Soviets had been simply refusing all applications for emigration from this group, especially if the individuals involved were well-educated, but we began to see some exceptions to this basic rule, partly as a result of the Helsinki event, and also because of Western pressures and public embarrassment resulting from the activities of the CSCE Commission and other groups.

Thru the new "Helsinki Commission" interested members of Congress sought to highlight these problems, and to take a leading role in supporting the dissidents in the USSR and Eastern Europe, while criticizing the outing Republican Administration for being inactive on such issues. The human rights and émigré groups wanted to use the Helsinki agreement much more actively on these matters, which were of concern to their members and constituents, who often had direct family relatives in these areas. The Commission could use the same sort of convening powers which are widely used by Congressional committees in Washington to hold hearings and to hear expert witnesses in public testimony. This sort of activity gradually had an effect, even in Eastern Europe and the USSR.

The Republicans, at least some of them, defended the Final Act half-heartedly, because they had suffered so much criticism when it was signed by President Ford. It is worth noting that both of the US Presidents who signed the two formative, summit-level CSCE documents—the Helsinki Final Act and the Charter of Paris—both of whom were Republicans, were defeated at the next election, and did not serve a second term. While there were certainly other factors, this remains a haunting political legacy in the US. Of course President Jimmy Carter, who pursued the most activist human rights policy in the CSCE context, also was not re-elected, so the legacy is mixed.

Other politicians, from both parties, wanted to use the "Helsinki commitments" more actively, and were unhappy that these were not being pressed harder. So the whole legacy of the Final Act became a sort of political football in Washington, and its real significance, along with the potential it offered for gradual change, was somehow overwhelmed by the politics of the debate. Political life has little room for patience. Many people, both in the government and outside, just wanted to forget about it, while others wanted to be much more active in using it as leverage for improving the situation of human rights in the East, collectively and in individual cases.

When Jimmy Carter was elected and took office as President on January 20, 1977, he initiated a much more active approach to demanding the full implementation of the human rights commitments contained in the Final Act. This approach was seen by human rights activists as having considerable potential for pressing for respect of human rights in the East. Carter's chief foreign policy advisor, already during his Presidential campaign, was Zbigniew Brezinski, an academic who was himself of Polish origin, and who was very much focused on relations with the USSR and Eastern Europe. Brezinski's view of the Helsinki Final Act was nuanced—he understood very well the background, the positions of the different players, and the overall bargain which had been struck, but he also thought that a more active policy of pressing for improvements in human rights was called for, in the USSR and Eastern Europe. The CSCE Final Act was perfect for this purpose.

Carter appointed Pat Derian, a human rights activist, to a new position as Assistant Secretary of State for Human Rights, and she immediately sought to control the State Department's implementation efforts related to the Helsinki Agreement, which were lodged in my office in the NATO section of the Bureau of European Affairs, traditionally the main author and executor of policies toward the Communist countries of Eastern Europe. The European Bureau was much more traditional in its approach, and preferred to consult and act in coordination with the NATO Allies, so there were differing views on how active and public the US government should be in pressing for full respect and implementation of what had been agreed in Helsinki. The Allies were reluctant to be openly and strongly critical of the countries in the East.

Carter's appointees all favored a much more active, high-level and public stance on human rights matters, and this was the core issue for the US approach to the follow-up to the signing of the Final Act. It was also an issue between the US and its NATO Allies, which were much more traditional in their approach, and were more reticent about using the Helsinki provisions to press the Eastern countries publicly. In the European Bureau of the State Department it was considered important to carry out broad policies, such as the approach to dissidents in the East European countries, in close consultation with the European Allies, and this had become a strong tradition in relation to the Helsinki commitments. So there was a difference of approach within the State Department, and I was seen as the official responsible for implementation of the policy which was to be followed on this set of issues, and therefor the focus of the pressures for these two differing policy directions.

I felt that by creating a system for tracking human rights cases, and coordinating this with our allies, and by using this information for raising individual human rights cases with the governments concerned, we had been innovative and had pushed the whole western approach forward, as a follow up to the Helsinki Final Act. But clearly our efforts were not enough for the human rights activists who were now in senior positions in the Administration, nor for the much more sweeping possibilities of the Helsinki Commission, with its large staff, the ability to hold hearings, etc.

By this time we were preparing for the first CSCE Review Conference, which was programmed to exchange national views on the implementation of the provisions of the Helsinki Final Act, and was to convene in Belgrade in June of 1977, just two years after the signing of the Final Act. Agreement on this one meeting, to review implementation of the Final Act, was the result of the work of the Working Group on the Follow-up to the Conference, in Geneva, where I had been the US representative. Control of the preparatory process for this review meeting became an on-going tug-of-war among different offices in the State Department, as well as with the CSCE Commission.

The Commission was in principle bi-partisan and included senior representatives from the Administration as well as its Congressional members, but as a practical matter it operated like a Committee of the Congress. I went regularly to the offices of the Commission to discuss all this, principally with Spencer Oliver, who emerged as the key staff official for the CSCE Commission, chaired by Congressman Fascell.

On several occasions I met with Fascell, but our approaches were very different—I had to take account of the need to coordinate what we were doing with our NATO allies, which naturally slowed things down. And the allies were reluctant to be very public in criticizing the USSR and its East European allies. Fascell thought I should be more active, but I was a junior State Department official and had to follow established policies, while Fascell was an elected Representative in the US Congress, with his own strongly-held views, in a new position which gave him a lot of freedom to be creative. I think he over-estimated my ability to affect policy, and also did not understand that I basically agreed with the idea of actively pursuing implementation of the provisions of the Final Act, though I preferred a diplomatic approach to such matters.

I was faced with the general reluctance of the whole internal State Department establishment about dealing with the USSR and its satellite countries on the basis of the Final Act, not to mention the views of our NATO Allies, all of whom favored a more cautious approach. The State Department's traditional establishment for relations with the USSR and Eastern Europe, with its long experience of fruitless dealings with communist regimes, where active support often brought about even worse treatment for the individuals involved, was much more cautious. Experienced Soviet and East European specialists had very little faith in the Final Act as an instrument for pressuring and influencing the regimes in the East. Experience had taught them that the communist regimes would only respond to real, concrete pressures, and that raising individual cases with governments could often make matters much worse for the individuals concerned. This was a long-standing debate, and was broader than just the question of using the Final Act and its provisions as leverage on human rights cases, but the Final Act was a new element, and was seen as potentially useful by the activists—outside and, with the election of Jimmy Carter, increasingly inside the Administration.

Career Planning

I was a career official, and I had to pursue my career. One of the principal career guidelines at that time was the need to serve overseas in different geographic regions. I was considered a political officer, and a European specialist, and this was something I wanted to maintain. But that meant I had to have at least one assignment in another world region, and in another career specialty. In consultation with my career advisor in the personnel department, and drawing on my experience as the French Desk Officer prior to my assignment to NATO, I identified a position which I thought would be ideal for my posting outside of Europe and outside of the political specialty. So I applied for the post as US Consul General in Martinique, and was selected for that post.
As is well known, Martinique is a lovely island—it has a wonderful climate, great cuisine, the culture and language is French, and you can read Le Monde over your morning café. It also turns out that the US Consul General has a very nice residence with a modest swimming pool, and a driver who takes him down the hill to his office in central Fort de France every morning. And of course it is an independent position, the nearest supervision being about five thousand miles away, and the heaviest issues being reporting on the possible development of potential independence movements. I was really delighted about this assignment, and began negotiating with my predecessor about various things like taking over the remains of his wine cabinet (I agreed to do this) or buying his sailing yacht (I had to refuse for financial reasons). And as the political situation in Washington heated up, I began to look forward with great anticipation to being able to climb aboard the flight which would take me away from all that, to the tropics and the Caribbean.
And then one day I was asked to cross the corridor to the office of the Assistant Secretary of State for European Affairs. This was still Arthur Hartman, but he was soon to leave to become the US Ambassador to Paris, an unusual and distinguished appointment for a

career foreign service officer and surely a recognition of his many talents. Replacing him would be none other than George Vest, my mentor from NATO who had originally gotten me into the CSCE negotiations. When I walked into Hartman's office, Vest was also there, as was Bud Sherer. Hartman closed the door and said "Sit down, Jack." So we all sat. And I was told that my assignment to Martinique had been broken, so that I could return to the CSCE for the first review meeting, which was to take place in Belgrade. I was to leave very shortly. Sherer was to be the head of delegation, and would join me there.

This struck me at the time as a very unpleasant development. Not only had I lost the dream-like assignment to Martinique—and I would once again have to look for an assignment in another part of the world, none of which were likely to resemble Martinique—but I would also have to continue to deal with the range of pressures which had been building up over implementation of the Helsinki Final Act, as well as the growing range of officials in the State Department and the CSCE Commission who were pressing for a more active US policy. But it was also clear to me that there was nothing—absolutely nothing—I could do about it. My assignment to Martinique had been broken, and instead I was being assigned (in principle, and as the place I would go to after the meeting in Belgrade was over) to a vacant position at the US Embassy in Paris, the position as Special Assistant to the Ambassador (Hartman). The deal had been cooked, all the responsible senior officials were there, and they had agreed on this scenario among them.

The idea was that I would carry out the Belgrade meeting, and then continue on to my assignment in Paris. I could move my family immediately to Paris, so that I would be able to go to Paris for weekends from Belgrade (which later proved to be virtually impossible). There was nothing I could do except to accept this fait accompli with as much grace as I could muster. So I started preparing myself for Belgrade.

Belgrade, 1977

The key event on the CSCE horizon was the first meeting which the CSCE had ever had to review how the provisions of the Helsinki Final Act had been implemented. This meeting had been a Western concept designed to keep some pressure on the East European regimes to carry out their Final Act commitments, which I had negotiated in Geneva, in the working group on Follow-up to the Conference. It was for this review meeting that my section of the State Department had been collecting data on our computer for the last two years, and for which the Allies had been comparing experience and plans in their regular meetings in Brussels.

There was, during this period, also a developing consultation process among the members of the European Union, which took place in parallel with the consultations at NATO, but which increasingly meant that US positions at NATO would face united or semi-united European views. This was a new and growing reality during this period, and became evident when the Belgrade meeting convened, and the US and its European Allies started to follow divergent tactics. The Belgrade CSCE meeting was, in fact, the first instance of close political consultations among the European Union members, and changed the dynamics within the CSCE considerably from the previous period, when the NATO group was the central coordinating body for the western group. And in the circumstances, as the US began to follow a policy of much more public criticism of the USSR and the Eastern European countries on their human rights policies, this difference in the way the main Western delegations consulted in the CSCE context became important.

Chairman Fascell, the Democrat Congressman from Miami, sought and obtained agreement from the newly-elected Democratic Administration that the CSCE Commission, which he presided, would be strongly represented in the US Delegation to this first CSCE review meeting, and that it would participate actively in the discussions and negotiations there. This was a highly unusual—perhaps unique—arrangement in the US experience, since the basic principle of government in America is the separation of powers between the Administration and the Legislative and Judicial branches. But the feeling among the Congressional members of the Commission was that it was not just a Congressional body but a joint Congressional-Administration organ, and therefor had a legitimate role to play in the formulation and even the implementation of relevant policies.

There was a good deal of reluctance in the State Department on this, but the US Delegation to the meeting in Belgrade, when it finally traveled to the Yugoslav capital, included staff people from both branches of the Government. In fact, the number and experience of the people from the Commission was greater than the group from the State Department, and they were not under the same discipline as was the case in an Administration-only delegation. I was once again the Deputy Head of the Delegation, so I had to find ways to manage this situation, while respecting my instructions and the overall State Department rules on such matters. Even the sharing of State Department instructions, or other papers, with people who were not from the Administration was something new; normally it was simply not permitted. We were breaking new ground.

The US delegation to the Belgrade Review Meeting was to be headed again by Ambassador Bud Sherer, who this time was to be a full-time Ambassador in this role, and was nominated by the President and confirmed for this position by the Senate. I was once again to be the Deputy Head of the Delegation. We also planned to have a small staff of experts. The CSCE Commission sent an equal number of staff people, headed by Spencer Oliver, to be full members of the Delegation. The Belgrade meeting was to review all aspects of the Final Act, and how the commitments it contained had been implemented, but the CSCE Commission people were naturally focused on Basket III and its human rights provisions. Some of them were true experts on these issues, and knew more about this field than our State Department people, so they really dominated that part of the debate, which of course became the central set of issues for the review meeting. They literally knew all the details of every specific human rights case, and when they learned of a new one they would dig in and learn those details. This gave the US delegation considerably more expertise than any other national delegation.

At first, when we arrived in Belgrade, things seemed to go pretty well. We all socialized together, and Bud Sherer was widely respected as the head of delegation. He resided in the guest house of the US Ambassador's residence. The Ambassador to Yugoslavia at the time was Lawrence (Larry) Eagleburger, a senior career Foreign Service Officer who I knew from my time in the State Department and who later became Secretary of State—a unique step for a career official. Eagleburger was very hospitable, but stayed away from the CSCE strategy sessions and meetings—being Ambassador to Yugoslavia was a more-than-full-time job, and he respected Bud Sherer's area of responsibility.

One day Sherer discovered a listening device in his apartment—it simply fell from his bedside table. We had a good laugh about how naïve the people who planted it there must have been—thinking that there might be some sort of state secrets discussed in Bud Sherer's bedroom, or that this CSCE review meeting would deal with any secrets at all! On the contrary, everything we were doing was intended to be public, and we had no secrets!

And the delegation got along well socially. We traveled together to different parts of Yugoslavia on the weekends—Dubrovnik, Split, the island of Hvar, etc., and there were many things we shared laughs about. But in Washington a major change was developing with respect to how strongly and publicly the US would present cases which we considered to be inconsistent with, or violations of, the provisions and commitments of the Final Act. The concrete question which had to be decided was whether or not accusations relating to specific individual human rights cases would be made public and would be handled publicly, or whether they would be raised privately with the country concerned, as was the traditional practice. Doing this publicly would mean public accusations of East European governments concerning their treatment of their citizens—a significant change in the way such issues had been treated up to that time. Some members of Congress who were interested in human rights issues in the USSR and Eastern Europe wanted the Administration to raise these issues more vocally and publicly, and President Jimmy Carter and his National Security team were evidently inclined in the same way.

As we were starting to organize our delegation in Belgrade, the decision was taken by the White House, in step with the growing Congressional and public interest, to pursue a much more political and public line in pressuring the Soviets and the East European governments for greater respect for human rights. This was a major change of policy, resulting from the strong political interest in Washington, and the President was committed in this direction from his strong statements during the election campaign. So decisions were taken at the highest levels to change the approach we had been following and to take a much stronger and more public line of criticizing the behavior of the Soviets and the other communist regimes on human rights issues, to cite specific cases publicly, and to press hard in the Belgrade meeting on these issues.

This was also a reflection of the dispute which had hovered over the relationship between the Congressional CSCE Commission and the State Department since the establishment of the Commission, but it had been raised to the Presidential level, and President Carter had decided to change the way the Belgrade meeting would be conducted, to be consistent with his campaign statements and his overall stance on human rights. And so one day I received a telephone call from John Kornblum, who had taken over my position in Washington, and who, many years later, became my successor as the US Ambassador to the CSCE, and after that was the US Ambassador to Germany.

Kornblum said jokingly, "Guess what. You're out." We often joked about such matters, and he knew that I was ambivalent about continuing my difficult role in managing the relationship with the Congressional side of what had become a very complicated CSCE process. It turned out that a hand-written note had been sent from the White House to Secretary of State Cyrus Vance, which read "Who is this guy Maresca who is screwing up our relations with Congress?"

This might have been a career disaster for me, as a junior career official, but as it turned out, it was not. Unusually, since the State Department is pretty big and I was a pretty obscure official, Vance knew me. He was the Chairman of the Board of Trustees of Kent School, a small school in Connecticut where I had been a bright scholarship student. Like Vance, I had gone from Kent to Yale. There were only a couple of "Kent-Yale men" in the State Department at that time (F. Scott Fitzgerald once described a character in one of his novels, completely, by stating that he was a "Kent-Yale man"). I had the backing of the European Bureau and was technically already assigned to the Embassy in Paris, so I simply took a plane to Paris and took up my position there as Special Assistant to the Ambassador, who was Arthur Hartman. Overnight, my whole professional and personal life was completely changed, as part of a much broader change of US policy regarding the Helsinki process.

A decision had come down from the White House that the Delegation to the Belgrade meeting was to be revised. Former Supreme Court Justice Arthur Goldberg was to become the head of delegation, with a mandate to speak out publicly and frankly about human rights violations in the East. Bud Sherer would be retained as an Ambassadorial Deputy to Goldberg, because he had been confirmed by the Senate, and this made his appointment difficult to un-do. As a part of the change of policy, I was being transferred, after four years of maintaining the US position in the CSCE. The US role in the CSCE was being significantly elevated, and the plan was to be much more active, contentious and confrontational during the Belgrade meeting, especially on human rights issues and specific human rights cases.

Human Rights Activists and the CSCE

"The Cold War, which divided both Europe and the international system for five decades, ended with the breaching of the Berlin Wall and the demise of Communist rule across Eastern Europe in 1989-90. These revolutionary changes were set in motion by the Conference on Security and Cooperation in Europe's establishment in 1975 of human rights as a formal norm for relations among European states. "

The Helsinki Effect, Daniel C. Thomas, 2001

There have always been debates in Washington between those who favored active, energetic and public efforts in favor of human rights and democratic values, and those who favored "realpolitik" in some form. During the long period of the Cold War confrontation, this debate was acute and on-going, and there were people in Washington, and among US political leaders in general, who supported, as a priority, vocal and public human rights advocacy, down to the level of individual cases of human rights leaders in the communist countries. And then there were those at the other extreme, who saw an over-riding interest in avoiding public confrontations which could, ultimately, lead to military conflict with the possibility of escalation to nuclear war. In addition, raising individual human rights cases, especially publicly, was risky for the individuals concerned. Such attention could bring much worse treatment for the people involved. Most people in the US were in-between, and favored some principled activity in support of human rights in the Communist countries while also wanting to avoid confrontations that could escalate into more serious forms of conflict, or could bring even worse treatment. The debate was on-going, manifested in individual cases that sometimes attracted publicity and became symbolic of the two sides of the discussion. Some events became watersheds for this debate, such as the case of the treatment by the Soviet government of Aleksandr Solzhenitsyn. The CSCE conference essentially came to a standstill while the world waited to see how the government of the USSR would treat Solzhenitsyn—whether he would be allowed to continue his active criticism of the government and the Communist system as a whole, or whether he would be arrested and sent back to the Gulag. When Solzhenitsyn was instead deported and relieved of his Soviet citizenship there was a sort of collective sigh of relief which settled over the CSCE negotiations in Geneva.

But the broader debate in the West, which pitted human rights activists against "realists," and against those who saw the possibility of nuclear war as an over-arching red line to be avoided at all costs, haunted the Western approach to the conference and the governmental decisions which were periodically taken on how it should be used, and what strategy should be followed in pursuing it as a major international activity.

During the Nixon and Ford Administrations, with Henry Kissinger as the guiding hand for US foreign policy, the US was prudent with respect to public use of human rights issues in the USSR. It was not totally inactive—the effort to get a Soviet commitment to permit Jewish emigration in large numbers, in connection with US signature of the Helsinki Final Act and the so-called Jackson-Vanik amendment, shows this. It was, I would say, coldly pragmatic and realistic, and efforts on human rights were principally made in private dialogue with the government concerned, focusing on specific cases that related in some way to US interests.

If there was indeed a conscious overall strategy with respect to the CSCE and its potential effect on human rights, it was that by putting the CSCE commitments in place, recognized and supported at the highest level of the Communist world, this would lead to an overall improvement in human rights in the East. The theory was that the easing of East-West tensions would have the effect of easing human rights abuses as well. The approach also was consciously designed not to alarm the Communist countries, and especially not to alarm the Soviet regime, and not to signal to them that there was somehow a Western plot to use the provisions of the Final Act to support human rights activists in the East. It was thought that such alarm would have made it impossible to obtain commitments on human rights principles or even the modest specific provisions contained in the Basket 3 section of the Final Act. The West European Allies were particularly keen to keep the debate with the East on human rights in an orderly, private, diplomatic context, and as a former NATO official I considered the views of our allies an important factor in the formulation of the US national position.

But this was a highly politicized, on-going debate in Washington, and when the Administration changed, with Jimmy Carter elected to replace Gerry Ford and the Republican government which had depended so heavily on the overall foreign affairs strategy of Henry Kissinger, many human rights activists came into the government, with a strong popular mandate. Policies and approaches changed rapidly as Democratic appointees were put into key positions and began to revise the overall approach which had been followed in the CSCE.

This sort of phenomenon is not unique to Washington, and happens in every democratic country when one political party replaces another. But in the case of the United States and the CSCE, it was something of an earthquake. The US had followed the "low profile" strategy in the CSCE for so long that it had become an assumption among the participating states that Washington would always play such a role. And the approach of getting the USSR to agree to commitments through patient, private discussion was assumed to be the standard working method in this complex negotiating body. So the appearance of a new US policy, with energetic, activist and public aspects, was nothing less than a revolution, and shook the whole CSCE process.

It should also be noted that a natural evolution was going on in the world during that period—there was greater access to information because of new technologies. Television, fax machines, early use of computers, etc. ensured the widespread availability of information in ways that were unheard of before. This dramatically broader availability of current information had an important affect on human rights throughout the world, because cases were known more widely and could be followed from a distance much more easily.

Looking back, one can see the full irony of the different phases of the CSCE/OSCE process: President Carter's approach of "speaking out" on human rights in the East would have made it impossible to negotiate and agree on something like the Helsinki Final Act, while the approach of Nixon and Kissinger, with its secretive diplomacy, and its "low profile" presence in the CSCE negotiations, drew the USSR into a broad negotiating process and surely led them to assume that they would not be subjected later to public criticisms. The USSR would certainly not have accepted international human rights commitments if they had thought those commitments would be used against them publicly. At the same time, once the Final Act was signed, the public efforts pursued on the basis of the commitments in the Helsinki Final Act, as thin as they were, became a major element in accelerating the process of emancipation in Eastern Europe. The Carter Administration was eager to pursue this, and it would surely not have been pursued as energetically and publicly by a second Ford Administration. Together, the public commitments obtained through careful private negotiation, combined with the subsequent public pressures for their fulfillment, had a major effect on the evolution taking place in what was then called Eastern Europe.

Leaving the CSCE

I did not suffer, in material terms, from being removed from the US Delegation to the CSCE Review Meeting in Belgrade. A couple of days after I got that call from John Kornblum I took a plane from Belgrade to my already-arranged assignment at the US Embassy in Paris, where I was the Executive Assistant to the Ambassador, Arthur Hartman.
Nonetheless, in Paris I spent a lot of time brooding about all this, and the politics underlying it, and I especially regretted having lost my assignment in Martinique. After my frantic and challenging efforts in Geneva, Washington and Belgrade I suddenly had time for reflection. On the one hand, of course, I felt that I had been the key person in developing the US role in the CSCE process over about four years, and that my removal was unfair. No one else in Washington understood all the complexities, etc. of the CSCE as well as I did, and I had influenced the course of events in countless ways, both large and small. Like most of my colleagues I thought the basic idea of working closely with our allies was an important one, basic to the whole US approach to its foreign policy priorities. And of course it seemed highly unfair to remove me so abruptly from the process I had constructed and led, following basic concepts of US foreign policy such as the guiding notion of solidarity with our NATO allies.
In addition, I had been building a unique set of approaches, plus a data bank of information on related individual human rights cases in the USSR and Eastern Europe, which were to be used at the review meeting in Belgrade. No one else at that time, in the government in Washington, had pursued anything like such an effort. I had also maintained close coordination with the NATO Allies, so there was a large degree of harmony between the US and West European approaches when we arrived for the meeting in Belgrade. The individual cases were all due to be raised, specifically and forcefully, using the commitments in the Final Act. The only difference was that

we had intended to do this in a diplomatic context rather than publicly.

At the same time I was also well aware that my personal, low-level dominance of CSCE issues in the State Department was resented by the Congressional people, who wanted this to be a high-profile issue, led by prominent public figures. They also wanted more political control over the way the US pursued implementation of the Helsinki Final Act, and to elevate it to a major element of national policy. I was viewed as a major obstacle for them to do this. Never mind that my "dominance" on this issue was due to the fact that very few other people in the State Department followed CSCE matters, or even cared about them. The fact that I was still a junior official was also relevant; the Administration was criticized for the fact that it did not have a much more senior person—a political appointee—with a large staff, larger resources, and policy clout, to pursue this area of activity. But the main point was that human rights activists wanted a more active and public US policy, and with Jimmy Carter as President, the Administration also favored such an active, vocal policy, which would be associated directly with the President and his political approach.

Looking back on these events after many years, my conclusion is that a number of different elements and political factors were needed to seriously challenge the human rights restrictions that characterized the Communist regimes in the East. The Kissinger approach of secretive negotiations to reach a deal with Moscow, plus the low US profile in public settings, was useful to bring the Soviet Union to an agreement which contained some basic written commitments on human rights. The public criticism by Washington of the way these commitments were implemented was also necessary, after they were undertaken, in order to press for implementation and to encourage the dissidents. Without both of these factors—the negotiations and the pressures for implementation—the Communist regimes would not have been so challenged, with the results we saw as time evolved.

I had been working in the main stream of this human rights activity, but at the same time, and from a career perspective, I realized that

I was lucky to be out. Working on the CSCE was not a promising career avenue in the US diplomatic service—far from it - while a position at the Embassy in Paris was an excellent step up in a classic Foreign Service career, sought by all my colleagues. Paris was right in the middle of the "main stream" of my chosen career, the sort of assignment all junior diplomats would die for.

I read or heard periodically about continuing difficulties within the US delegation in Belgrade, and they seemed considerable. Washington's decision to "go public" on specific human rights cases was not very welcome among the NATO allies, who preferred a more discreet approach, and who believed that governments were often more able to change their position on cases of individual dissidents if the case was raised privately, rather than thru public accusations. There was a continuing, basic disagreement over the extent to which disputes regarding specific human rights cases should be made public, and to what extent they should be discussed privately with the representatives of the government concerned. This was a classic dispute, to which there would never be a final answer, and the experts on the USSR and Eastern Europe would always be more prudent about such matters than the human rights activists. And the reality was that each case was different; sometimes public pressure made sense and could help, while in other cases it just made matters worse. Experts knew this.

This broad set of issues had been a major focus for me, but international relations are made up of many other elements, too, and it was actually beneficial for me as a career diplomat to shift my focus to other matters, so my assignment to Paris turned out to be a very useful step.

President Jimmy Carter's appointment of former Supreme Court Justice Arthur Goldberg to be the Head of the US Delegation in Belgrade reflected Carter's intention to use the CSCE as a highly provocative public lever for his active human rights advocacy concerning the USSR and Eastern Europe. This was a very sharp change of general policy from the Kissinger years. Bud Sherer was retained as Goldberg's Deputy, but Goldberg completely overshadowed him, and made human rights in the Communist countries into a banner public policy of the US Administration. With Goldberg as the leader of the US delegation the famous US "low profile" in the CSCE was a thing of the past, and the Belgrade meeting became very contentious as he raised specific names and cases, and did not hesitate to address issues publicly. And since he was already a well-known public figure, with the obvious credentials of being a former Supreme Court Justice, he routinely made headlines pursuing human rights issues in Belgrade.

For many years—before and after the Helsinki negotiations—there was an on-going debate in Washington about whether it was more advantageous to try to handle delicate matters with the USSR privately or publicly. The same sort of debate comes up periodically with respect to other sensitive international issues. There were solid arguments on both sides—by handling an issue privately it might be possible to find a private, but satisfactory, solution, while handling an issue publicly is always risky—it can create pressures for the other side to be more forthcoming, or it can close the matter completely and render any solution impossible. There have been good examples on both sides of this debate.

Also, the discussion with regard to publicly raising issues related to the USSR and Eastern Europe does not completely depend on party lines; there are Democrats and Republicans on both sides of this debate. During the Kissinger era it seemed that the Republicans were more favorable to using private dialogue to reach their objectives. At the same time, the human rights activists and the activist organizations tend to be Democrats, or on the left side of the political spectrum. But this has always been more a matter of personal inclination than of strict party policy, and also depends on the specific case as much as a general approach. And there have always been people in both parties who favored one approach or the other. Among the activist human rights organizations, most people favored using public pressures, but many would also recognize the advantages of using "private diplomacy" in certain situations.

When Jimmy Carter was elected President, those favoring "public diplomacy" on human rights issues came into the Administration, and so this became the official Washington strategy, replacing the secrecy and back-channel "private diplomacy" used by Kissinger under Presidents Nixon and Ford. It is worth noting here that it was two Republicans who came up with the idea of the US "Helsinki Commission," and the legislation on this was signed into law by President Gerry Ford. But the changes which took place in the US strategy for the CSCE review meeting in Belgrade reflected a broader change from private to public handling of CSCE issues, resulting from the change in the White House.

I was not a member of any political party, and I believe my approach to these matters was basically pragmatic, trying to find the best combination of tactics and strategy which would work to attain our objectives, and not excluding any possible type of action or activity. But one becomes linked to one's associates, and in the US system it is often the case that career officials become associated with one political party or the other simply because they serve in policy-related positions in a Republican or Democratic Administration. And that is more-or-less what happened to me. I became identified with Republican Administrations, and despite my basic independence, this identification followed me throughout my career.

The arrival of Justice Goldberg, and his readiness to "speak out" on individual human rights cases, inevitably made for a very messy meeting in Belgrade, with the US delegation "naming names," and many of the Europeans surprised and even dismayed by the frank and sometimes openly hostile discussions. The approach probably did have some positive effect on the way the Soviets treated their dissidents, especially over time, as the Soviets realized that they would suffer from public accusations in such review meetings, and began to worry about the overall effects of such accusations. But this was balanced by the fact that some individual cases were resolved privately.

In addition, and more importantly, dissident activities were strengthened and encouraged throughout the Communist countries, as became evident years later when the Communist regimes in the East came under pressure precisely in relation to their commitments in the Helsinki Final Act. This was a key element in the way "Helsinki" affected the situation in Europe over time.

I was watching the Belgrade meeting, and the CSCE, from a distance, as I went about my work in Paris. Many of my friends, who were still involved in the negotiations, told me how lucky I was to have moved on, and this was certainly true in career terms. But for a long time I was bitter about how I had suddenly been removed from something I had worked so hard to build. It is not an exaggeration to say that I was the American most closely involved in the development and the evolution of the CSCE process from about 1973 to the moment when I left Belgrade for Paris, in 1977.
Then, one Paris evening, in the middle of winter, I came out of the Embassy late. It was snowing, and the thick, fresh flakes rapidly covered the sidewalks, the lawns, and the streets, as far as one could see. The falling snowflakes imposed an unusual silence on the busy corner of the Place de la Concorde where the US Embassy is located. I crossed the Embassy courtyard and pushed open the heavy gate from the dark courtyard onto the sidewalk outside. Just then—exactly then—the streetlights of Paris came on, illuminating the frail beauty of the entire scene. As always, all the lights came on at once—across the Place de la Concorde, and all the way up the Champs Elysees, as far as one could see, and in the other direction down the Rue de Rivoli. I looked up the Champs Elysees, and across the Place, to see who else was there to appreciate this unique and sudden spectacle, this magical moment when the snow was suddenly illuminated by the many lights of Paris. But, uniquely on this busy corner of this very busy city, there was no one around to share the moment. So I said to myself "that was for you, Jack, just for you!" My spirits brightened, and after that I did not look back.
Within the Embassy I became the Deputy Political Counselor, under Warren Zimmermann, who I had known socially in Washington. Warren had a beautiful house in rural Virginia, with a tennis court and a pond for rowing small boats. He and his wife invited numerous people on Sundays, and I had occasionally benefitted from their generous hospitality. They seemed to know everyone worth knowing. In Paris we collaborated on several reflective analytical papers which we sent to the State Department—we shared an interest in viewing events "strategically," and in writing such analyses. Warren

later became the head of the US delegation to the Vienna CSCE Follow-up Meeting, and I replaced him there when I first arrived as Ambassador to the CSCE. After that he became the US Ambassador to Yugoslavia, as that country fell apart in civil war. Unfortunately, Warren passed away some years ago. He was regarded by all who knew him as an unfailingly nice and intelligent person, and I always valued his friendship.

I learned a great deal about the diplomatic profession in that position in Paris—it was the first time I had a normal assignment in an American Embassy, and Paris was an orderly, model European society where the US Embassy had an important role. And then, years later, when I replaced Zimmermann in Vienna, I was arriving to take up a different role, as the US Ambassador to the CSCE Negotiations on military Confidence and Security-Building Measures (CSBMS). But we were both operating within the broad scope of the CSCE. And Zimmermann later came back to Vienna, as an observer, when Yugoslavia was coming apart because of the civil wars there, and in the CSCE we were being lobbied by representatives of the different Yugoslav republics who were clamoring for recognition and acceptance into the CSCE as individual states. Zimmermann's book, "The Last Ambassador," is about that period; he was the last US Ambassador to Yugoslavia.

Europe and the Communists, 1977-85

I have never been very ideological; I am more of a pragmatic sort of person, looking for what seems best, finding solutions that work, developing relationships with people who seem worthwhile and friendly, respecting the views of others. I have never belonged to a political party, though I have held more significant positions, in Washington and overseas, under Republican administrations. My basic political independence has usually worked for me, though, I readily admit, not always. It is sometimes useful to be identified with one political party or tendency.

In Paris I realized that I was in the real world, unlike the isolated diplomatic world of international negotiations, and that it was, as the CIA Station Chief once told me, "a city of dangers, a city of temptations." Things were very political there, and I could see the politics evolving before my eyes. My French was very good, and became better—there were times when I was assumed to be French. And the result of all this was that three years later I returned to Washington as the Director of the Office of Western European Affairs, the "Harvard of the Regional Offices" as it was known in the State Department at that time. It is the office which oversees US relations with many of the countries of Western Europe, with a focus on the Latin countries.

It was the period when Washington was warily watching the rising popularity of the Communist parties in many West European countries—France, Italy, Greece and Portugal—and there was widespread apprehension that Communists would enter governments somewhere in the region. Time magazine did an anxious cover story on the phenomenon, showing a map with much of Europe colored in red.

It had been a long-standing pillar of US policy toward Europe that Communist parties should not enter governments anywhere in Western Europe. US policies were shaped to oppose such a development, which many people in Washington thought would lead to further Communist advances. We actively discouraged the West European governments from including Communists. And then, suddenly, Communists did indeed enter a West European government, when Francois Mitterrand was elected President of France and included several Communist ministers in his cabinet. And this was not just any country—it was France, a Permanent member of the UN Security Council, a (somewhat maverick, it is true) NATO Ally with its own nuclear weapons, and with broad influence throughout the world.

In the new Republican Administration of President Ronald Reagan, many people were perplexed and concerned; some American companies in France were nationalized, and new investors hesitated or simply cancelled out. I was often called upon to "explain" this new political phenomenon; many Americans simply could not understand this French move, and considered it somehow directly hostile to the US. The period seemed to echo the post-war Communist takeovers in Eastern Europe, and this caused real concern in Washington.

President Ronald Reagan nominated a conservative Republican banker, Evan ("Van") Galbraith, who was right-wing icon William F. Buckley's life-long best friend and co-founder of the conservative National Review magazine, to be his Ambassador to France, and Galbraith walked into my office in Washington to prepare for his assignment in Paris.

Van Galbraith and I hit it off personally right away, and I even got to know Buckley on a friendly basis when he organized an elaborate swearing-in party for his friend, who he had proposed to Reagan for the post in France. Galbraith and I were both from Yale, we talked the same language, laughed at the same things, and had the same sense of bemusement about the human condition—or something like that. And in the end he refused all the distinguished candidates for the very senior career position as his deputy, and invited me to go back to Paris as the Deputy Chief of Mission (DCM), the US Minister to France. This was the title held by Benjamin Franklin and Thomas Jefferson during their time as representatives of the USA in Paris, and the US mission in Paris was America's biggest overseas post. It was an offer I could not refuse, the State Department grudgingly accepted the idea, and I went back to Paris just two years after I had left, this time as the supervisor of the entire US Mission.

Two days before I arrived in Paris, my predecessor there was the subject of a full-fledged assassination attempt. The would-be assassin emptied his pistol at his target, just outside the official residence of the Deputy Ambassador, which I then took over as my home. As a result of this attack, the whole time I was in Paris—all three years—I circulated in an armored limousine and was followed everywhere by a follow-car with two French police inspectors armed with sub-machine guns. While I was the Deputy Ambassador, our senior military attaché was assassinated in a pistol attack outside his apartment, and our Consul General in Strasbourg was almost killed in a similar attack. There were also bombings, and other incidents, including a mysterious plot to introduce a bomb into the Embassy's underground garage—the bomb exploded in the street, killing two French police explosives specialists.

The fact that the Communists were included in Francois Mitterrand's government turned out to be a non-event, historically speaking. They made mistakes like anyone else, and were widely criticized, and in the end the Party did not gain anything from the experience. Washington's fears turned out to be unfounded. In fact, the French communists lost popularity by participating in the government—it was a period when Communist regimes were having their problems everywhere—and they never really recovered. Participation in the Mitterrand government was a sort of high-water-mark, not just for the French Communists, but for Communist parties throughout Western Europe; afterwards they were all marginalized, and later the disappearance of the USSR left them without any credibility at all.

While I was in Paris I was host for a visit by the Vice President, George H. W. Bush, because Galbraith was away sailing across the Pacific, and we also had a visit by President Reagan, so I had occasion to meet him. Paris is one of those places where everyone visits eventually, and I got to know a lot of people.

Washington and the Pentagon

My tenure in Paris was a significant experience in many ways—both political and managerial—and when Galbraith left the government I was recruited by the well-known conservative US defense official, Richard Perle, who was sometimes called the "Prince of Darkness" because of his deep suspicions of the hostile intentions of America's enemies, to take a senior Pentagon position as Deputy Assistant Secretary of Defense for Europe. I knew Perle both from Chevy Chase Village, the elegant Washington suburb where we both lived, and also from his many visits to Paris for consultations with the French on defense issues. My predecessor in the Pentagon position, Ronald Lauder, was going to Vienna as the US Ambassador to Austria. So I spent a year as a resident fellow at Georgetown University revising my book, "To Helsinki," for publication, became friendly with Ron Lauder, and then moved to the Pentagon to replace him when he left for Vienna.

One day while I was the Deputy Assistant Secretary of Defense for Europe, the Soviets shot a US officer on an official patrol in Berlin, and prevented his Sergeant from giving him emergency assistance. The officer died, needlessly, from loss of blood, and officials in the Defense Department—and throughout the US Government—were outraged. We sought, but never received, an apology from the Soviet Union for this totally unjustified shooting, and the whole episode left bitter feelings throughout the US military.

This incident later became a building block for me, as I put together the first "Military Doctrine Seminar," in the context of the CSCE discussions of what had come to be called, by this time, "Confidence and Security Building Measures (CSBMs)" as opposed to simple "Confidence Building Measures (CBMs)," as we had called them during the original CSCE negotiations.

I served for two years as the Deputy Assistant Secretary of Defense for Europe, the key Pentagon official for Europe. I made many useful contacts in the defense world, including Cap Weinburger, the

Secretary of Defense, and Will Taft, his Deputy—I traveled frequently with each of them. And after a couple of years in my position I was held in some respect in the defense establishment. At one point I was invited to go over to the State Department for a meeting with John Whitehead, the Deputy Secretary of State, who I did not know. Whitehead had been Chairman of Goldman Sachs for many years, and was very widely respected as Deputy to George Shultz, the Secretary of State. Whitehead asked me to return to the State Department to take up a new position, which would have Ambassadorial rank, and which would be responsible for policies with respect to technologies—how to follow their development and control how they would be used, whether and how they could be exported or shared with other countries, etc. The position was, it must be said, very much in advance of its time—later this function became crucial as new technologies began to be the very cutting edge of economies around the world. Somehow people in the State Department thought that my position in the Pentagon (or perhaps my pioneering use of computers to track CSCE performance in Europe?) had given me an understanding of this field of high technologies, which was not entirely wrong. I hit it off personally with Whitehead, and asked him if I could think about the idea, and he gave me some time to do that.

Almost immediately after I got back to the Pentagon from that meeting I had a call from Weinburger. He must have been informed, somehow, of my meeting with Whitehead, and dialed the number himself, because when I picked up the phone in my office he was on the line. He said he knew I was being recruited to go back to the State Department, and asked me to stay on in the Pentagon. He said basically that he needed me there. I had traveled several times with Weinburger—I was, after all, responsible for Europe, and he loved to travel to Europe, where the US had a huge range of defense interests. He also liked to discuss defense issues with intellectuals who had original views on them, and had on occasion asked me to set up discussion sessions with "defense intellectuals" in Europe. This was something interesting to do in Paris, because the French tended to have more out-of-the-box ideas on defense issues than other people in Europe. One time we had a dinner in a private room at the famous Parisian restaurant-night club, Maxim's, where I assembled a small group of French "defense intellectuals," for a free-wheeling discussion of defense issues with only Weinburger and myself on the US side.

I felt I could not walk out on Weinberger after he had made such a personal appeal for me to stay. So I called Whitehead back and said that unfortunately I did not think I could accept his offer at that time. This was a major career mistake—one of many I have made and regretted over the years—but I did make friends with John Whitehead, and maintained a friendly relationship with him over many years, until he passed away recently. He was one of the two Honorary Co-Chairmen—along with my longtime friend George Russell—of the organization I founded in Geneva many years later, called the "Business Humanitarian Forum," which advocates responsible and sustainable business management practices.

As it turned out, Weinburger left the Pentagon shortly after this episode, as did Richard Perle, and I was left in a situation where there was a lot of fierce, unpleasant, bureaucratic competition for influence. Fortunately I knew Will Taft, the courtly Deputy Secretary of Defense, quite well from traveling with him, and as the Acting Secretary of Defense he named me, briefly, to be the Acting Assistant Secretary replacing Perle. I also got to know Frank Carlucci again, when he came into office as Weinberger's successor; years earlier we had served on a State Department panel together when he had been in the Foreign Service.

While I was in the Pentagon I became friends with General Colin Powell, the Chairman of the Joint Chiefs of Staff, Condoleezza Rice, who at the time was the senior Pentagon expert on Soviet military forces, and Mike Huffington, who was my direct colleague as another Deputy Assistant Secretary. I also saw Ron Lauder when traveling in Europe with Fred Ikle, and got to know Richard Armitage, another senior Pentagon official at that time. But when Weinburger left the Pentagon, and the other officials I had been working with—including Fred Ikle and Perle—also started leaving, I realized that I had to get back to my regular career path.

I knew that an Ambassador would have to be appointed to carry out the next round of negotiations on Military Confidence and Security Building Measures, a key item on the CSCE agenda, so I went to see a friend in the State Department's European bureau, Charlie Thomas, a wonderful person and loyal colleague who later passed away, and asked if the bureau would support me for that position, or if they had another candidate in mind. With my past experience in the CSCE, plus my recent job in the Pentagon, I thought I would be unassailable as a candidate to head the US delegation to this new negotiation on CSBMs. I got the job, was confirmed by the Senate after a perfunctory hearing (this was a pretty obscure position from the Congressional perspective) and was sent to Vienna as Ambassador and negotiator on the CSCE's Military Confidence and Security-Building Measures (CSBMs). I was back in the CSCE after almost ten years' absence.

Vienna, 1989

When I arrived in Vienna I paid a courtesy call at the Austrian Foreign Ministry, a mini-version of the sort of presentation of credentials which Ambassadors do when they first arrive in the capital where they are accredited. I was received by a senior Austrian official and we chatted politely about the CSCE and the prospects for a new agreement on military confidence-building measures. When it was about time for me to go, my host surprised me by saying: "You know you are not the first Ambassador Maresca to present his credentials to the Foreign Ministry in Vienna." I confessed that I did not know of any other Ambassador Maresca. The official told me that a previous Ambassador Maresca had come to Vienna in 1815 to represent the Kingdom of Naples at the Congress of Vienna! He had been transferred to the assignment in Vienna from St. Petersburg, where he had been the Ambassador of the Kingdom of Naples to Russia. I left this meeting with a feeling that, after all, perhaps I was not as badly suited for a diplomatic career as I had thought!
I had an excellent delegation in Vienna, including Bob Frowick, a senior foreign service officer who could well have been the Head of Delegation himself, and who later became an Ambassador and a key senior official in the effort to rebuild from the physical and social destruction following the wars in former Yugoslavia. Bill Harris was also a big support, and later we were joined by Rudy Perina, who I knew from the NATO office in the State Department. Perina went on to be Ambassador to Moldova, and Harris became a key senior official, advising the US commanding general during the post 9/11 war in Afghanistan.
Things started slowly in Vienna, but as summer approached we began to hear stories of unusual events in the East. And soon these events became clearer. There were hundreds of East German vacationers in Budapest, seeking exit visas to cross the border into Austria. They were demanding their rights under the Helsinki Final Act, which reaffirms the commitments of the Universal Declaration of

Human Rights, including the provision that "Every person has the right to leave any country, and to return to his own." Hungary had a bilateral treaty with East Germany under which it could only grant exit visas to East German citizens after requesting the approval of the East German government, which never granted it. But after careful consideration the Hungarian Government decided on this occasion that its obligations under the Helsinki Final Act over-rode its bilateral agreement with East Germany, and granted the visas requested by these hundreds of East German citizens!

And so these East Germans hurried across the border into Austria as quickly as they could, even abandoning their miniature East German Trabant cars by the side of the road and hitch-hiking to the border. Once in Austria, they made their way as fast as they could to the West German Embassy in Vienna; the West German policy was to grant a passport to anyone who was German. So all these East Germans immediately became West Germans, and entered whole new lives! The queue at the German Embassy in the center of Vienna stretched around the corner, and the joy of these people was astonishing, even though they had left everything behind—homes, possessions, careers, relatives. There was a clear sense that something important was beginning in Europe, and that things would be changing very fast. I later described this incident, and something of its significance, in an article called "The CSCE at its Inception; 1975 in Myth and Reality," (2) which I wrote in 2005 for the "OSCE Yearbook," published at the Center for OSCE Research at the University of Hamburg. (This article is included as an Annex to this book.)

This incident was followed by a huge assault by East German tourists on the West German Embassy in Prague, where they climbed over the walls, and were sheltered for a period of time in the Embassy gardens before they were granted safe passage by the Czech government to exit the country with their new West German passports. These people, too, immediately became West German citizens.

In the midst of these stirring events, there was a meeting in Berlin of all US Ambassadors in Europe, to exchange observations and experience, and to review developments in the East. Almost all the

Ambassadors present thought this was a passing episode, similar to some previous occurrances. But there were three dissenting voices—Henry Grunwald, Vernon Walters and myself. I was pleased to find myself in agreement with these two senior figures, since they were the most experienced observers of the USSR and Europe at the meeting. Grunwald, who was Jewish and born in Vienna, had fled with his parents when Austria was annexed by Hitler. He had been the long-time Editor-in-Chief of Time magazine, and a respected expert on Europe, who was serving as the US Ambassador in Vienna. Walters was a legendary linguist and figure in US foreign relations, who served as Director of the CIA and Ambassador to the United Nations. At the time of this meeting he was Ambassador to the Federal Republic of Germany. We three thought there were important differences in the current episode, and that the Soviets would be unable to contain it. Since I was a negotiator on military issues I had the right to use Air Force planes for official travel, so I offered Grunwald a lift on my plane and we returned to Vienna together.

Back in Vienna, I proceeded with my colleagues to organize the first CSCE "Military Doctrine Seminar," to be conducted in the context of the negotiations on military confidence-building measures. I went to Washington and had a private meeting with General Colin Powell, the Chairman of the Joint Chiefs of Staff, who by that time was an old friend. He joked when I walked into his office that his staff had warned him to be cautious and not to accept anything I might propose. But I persuaded him anyway, and he agreed to come to the military doctrine event. And because he agreed to come, all the Chiefs of Staff, of all the military forces of the CSCE participating states, accepted to come, and the event looked like it would be a truly ground-breaking experience.

It also appeared to be somehow in tune with what was going on at the popular level; the Cold War was clearly winding down—people on both sides of the division between East and West in Europe were tired of it, and wanted more normal relations. The whole of the East was in turmoil, and the Communist regimes were facing the most serious threats to their existence that they had ever known. It seemed very timely that the chief military officers of the countries of Europe and North America should come together, in professional respect and even friendship, to exchange views and experience, and to create an atmosphere of mutual respect and a new concept of cooperation among themselves. The context of the CSCE was uniquely relevant for the kind of East-West dialogue which everyone wanted and considered necessary at this time, and our negotiation in Vienna was an appropriate "venue" for such dialogue and face-to-face discussion, particularly about military issues.

Everything in Europe was changing rapidly. I traveled to one East European country for an official visit, and paid a call on the Chief of Staff of the armed forces. He said to me, "We are a small country which has been badly used by history." This seemed to reflect opinions throughout Eastern Europe. And at the same time the ability of the USSR to control these areas was crumbling. We knew, for example, that Soviet troops stationed in Poland were sneaking out of their bases at night to steal cabbages from farmers' fields. They were hungry. How could an army in such condition be in control of half of Europe, and threatening the other half?

I took the train back to Vienna from that visit, alone, leaving my plane to take my delegation colleagues home a day later. It was refreshing to cross this still-divided Europe, where I had been born and where I had spent so much of my adult life, and to appreciate its special atmosphere. The train slowed and stopped at a small town just before the border with Austria, and young girls came to the windows with flowers in their hair, selling bunches of lilacs. It was spring. I was almost in tears; this was the timeless Europe I was so fond of, which I have carried with me, always. And one could feel that the long-standing division of this Europe was coming to an end, that it would soon, once again, be one continent, with its many languages and nationalities and its somehow common culture.

The author in Vienna in 1990.
© John J. Maresca, 1990.

When General Powell arrived in Vienna I arranged a private dinner at my residence for him and the Soviet Chief of Staff, a unique event recounted in Powell's autobiography, "An American Story". The next day, to ensure that Powell met privately with each Chief of Staff from every Warsaw Pact country, in the short time he had available, I arranged at my residence a very special sort of luncheon, with a separate table for each Warsaw Pact country (except the USSR, which was not invited in view of the private dinner I had arranged the previous evening). I had one course served at each table, and by pre-arrangement, Powell, Condi Rice, and I moved from one table to another for each course. These senior generals were amused, and also very proud to have private meetings with the Chairman of the Joint Chiefs of Staff of the USA. Powell was graceful and friendly, and everyone present understood the significance of this ritual. The European equation was changing before our eyes, and nothing would stop this accelerating change.

And this first Military Doctrine Seminar, held from January 16—February 5, 1990, was a great success. I published an article on it, called "Thinking Beyond the Assumptions of the Past," and that title pretty well captured the spirit of the meeting. We looked at many basic military issues, such as how soldiers are instructed to control their weapons (Loaded or unloaded? Pointing forward or pointing down? Pointing down, which was the basic Western rule, is far safer), and we reviewed how defense budgets are presented to national legislatures for explanation, questioning and political control. The Eastern countries did all this in a very secretive way, and this discussion, with presentations by Western experts, was an eye-opener for them. I invited the official from the Pentagon who was responsible for presenting to Congress the proposed budget of the Department of Defense—which consists of many volumes of facts, figures and justification for necessary expenditures—and his presentation was fascinating for the defense officials from other countries.

There were two negotiations going on in parallel in Vienna at that time. The one which was considered the more important one in Washington was the negotiation on Mutual and Balanced Force Reductions (MBFR) in Europe, which was seeking concrete agreed force reductions on the basis of "balance" between the two sides. This was very difficult because it meant essentially that the Eastern side would have to make bigger reductions than the Western side. Military planners are always loath to have smaller forces in proportion to their potential enemies, or to reduce their forces more than their potential opponent does. The US Delegation for those negotiations was headed by a political appointee, Jim Woolsey. Woolsey and I were both from Yale, but I think he felt there was a kind of professional competition between us. He later went on to be the Director of the CIA, while I left the government. The MBFR negotiations included only the delegations from the member countries of NATO and the Warsaw Pact.

And the other negotiation in Vienna was the one in which I was the head of the US delegation. This was about military Confidence and

Security-Building Measures (CSBMs), a subject which had been included in the Helsinki Final Act and was the established military component of the CSCE agenda, having produced more than one agreement since Helsinki. This negotiation included delegations from all the states which were participants in the CSCE, even the neutrals and the mini-states. The membership in these two negotiations became relevant later, as developments in the East evolved into a more important denouement, requiring the attention of the highest levels of government and a high-level political, even historic, response by the members of the two military alliances in Europe.

And, indeed, it soon became apparent that the Europeans wanted the full CSCE to be re-convened, to take account of the changes which were happening before our eyes, to prepare a new Summit-level gathering to reflect the significance of the historical moment we were seeing taking form, and to lay the basis for peaceful relations in Europe. Phrases like "a common European home," and "creation of a peaceful order in Europe," were used to describe the objectives of such a meeting.

The Soviet President, Mikael Gorbachev, proposed such a new summit meeting of the CSCE to President Francois Mitterrand at their meeting in Kiev in December of 1989, and Mitterrand immediately supported this idea. There was recognition all around that events were moving swiftly, that the issue of possible German reunification was looming up, that the entire European balance was changing, and that measures were needed to ensure that the coming evolution would happen peacefully.

So the CSCE was indeed re-convened, taking advantage of the existing format of delegations accredited to the CSBM negotiations, to prepare for a new CSCE summit, to take place in Paris. My responsibilities were expanded to represent the US in this broader negotiation as it took form. The new set of negotiations was amorphous at the outset, but we soon learned that we were headed toward a new Helsinki-style summit signing, where the participating states would recognize, at the highest level, the changes which were taking place in Europe, and prepare the ground for a new chapter in the history of the continent.

The French, who were planning to host this new CSCE summit event, sent a senior-level negotiator to Vienna to encourage the delegations there to think in the lofty terms of the end of the Cold War, to draft a document which would fit the historic nature and context of the coming conference and would be signed at the summit level in Paris. The new French negotiator was Pierre Morel, a senior diplomat with historic perspectives, who made it clear from the time of his arrival that Paris wanted a forward-looking and inspiring text for President Francois Mitterrand, and the other Chiefs of State, to sign. In fact, before the end of the negotiations Morel sent around to all the heads of delegation in Vienna a copy of the poem by W.H. Auden entitled "Embassy," which focuses on the essential role of diplomats in negotiating and preventing wars. The French clearly wanted the Paris Summit meeting of the CSCE to become known in history as the meeting which would end the possibility of war in Europe.

The challenge presented to the negotiators was stunning: in a few months we were to produce not only the text of an historical declaration reflecting the extraordinary changes taking place and the commitment of all the Chiefs of State to cooperate in ensuring that these changes would be peaceful and would be respected by all the states of Europe and North America. In addition, we were also to develop some on-going institutional elements which would stabilize this process and permit cooperation on common problems. The evolution which was about to start would unfold over the following years, dramatically changing the European map, and the Chiefs of State wanted to ensure that it would take place peacefully and democratically.

We, the negotiators in Vienna, began this work from point zero; we had no existing guidelines or concepts to work with at the opening of this challenging process, so we all probed our capitals for inspiration and ideas. In Washington my key point of contact became Bob Zoellick, who was a special assistant to Secretary of State Jim Baker, and was responsible for watching over a number of on-going issues of special interest to the Secretary. Zoellick was new to the State Department, but understood very well the complexity of the negotiations and the key issues involved, and he was able to ensure a close connection to the political leadership in Washington. He perceived the potential significance of the work we were doing in Vienna. Without such a channel it would have been difficult for me to confidently move the negotiating process forward, since once again I was negotiating without any real instructions. But I was used to this, and to being creative and working with only minimal guidance. Zoellick was the ideal connection in these circumstances, and of course over the years he became a senior figure in Washington and ultimately served as President of the World Bank.

On November 9, 1989, the East German government opened the gates in the Berlin Wall, and Germans from both halves of Berlin poured joyously through the gates to see the other side. Half of Berlin was sitting on the Wall, chanting slogans, and there were heart-rending reunions among relatives who had not seen each other for decades. The population began hacking away at the wall, which tumbled into pieces that were carried away as souvenirs.

The barbed wire fence which had cut across farmers' fields to form the border between Austria and Hungary was demolished and removed. One day my Austrian colleague and friend, Helmut Liedermann, sent me a souvenir—a box in which I found a tangled spool of the barbed wire which had formed part of the barrier between East and West throughout the Cold War, stretched along the border between Austria and Hungary. Many years later I installed that tangled bit of barbed wire in the library of the United Nations University for Peace, in Costa Rica, where I was the Rector, with an inscription recounting that it had been, for so long, a part of the barrier dividing East and West in Europe.

Slowly, farmers on both sides of the frontier began again to plow their fields which crossed over to the other side of what had, since the end of the Second World War, been the East-West dividing line, crossing Europe from the Baltic Sea to the Mediterranean.

At the same time, and in reaction to these events, we began negotiating another document, which eventually was called—very modestly—the "Joint Declaration of 22 States." This was to be a simple declaration, by the member states of NATO and the Warsaw Pact, that the Cold War was over. It would be a kind of low-key, ersatz peace agreement whose significance would be that it would officially conclude the Cold War. This negotiation was limited to the countries that belonged to the two military alliances which had confronted each other throughout the Cold War, and was built on the broadly-shared view that the Cold War had, in fact, ended.

This declaration states that the countries concerned affirm "the end of the era of division and confrontation," and "are no longer adversaries." The document commits the signatories to peaceful relations: "None of their weapons will ever be used except in self defense." Although this was not known when we began this negotiation, one of the national delegations at the table, that of the German Democratic Republic, would not complete this negotiation, nor the Vienna conference as a whole, because during the course of our negotiations it would be reunited with the other half of Germany—that seemingly impossible event for which the door was held open in the negotiation of the Helsinki Final Act, many years before.

The "Joint Declaration of 22 States" was thought of by its negotiators as a CSCE-related document, but was attached to the MBFR Agreement because of the more limited list of signatories, and it became separated from the CSCE historical track. But re-reading it, even today, makes its origin in the CSCE negotiations clear, and its relationship to the CSCE should not be lost. It is a unique historical document, as important historically as the peace agreement concluding any other war.

The Cold War was a long and difficult period which fortunately never burst into a major military confrontation. But millions of people suffered during this confrontation, and some died because of it, so the act of concluding the conflict was as important historically as other peace agreements of the past. Because this document is not well known, I am including it as an annex to this book. It is interesting to read it, these many years later, and to be reminded of just how significant these changes were for Europe at the time. (3)

The disappearance of The German Democratic Republic meant a small change in the area where the US delegation was seated in the CSCE. The seating of delegations in the CSCE has always been something of an anomaly. At the outset, at Dipoli in Helsinki, the two German delegations let it be known, privately, that they wished to sit next to each other. However, in the French alphabetical order which is normally used for such seating, this would have meant that the two Germanies, known by their French name of "Allemagne," would be seated immediately next to Austria, known as "Autriche," which understandably did not want to be seated in a row along with the two Germanies. To resolve this problem, George Vest, on behalf of the United States, offered to have the US delegation known, in the French alphabetical order, as "Amerique, Etats-unis de." This put the US in between East Germany and Austria, and everyone was happy. So for years the US delegation had been sitting next to the delegation of the German Democratic Republic—without any negative effects. In fact, we always got along quite well with our GDR diplomatic neighbors—sharing jokes and useful conference information.

But one day, at the end of a regular session of the conference, my GDR colleague shook my hand, saying in a very courteous tone how much he had appreciated working with me. I told him the same thing. Diplomacy is a peculiar profession; feelings of mutual respect—even friendships—take form in the most unlikely and inhospitable circumstances, and among the most disparate partners. We went thru a moving goodbye, and the next day, October 3, 1990, Germany was reunified, and my neighbor, along with the sign in front of his place at the negotiating table, had disappeared. Overnight, the German Democratic Republic, one of the original signatories of the Helsinki Final Act, which was, importantly, about Germany, had ceased to exist.

Europe at the time of the Paris CSCE Summit of 1990: The member states of NATO are shown in blue, including reunited Germany, and the member states of the Warsaw Pact are shown in red.
© Kolja21. Source: Wikimedia Commons. Licensed under CC BY 3.0
(s. https://creativecommons.org/licenses/by/3.0/deed.en)

Preparing the Paris Summit of 1990

The broad CSCE negotiations which were aimed toward the anticipated summit-level conference in Paris soon fixed on a name for the document we were developing. At the suggestion of the French, it was to be called the "Charter of Paris for a New Europe," which pretty well captured the sense of history we all thought was appropriate.
The focus of the negotiations was very different from what it had been during the negotiation of the Helsinki Final Act; there was now broad agreement on the basic underlying concepts, both within national societies and among independent states. But it was assumed that the "New Europe" which was emerging—one based on universal concepts of human rights, independence of states, and representative governments, would need some new structures to ensure stability, especially during what would surely be a period of adjustment following the long decades of the Cold War.
Ideas for such structures were developed hastily, without a lot of prior planning or consideration, and were put forward by a number of national delegations. We did not have time for the sort of careful preparatory process which I had observed at NATO before the original CSCE, and we basically had to pick and choose among the ideas which were put forward, and try to identify the ones which seemed most likely to be both useful and also achievable. That is, they had to be concepts that would gather a full consensus in the short time we had available to prepare for the Paris meeting. They could not duplicate existing structures, and they could not infringe on any sensitive areas, since that would make consensus impossible, and consensus was the single decision-making procedure used in the CSCE.
I was in a unique position, since all delegations looked to the USA to take the lead in this situation. So I learned to be creative, and asked a number of delegation heads—the ones who were clever,

honest and respected—to take on different leadership roles, on specific issues which had to be resolved in concrete agreements. In the end, and with some compromising all around, these new CSCE structures and institutions were born, and have grown into substantial organizations pursuing a wide range of international efforts, from election monitoring to observing of military activities, to special functions of all kinds. Some of these have proven to be more useful than others; for example, the possibility for the OSCE to send observers to conflict regions, or regions of potential conflict, has become very useful and appropriate, and this possibility has been used, importantly, in the events that have taken place in Ukraine. The fact that the OSCE could supply observers in this situation, and that they were accepted as legitimate by all the parties involved, was perhaps unique, and resulted from the agreements reached in these negotiations.

In Vienna we began to receive representatives of the Baltic States, requesting recognition of their independent statehood through their admission to the conference. The Soviet Union was in turmoil, and the three Baltic States, which had never accepted their forced incorporation into the USSR, were making various moves to establish, confirm or reassert their independence. They were soon to formalize their independent status, as the Soviet Union began to crumble.

The Soviets were, of course, hostile to any such efforts, and maintained a strict opposition to any contact with the Baltic State representatives, and especially to any form of participation by the Baltic States in the work of the CSCE. But the positions of other countries were more nuanced, and the US position of principle was very clear: Washington had never recognized the forced incorporation of the three Baltic States into the Soviet Union. From the time when the Baltic States were absorbed into the Soviet Union the US had continued its principled position. This position had been reiterated on several occasions by senior-level government statements in Washington, and these states even continued to maintain diplomatic missions in the US capital, which were officially recognized as such by succeeding American Administrations.

One of the senior representatives from the Baltic countries who came to Vienna, and to the Paris CSCE Summit meeting, was Lennart Mery, who later served for many years (1992-2001) as the President of his country, Estonia. He was the natural leader among this group who were basically lobbying for broader recognition of their independent statehood. Since the United States had never recognized the absorption of the Baltic States by the USSR, Mery and his colleagues were, for us, legitimate national representatives, as a matter of principle. The Scandinavian countries had accepted the takeover of the Baltic states, but regretted this and felt a Nordic solidarity with them. My Swedish colleague, Rolf Ekeus, and I, along with the Norwegians, Leif Mevik and Jakken Bjorn-Lian, created a unique format for keeping the representatives of the Baltic States informed of developments in the Conference, which we called simply "The Friends of the Baltic States." This was an on-going device under which we regularly briefed the Baltic States representatives on developments in the Conference, got their views, and took them into account in our own national positions. Of course this was a purely informal arrangement; there was no way we could bring the Baltic States into the full CSCE, since all decisions were based on consensus, and the Soviets maintained their position that the Baltic states were part of the USSR.

Later, as the breakup of Yugoslavia advanced, we also faced diverse representatives of the different Yugoslav republics, all seeking to be recognized as sovereign states in the context of the CSCE. Some of them had previously been Yugoslav delegates in the CSCE, and knew the context very well—and we knew them personally. But we could not admit them to the conference because Yugoslavia was a member state. Early on, the CSCE sent observers to the combat zones in Yugoslavia, when fighting began, but there was little experience of such efforts, the observers were powerless to do anything, and this experiment was quickly terminated after some negative articles appeared in the European press, with photos showing the observers sitting comfortably on a terrace, "observing" the shelling of Dubrovnik.

We assembled for inclusion in the document we were preparing for the Paris summit a mix of commitments and mandates for new institutions, to monitor and support the kind of Europe which seemed to be emerging. Since the underlying political values had been established in the Final Act, they did not need to be re-negotiated, and the central concept for the Paris meeting was to make the CSCE into an on-going organization, or at least the beginning of such an organizational structure, and to give it the means for watching over events in Europe which were relevant to its recognized areas of interest, and where on-going watchfulness would be useful to Europe as a whole.

There were a variety of ideas for monitoring of human rights, free elections and democratic values, as well as a nascent concept for responding to conflicts or potential conflicts in the region, and for the use of observers in relation to such conflicts. It was assumed that there would be regular meetings of the CSCE at senior level, with some sort of standing group which would be available periodically and at short notice. Since that time these institutions have begun proving their value, with OSCE Observers now taking important roles in the events in Ukraine, as they have in other challenging conflict areas, and OSCE election monitors now routinely watching over elections in the OSCE area, including the USA. These missions are valuable even if they perhaps cannot always prevent wars from happening. The establishment of a special position of High Commissioner for National Minorities, with a permanent staff in The Hague, was intended as a mechanism for discreet political intervention in situations which look like they might lead to internal conflicts, in countries where there are ethnic or nationalistic tensions.

Surrounding these concepts were the usual national rivalries, competition for hosting of new institutions, and even fixed, sometimes competing, ideas about the titles of the new organizations, which derived from the original national proposals. All these factors required compromise and give-and-take.

At one stage during the preparations/negotiations for the Paris summit meeting of the CSCE, I received a visit in Vienna from Spencer Oliver, my old colleague from Washington and the Belgrade review meeting of the CSCE, who was the senior staff person for the Joint Congressional-Administration Helsinki Commission. Spencer and I were the same age, and were friendly veterans of many bureaucratic episodes. I gave a dinner in his honor at my residence, and invited a group of key Ambassadors.

During the dinner I spoke about the activities of the Helsinki Commission, which by this time had an extensive record of work related to the CSCE process which was very worthwhile, and Spencer had become one of the established figures in the overall CSCE landscape. At a certain point in the dinner conversation I proposed that the CSCE should have a parliamentary assembly, along the lines of the NATO parliament, a well-established element of NATO's political support which I had observed during my time in Brussels.

The idea immediately gained some backing around the dinner table—the Ambassadors clearly liked it. And as a result this body was indeed created by the Charter of Paris, and came into being shortly after the Paris summit. Spencer, who has for many years been the Secretary General of this parliamentary body, based in Copenhagen, recently invited me to sit in on one of their sessions as an observer, and I was fascinated by the lively debate, unvarnished criticism and innovation which I saw happening before my eyes. I think this Parliamentary Assembly is an under-appreciated asset for the OSCE process, and some thought should be given as to how to make better use of it, so that it can have more direct effect on the work of the OSCE.

The negotiation of the Paris document was much smoother than the negotiation of the Helsinki Final Act had been, many years earlier. For one thing the Soviet delegation, headed by Ambassador Yuri Deryabin, was much more civilized and easier to deal with. The objectives of the Soviet Union were also far closer to those of the Western countries than they had been during the original CSCE in Helsinki-Geneva-Helsinki. And the negotiations were more open, with a broad sense that we were all working together to construct something solid and in the interests of all the member states of the CSCE. In this situation the NATO group had a much smaller role, and met only to maintain the principle of Allied unity. And of course the European Union (EU) group was much more important, and sought to align their positions on all conference issues.

In fact, the final negotiating difficulties were not at all between East and West, as they had been during the Geneva negotiations, years before, but rather among Western countries, each of which had its pet ideas for the shape of the new international organization which was going to emerge after the Paris summit, and which would be the center for the CSCE's anticipated role as a broadly-based all-European organization. Some delegations were stuck on their national proposals and were unable to compromise easily, and the main compromising which was required was among the NATO member states. The issues which were disputed were not related to basic political differences, but were really more cosmetic—what to name a new institution, where it would be headquartered, etc. Each country had its own ideas on such matters, and political authorities back home wanted to claim credit. But these differences were just as strongly held as basic political positions, and agreements were surprisingly difficult to find.

So before one of the last meetings of the NATO group I devised a complex compromise arrangement among the varied positions of the Western allies, which touched on every significant part of the CSCE's broad agenda. My compromise proposal conceded certain things in some areas and took away things in other areas, and was designed to give every delegation something in the area that was most important for them. It was a delicate balance, involving all the remaining issues on the conference agenda, but if it worked, we would be able to conclude the negotiations.

I asked for the patience of the group while I explained all the elements of my complicated compromise proposal. Then I said that this was a package; if anyone tried to change some elements, the whole compromise package would fall apart. But if we could all accept it, we could conclude the negotiations and go to Paris. There was a moment of silence. I asked if the silence meant that we could all accept this compromise proposal, and there was a movement of nodding heads around the meeting room. The rotating Chairman asked if there was any objection to the proposal, and again there was silence, so he concluded that it was approved and the various elements would be presented in the different conference committees. In that moment we had resolved all the final problems, and the way was open to the Paris Summit.

On our way out of the meeting room I had a word with my British colleague, a brilliant but sometimes sharp-tongued diplomat who was creative and active in all aspects of the negotiations. I said to him, "Thanks for not suggesting changes in that compromise package—any changes and it would have fallen apart." And he replied: "I know a masterpiece when I see one."

1990—Bush and Gorbachev Go To Paris

Going to Paris for the summit-level signing of the "Charter of Paris for a New Europe," was of course a very rewarding moment—not just personally for each of us who had negotiated the document which was to be signed, but, more importantly, because of the very positive development we would celebrate there—a time when Europe was once again becoming a single continent, undivided by the political division which had been its central feature for almost half a century. The Paris document would specifically declare that the Cold War was over: "The era of confrontation and division of Europe has ended . . . The power of the ideas of the Helsinki Final Act have opened a new era of democracy, peace and unity in Europe."
The occasion would be very different from the somber mood which had dominated the Helsinki Summit in 1975. And for me, personally, it would not only be a satisfying return to the CSCE at Summit level, but also a return to a city where I had some previous experience. I knew President Mitterrand, and many of the senior French officials, personally from my time as American Minister to France.
But just before I left for Paris I got a telephone call from a senior official in the White House staff. He said that the White House would appreciate it if I would yield my place at the signing ceremony which was to take place at the Elysee Palace, so that a key US Senator could be present at that ceremony. In fact, there were to be three signing events in Paris: the signing of the "Charter of Paris for a New Europe," which would take place at the Kleber Conference Center being used for the 35 nation summit meeting and would include the chiefs of state or government of all the CSCE participating states, and two events which would take place at the Elysee Palace, the official residence of the President of France, to include only the member states of the Warsaw Pact and NATO. This second event would be for signature of the MBFR agreement, negotiated for the US by Jim Woolsey, and also of the "Joint Declaration of 22 States," which I had negotiated.

The "Joint Declaration of Twenty-Two States," which can only be found these days in conjunction with the "Treaty on Conventional Armed Forces in Europe," forms the link between the concrete commitments of the signatory states of that Treaty, and the larger political context of the CSCE/OSCE which is laid out in the Helsinki Final Act and the Charter of Paris. The "Joint Declaration of Twenty-Two States" has been obscured, but should rightly be attached to the Charter of Paris because it extends the significance of that document in a most important way—to the reductions in the military forces of each of the two alliances which had faced each other throughout the Cold War. But the Joint Declaration is usually left out since it is thought (incorrectly) to be unrelated and somehow not properly a document of the CSCE/OSCE, in view of the more limited number of signatories.

Insofar as what was called the "Cold War" was indeed a conflict, the Joint Declaration of Twenty-two States is the document that formally ended that conflict. It was signed at the Elysee Palace on November 19, 1990, officially ending the confrontation which had been maintained between the countries of the Warsaw Pact and NATO since the end of the Second World War. So it was a sort of peace treaty ending the Cold War.

I told the White House staff member who called me that it was a fundamental diplomatic tradition that the negotiator should be present when his Chief of State signs an international treaty or agreement. It has always been universally assumed that the negotiator should be there, just in case there are last-minute questions, or there is a need for clarification of some negotiating point. But the White House staff person who had called me insisted, saying the President would appreciate it, etc. (I actually doubt that the President even knew this was going on!) So, what could I do? I accepted the situation, and this White House request, as gracefully as I could, and was therefor not present when the Joint Declaration of Twenty-Two States, which I had negotiated on behalf of the United States, was signed at the Elysee Palace by President George H. W. Bush and all the other Chiefs of State of the members of NATO and the Warsaw Pact.

I have always thought that the White House Staff, to cover their tracks, then took my name off anything which had to do with that ceremony. I recently looked at the list of the US Delegation, for example, and found to my great surprise that my name was not listed! Of course I should have been there, as the person who had negotiated the document, and should have sat with the President during the proceedings. President Bush, who I knew personally from a number of meetings and events in the past, was always very courteous and friendly toward me, for example when he was Vice President and I hosted his visit to Paris because the Ambassador, Van Galbraith, was at the time sailing across the Pacific with Bill Buckley.

But Bush was famous for sending hand-written thank-you notes to people who had assisted in his visits, etc., and I never received anything from the White House acknowledging my role in negotiating the "Joint Declaration," which he signed, and preparing the "Charter of Paris," and the Paris Summit, a major international—even historical—event under his presidency. This was in spite of the fact that I corresponded with him, another fellow Yale man, on a number of occasions, after these events. So I think my name was just taken off the relevant documents in the White House as part of my incorrect exclusion from the "other" signature event which took place at the Elysee Palace. I am still just a little bitter about how this was handled, and how I was omitted from that signature event, especially since I knew Mitterrand and his associates from my days as the US Minister in Paris. So for me it would have been an important return. Regardless of this not-very-pleasant matter, the ceremonies for the signing of the "Charter of Paris," were very celebratory, and in retrospect perhaps overly optimistic. As President Bush said in his speech, "A continent frozen in hostility for so long has become a continent of revolutionary change." But, he added, "Europe is entering unknown waters." And indeed, many long-standing pillars of the European structure were crumbling. The USSR's stature had been reduced and it was entering what would prove to be a difficult period of post Cold-War adjustment, complicated very soon by the breakup of the country as it had existed for two centuries and more.

Gorbachev tried to put the best face on the situation, and the language of his speech echoed the same ideas the Western leaders were expressing. But the reality was that the USSR, and Russia, was entering a period of greatly diminished stature. The Warsaw Pact, Russia's key military alliance, was disappearing or even had already disappeared, Germany had been reunified, the Communist systems which had sustained Soviet domination of Eastern Europe for almost half a century were crumbling, and although we did not know it at the time, the USSR itself was about to break apart.

The general concept of adding to the CSCE's monitoring and oversight possibilities through the establishment in the Paris document of the first elements of an on-going CSCE organization with several new all-European institutions to strengthen democracy and peace, was a reaction to the way Europe was changing as the Cold War ended. These new institutions included an on-going CSCE Secretariat, at first located in Prague (and later moved to Vienna), a Conflict Prevention Center in Vienna, an Office for Free Elections in Warsaw, and the Parliamentary Assembly, based in Copenhagen. In addition, there was agreement that there should be regular meetings of a new "Committee of Senior Officials," as well as periodic meetings among Foreign Ministers. The general idea was to use the CSCE's new institutions to strengthen democratic forms of government (for example, thru election observations), and to be prepared to contain local violence and conflicts, if that should occur (for example, through the use of CSCE observers). Some local offices were later established in areas which were distant from the CSCE's center in Vienna, and these Missions continue to carry out a number of useful functions, reminding the local populations, as well as the political elites, of the Helsinki principles, and the follow-up functions of the OSCE.

The CSCE's Paris Summit saw a series of positive and optimistic speeches by national leaders, but at one point during the Summit events, Gorbachev recognized, the Estonian Leader, Lennart Mery, in the lobby of the great Parisian hall where the ceremonies were taking place. Mery was there as a specially-invited guest, along with representatives of the other Baltic States, under a special arrangement we (the so-called "Friends of the Baltic States") had negotiated with the French, and which the Soviet delegation head in Vienna, Yuri Deryabin, an expert on the Nordic countries, had accepted (the Soviet delegation, though they were informed, simply turned a blind eye to what was going on). Under this arrangement, the delegations of the three Baltic States were admitted to the public spaces of the Kleber Conference Center (but not to the conference hall itself) using name cards on which their country name was not specified—the space for "country" was simply left blank. The leaders of these Baltic States were therefor present in the hallways and outer reception rooms of the ornate Kleber Center, the location of the Conference, mingling with delegates and representatives of the press, and Secretary of State Baker met with the Foreign Ministers of the Baltic states on the Sunday before the conference.

However, when Gorbachev saw Mery, who was a well-known figure in his country, he immediately asked Mitterrand to have him and his associates from all three Baltic States, removed from the premises. Mitterrand directed his Foreign Minister, Roland Dumas, and the French security service to expel these representatives. From across the huge entry hall I saw the French security agents escorting the Baltic State representatives out of the conference building, and Mery shouted to me, saying they were being expelled. But there was literally nothing I could do about it, because it had been Gorbachev himself who had asked for their removal. Everything in the CSCE was subject to the consensus rule, so if one country objected to the presence of the Baltic States' representatives, the French hosts could not permit them to stay.

This incident took place quickly and was unannounced, and no head of state even had time to object. These senior representatives of the Baltic States were taken from the conference site to the French Foreign Ministry, where they met with Dumas. The Minister explained that the Soviet Union had objected to their presence in the conference, and under the CSCE's rule of consensus France, as the host country, was obliged to exclude them. This was done, and even the reception which the Baltic States organized near the conference site saw a limited participation.

Gorbachev reportedly cancelled a planned meeting with Vaclav Havel simply because he had met with a Baltic State representative. Other leaders were reluctant to challenge the Soviets over the status of these countries, even though some of their countries, including the US, maintained as a matter of principle that they had never recognized the Soviet annexation of these states, which had been independent before the Second World War.

In fact, however, the political situation in each of the Baltic states had been evolving rapidly during this period, and political elements in the Baltic capitals were organizing themselves against the continuing Soviet occupation. The local press was already very vocal and active, and these countries were openly challenging the continuation of their forced status as parts of the USSR. Their activities with respect to the CSCE were just one reflection of how events were evolving in the Baltic capitals.

The incident when Gorbachev insisted that the Baltic State representatives be expelled from the Conference was reported in some detail by newspapers in the region at the time, and was later recalled in the bimonthly publication "Diplomaatia," in 2005 by Riina Kionka, an associate of President Mery, who is now the Foreign Policy Advisor to the President of the European Council. Some Estonian press reports of the time are included in an annex to this book. (4)

It is worth noting that less than one year after their exclusion from the OSCE Summit in Paris, all three Baltic States were admitted as full members of the OSCE, and of the United Nations, following months of turmoil as the USSR crumbled and was dissolved. I believe our little-known efforts to bring the representatives of the Baltic States into the periphery of the Conference were timely and foresighted, and that this was one of the elements which encouraged them to pursue their struggle for recognition of their independence. Nonetheless, it remains that their treatment in Paris was disgraceful.

At the vast reception which followed the signing event for the Charter of Paris, I ran into my Swedish colleague, Rolf Ekeus, and we toasted, congratulating each other on what had been achieved in such a short time. "We all knew," he told me, referring to the negotiating process which led up to the Paris Summit, "That we were puppets in the Maresca Theatre."

Ekeus later arranged for me to be invited to Sweden to observe some special field activities by the Swedish Army, Navy and Air Force, a fascinating experience and an impressive demonstration of the capabilities of the very independent Swedish armed forces. He subsequently became the OSCE's High Commissioner for National Minorities.

As the Los Angeles Times reported on the eve of the Paris meeting, "'The Paris summit,' commented U.S. Ambassador Maresca, 'will really be a celebration of the end of the Cold War.'"

Presidents George H.W. Bush and Mikhail Gorbachev in 1990.
© RIA Novosti archive, image #330109. Foto: Yuryi Abramochkin.
Licensed under CC-BY-SA 3.0 (s. https://creativecommons.org/licenses/by-sa/3.0/deed.en)

Part III

Part III

Dissolution of the USSR—1991

Beginning in August of 1990, and continuing until December 12, 1991, all the republics which comprised the USSR declared their independence—one by one. The only exceptions were the Baltic States, which held to the principle that they had never ceased to be independent. But the Baltic States were increasingly treated as fully-independent states and were soon admitted to the OSCE as full-fledged members under a special and hastily-organized procedure. The situation with respect to membership of the OSCE became further complicated later, because of the disintegration of Yugoslavia, which was also beginning during this period, and which descended rapidly into a complex and vicious conflict.

On December 16, 1991, just one year after the Paris Summit meeting of the CSCE, it was finally confirmed officially that the Union of Soviet Socialist Republics (the USSR) had ceased to exist, and that the individual Republics from the USSR were independent states. This was the result not only of the general deterioration of the political unity of the USSR and the rejection of its Communist ideology, but also of the political and personal rivalry between Boris Yeltsin, President of Russia, the dominant republic in the USSR, and Mikhail Gorbachev, the President of the USSR. By withdrawing Russia from the USSR Yeltsin left it a hollow shell, and the official dissolution of the union was the inevitable result. As a practical matter Gorbachev no longer had a position, and he was the one who officially announced that the USSR had ceased to exist. Two days later Yeltsin moved into the office in the Kremlin which had previously been occupied by Gorbachev.

The break-up of the USSR came after a long period of decline and growing recognition that the Communist system, as well as its ideology and rationale, had lost its meaning, and that the ties which held the vast space together as a single state no longer had any purpose or validity. Each of the newly-independent states had its own identity, which was recognized and felt by the majority of the people. There was virtually no such feeling for the USSR, even though many people identified with the USSR, understood its importance, and took pride in its role as a world power.

This break-up was a totally unforeseen development, and it took years for the world to adjust. For those of us who were working directly with the Soviets, and then with Russia and the other newly independent states, it was a particularly challenging time, when almost anything, positive or negative, was possible. The world is very fortunate indeed that the worst possibilities—such as widespread civil war, or some nuclear incident—did not occur, and that the Russian leadership, and people, remained calm and controlled as a series of delicate and potentially catastrophic events unfolded. Miraculously, this historic change took place without developing into an East-West conflict, although smaller conflicts did emerge in different parts of the former USSR over the next decade, and later.

The restraint and steadiness of the administration of President George H.W. Bush, as well as the existence of the CSCE, were important factors which helped to ensure that this evolution took place peacefully. But there were many other side effects and adjustments that had to be made, and events in the region, even today, can be seen as parts of a continuing story which began with the break-up of the USSR, and had its roots in the history of the Russian Empire, how it was built, and how it evolved into the Soviet Union.

In my own area of responsibility the break-up of the USSR immediately posed the question of whether the "Newly Independent States from the Former Soviet Union"—or simply the "Newly Independent States," an appellation which sprang into use during the process of break-up and continued in use for a couple of decades after that— had the right to be members of the CSCE. Some delegates in Vienna, where the CSCE continued to meet regularly, as the "Committee of Senior Officials," took the view that this was an open question, and that each newly independent state would have to apply for membership in the CSCE, if they wished to do that. Others argued that some of these new states, which were not clearly "European," could not belong to the CSCE, which was, after all, a European body. This view would have split these newly independent states into "European" and "non-European" groups, with great potential for difficulties. And there were some diplomats who thought there should be tests or benchmarks for these new states to qualify for membership—regarding human rights practices, etc.

It had been agreed at the Paris summit that there would be regular, periodic meetings of the Foreign Ministers of the CSCE member states, and the second of these meetings was held in Berlin on June 20, 1991, just six months after the Paris Summit. The situation in Yugoslavia had deteriorated dramatically by then, and for the first time it looked very possible that the country would break up. The US position at the time was to support the continued unity of Yugoslavia, and I was instructed to get the CSCE meeting to issue a statement to this effect. But—here was the hooker—I was not to table a draft of such a declaration myself—it was not to be a US proposal. Instead, I was instructed to get the European Union countries to table it as their proposal, based on our US draft.

This looked challenging, but I set up a series of private meetings with the Ambassadors of each of the member states of the EU, one by one, mainly in my hotel room. In each case I handed the Ambassador our anonymous draft of such a resolution. That evening the EU Ambassadors had a working dinner, along with their Foreign Ministers, and agreed on our draft with just one word changed. The next day they tabled it in the full CSCE, and it was approved and issued as a CSCE statement.

But of course the effort to preserve Yugoslavia as a single state proved to be futile, and shortly after the EU had announced its support for a continuing state of Yugoslavia the German Foreign Minister, Hans-Dietrich Genscher, unilaterally recognized the independence of Slovenia, Austria's next-door neighbor, thus breaking the unity of the Europeans (and Washington) in favor of a continuation of the Yugoslav federation, and making the complete breakup of Yugoslavia only a matter of time. This episode reflected the confusion and disarray of the NATO allies, and the EU member states, at the time as to what might be the most desirable and least controversial way forward, in response to the Yugoslav wars.

And as we all know, the next few years were filled with savage warfare and horrific human suffering throughout the former Yugoslav lands.

An additional meeting of the CSCE Foreign Ministers was arranged in Moscow on September 10, 1991, on the eve of the previously scheduled CSCE meeting on the human dimension, also presided by Foreign Minister Genscher, for the purpose of accepting the three Baltic States as members of the CSCE. This was done by a simple exchange of letters, in view of their special status and strong support among the CSCE member states.

The next meeting of the CSCE Foreign Ministers was scheduled to take place in Prague on January 30-31, 1992, and the overall issue of the status of the newly independent states had to be resolved prior to that meeting so that any new foreign ministers who might be invited to participate could make their travel plans. As the meeting approached and discussions continued there was a growing assumption that, one way or another, these new states would send senior representatives to participate as they were accepted as CSCE members. Many national representatives took the view that, as a practical matter, these newly independent states were already members of the CSCE, since they had been a part of its establishment and history as component parts of the USSR, and this was also my personal view. The precedent of the Baltic States' admission was relevant, but not exactly the same, since some CSCE member states had never accepted that they were legally part of the Soviet Union. For this reason the acceptance of the Baltic States into the CSCE could not be considered a precise precedent.

In the lead-up to the Prague meeting I was visited by one Ambassador who told me that he had instructions to oppose the membership of one of the newly independent states in the CSCE. When I asked him why, he referred to reservations about the existing borders. I reminded him that these were the same borders all the member states had recognized throughout the history of the USSR, but he said that his country's position on the matter had always been subject to reservations.

I suggested that he seek urgent instructions which would permit him to join a unanimous decision in favor of admitting all the newly independent states to the CSCE at the same time. A decision on this would have to be taken the next day, and a national reservation on the membership of one new member would open a "Pandora's Box," leading to reservations of various kinds on all the new members. I argued that the interest of the conference and its participants was to retain all these new countries, which effectively had been members of the CSCE from the beginning because they had been parts of the USSR, one of the founding member states of the CSCE. Their continuing membership in the CSCE would be the best way to influence them, and to encourage them to adopt the same values and commitments which all other CSCE member states had already subscribed to. All of this would be important for the continuing stability of the region. The Ambassador left to seek instructions on the matter.

After he left I tried to find representatives of each of the newly independent states, as well as key Ambassadors from member countries, in order to ensure that there would be a smooth acceptance of these "new members" at the CSCE Meeting of Foreign Ministers which was to take place the next day. I informed Washington of what was going on, and of the assumption that all possible new members which had been parts of the USSR were eligible to belong to the CSCE as fully independent states if they chose to belong.

I spoke to most of the new Ambassadors, and there did not seem to be any other major potential problems. And the following day the Foreign Ministers of the existing member states unanimously decided to admit all of the newly-independent states from the former USSR as full members of the CSCE, at the same time. It was a significant moment; all the representatives of these new states were ceremoniously invited to join the meeting. There was a short break while national placards were arranged for each of the new members, and then the meeting re-convened with the representatives of the new members at the table. This was accompanied by loud and prolonged applause. A new Caucasus-Central Asian dimension had been created within the CSCE, which had previously been obscured by the fact that these new states were parts of the USSR, which clearly had its head and shoulders in Europe. The implications of this opening to the Caucasus and Central Asia were far-reaching, and even now, more than twenty years later, they have not yet been completely explored.

I did not specifically ask Washington for instructions on the question of membership in the CSCE for these newly-independent states—whether they should be accepted as members or not. Of course I kept the State Department informed of the steps which were going forward, the arrangements for acceptance of new members, and the fact that some of their Foreign Ministers were planning to come to Prague for the event. But my view was that these newly independent states had already been members of the CSCE, as parts of the USSR, one of the leading countries in the development of the Final Act, so they could not be excluded at this point. There was thus no policy issue for consideration, though Washington was informed and could have taken a different view at any time. But it was clear to me that membership of these newly-independent states in the CSCE would open many new possibilities for direct relations with them, something which was very much in the Western, and US interest. So the acceptance of these new members went forward, and some years later, in 2012, even Mongolia—which was never a part of the USSR—joined the OSCE, consolidating the Central Asian dimension of the organization.

Some in Washington were not happy with the admission of these newly-independent States to the CSCE, but when the war in Afghanistan obliged the US Army to use Central Asia for transit routes to supply US forces there (the army's "Northern Route"), it was useful to have a good basis for positive relations and cooperation with all these states. Central Asia is a "new" world region, with enormous potential for development, and the West has an important role to play there. I am attaching as an annex to this book my recent article about Central Asia, called "Foreign Devils on the Silk Road, Take Two," which appeared in Chinese in the Strategic Studies Report at Peking University, and in English in the "Baku Dialogues" review, published at ADA University in Baku, where I have been teaching

for the last year. This article is included as an annex to this book.
(10)
Following the decision to admit the newly-independent states as CSCE members, and the ceremonies as they took their places around the huge meeting table in the (now revised) alphabetical order, each one of the new representatives made a few remarks about being pleased to be a part of the CSCE, and about their country's commitment to respect the provisions of the Final Act. It was clear that the CSCE had opened a new dimension for its international role.

Just before the closing of this meeting the British delegate, whose Minister had already left to return to London, asked for the floor and noted that there was a conflict going on in the area, between two of the newly-admitted members—Armenia and Azerbaijan—that this conflict was over control of the territory of a mountainous region called Nagorno Karabakh, and that it was the CSCE's principal responsibility to seek to resolve such conflicts. All the representatives around the conference table immediately agreed, and there was a good deal of nodding of heads. There was a suggestion that the CSCE should organize a peace conference to settle this conflict. The delegate from Belarus offered his country's capital, Minsk, as the site for such a peace conference, which was unanimously accepted. The Chairman called for countries to volunteer to participate in the preparations for this peace conference in Minsk, and a number of country representatives, including myself, raised their hands. Thus it was that the so-called "Minsk Group" took form as the group of states which would prepare the conference on resolution of the conflict over Nagorno-Karabakh. Italy volunteered to provide a chairman for this group, which included Armenia, Azerbaijan, Belarus, Finland, France, Germany, Italy, Netherlands, Portugal, Russia, Sweden, Turkey and the USA.

Ambassador to the "Near Abroad"

On December 12, 1991, Secretary of State James Baker made a speech at Princeton University, where he had been a student from Texas, many years before. In this "Princeton Speech," he reviewed the implications of the break-up of the Soviet Union, which, along with the collapse of Communism, was a truly history-changing event, and the ways in which the US would move to ensure stability in the unpredictable period which was to follow, to promote democratic values and offer cooperation and support. It was important that the US response to the break-up of the USSR should be as calm and supportive as possible, and this speech was a significant review of the elements of this policy of restraint and supportiveness during an unpredictable period of change.

During this speech Baker said that the United States would "send our CSCE Ambassador" to the newly-independent states from the former USSR, to discuss their relations with the US, and to encourage them to cultivate democratic values.

I called and asked John Kornblum, who was then again my main contact in Washington, who Baker was referring to, since I had heard nothing of this idea. Kornblum told me that this special envoy would be me—that it was intended as a reward and a recognition of my role. So I began planning for this heavily symbolic mission, for which I never did receive any real instructions or guidelines. I was told very simply to explain the commitments of the Helsinki Final Act, which these new governments had just signed up to as independent states (but which they had been committed to from the beginning as parts of the Soviet Union, one of the original signatories), and to tell them that we would base our new bilateral relationships with these states on their respect for the commitments and values represented in the Helsinki Final Act.

And so I became the US Ambassador and Special Envoy to the Newly Independent States from the former USSR—the Ambassador to the Near Abroad. I was again given the use of an Air Force plane, this time big enough to carry a staff of specialists, and we planned to travel to all the new capitals in the vast former Soviet space—except for the Baltic states. Since Washington had never recognized the Soviet absorption of the three Baltic countries as legal, these were not "new" relationships for the US. So there was thought to be no need for such a visit to those countries. But other than these exceptions, I was instructed to visit all the "Newly Independent States" from the former USSR.

I undertook this mission in a spirit of adventure. As parts of the USSR these countries had been visited regularly by officials from the US Embassy in Moscow. The Embassy staff included diplomats who were assigned to cover events in each of these Soviet republics, and who visited them regularly. But now the situation was different, and the emphasis shifted toward the individual identities of these peoples and countries, and to the possibility of developing true bilateral relationships with each of them. Some of these new countries had well-established national identities of their own—for example the three "South Caucasus" states (i.e. south of the Caucasus mountain chain, and south of the Russian border)—Armenia, Azerbaijan and Georgia—were distinctive peoples with their own national characters, histories, languages and cultures. Others were less distinctive and in some cases were closer to the Russian identity, such as Belarus and Ukraine. And some had never really existed as independent countries, and needed to establish their own national identities.

My visit was not particularly welcomed by the tight group of Soviet specialists in the State Department, who saw me as an outsider. I did not even speak Russian, and I had the reputation of being something of an independent maverick. The Soviet specialists had their own close fraternity, which considered the whole of the former Soviet space as their area of focus, and they did not particularly trust people who were not a part of their disciplined group. The new and hastily-established US posts in these newly independent states were largely staffed from this group of specialists and did not yet have resident Ambassadors.

Needless to say, this unique mission was one of the most challenging and original undertakings I have carried out in my entire career. It was filled with individual adventures and episodes which could fill a book all by themselves. Each country visit was different, and I had to be ready for new challenges at each stop. The value of the ruble—still the universally-used currency in this vast region—versus the dollar was unpredictable from one day to the next. One day the hotel bill would amount to about 10 US cents, while another day I found myself carrying an armload of Russian rubles away from a currency exchange booth in order to settle my hotel bill.

And there were many unforeseen adventures. In some cases I was warmly received by the Chief of State, who would spend ample time in broad-ranging discussions with me. This was the case, for example, in Almaty, where the Kazak President, Nursultan Nazarbayev, spent a couple of hours in animated discussion with me. Some years later I participated in a small dinner for Nazarbayev, given in Geneva by my old friend from the CSCE, Vladimir Petrovsky, at his official residence, the Villa La Fenetra, overlooking the lake. Petrovsky took Nazarbayev around the circle of guests, introducing the President of Kazakhstan personally to each of us—key bankers and senior officials from Geneva and the United Nations. When he came to me, Nazarbayev's eyes lit up and he immediately recalled our meeting, years earlier in Almaty. He dashed out of the room and was gone for several minutes, to the general consternation of everyone present. When he returned he presented me with a huge book of photos of Kazakhstan, with his personal dedication inscribed to me.

But in some capitals I was less warmly received. It usually depended on the local U.S. Embassy staff more than the host government. In some cases the embassy personnel were suspicious of visitors like myself. It was a long-standing tradition in the US Foreign Service that the Russian-speakers considered themselves the best analysts of what was happening in the USSR, and would-be analysts who were not members of this fraternity were not taken seriously. Since I was an outsider for this group they thought I knew nothing, and treated me almost like a foreigner. So in some places my visits were pretty perfunctory, and if the local US Embassy treated me as a perfunctory visitor, the local officials of course did the same, and there was nothing I could do about it.

And there were a few countries I could not visit because of events or a lack of time. I did not get to Moldova because of travel requirements, and I had to cancel my trip to Tajikistan at the last minute because, on the day of my planned visit there my party received a report that there was fighting going on between the airport and the capital, Dushanbe. My Air Force pilots said they could not land in those circumstances.

We were having breakfast in our hotel in Tashkent when one of the pilots came in with this news. My whole delegation—an economist, a military officer, an interpreter, and a couple of support staff—were sitting at a round table when the pilot arrived and said we could not travel to Dushanbe. We all looked at each other in some consternation, and there was a moment of silence as our pilots fidgeted, clearly awaiting some sort of decision and instructions as to what they were to do. I asked my colleagues for their thoughts on what we should do in the circumstances, and addressed this same question to the chief pilot, who replied, "It's up to you; it's your plane."

So we discussed how to use the next couple of days in some constructive manner, and consulted with our local hosts. Tashkent is at the Eastern extremity of Uzbekistan and our hosts strongly recommended that we visit the other main cities of the country, to get a full understanding of the historic civilizations of Central Asia. Professor Fred Starr of Johns Hopkins University has captured very well the importance of these cities in his recent book, "Lost Enlightenment; Central Asia's Golden Age," and it is true that to see them helps to understand not only the past, but also the present and the future of the vast region between China and the Caspian Sea. Based on the urging of our hosts, we decided to do this.

I asked the pilots to file a flight plan which would take us to Samarkand and Bukhara, and that was how we made use of the days when we had planned to visit Dushanbe. And this was a very useful substitute side trip, for it gave us all a real understanding of what Central Asia was all about, something which has stayed with me to this day. My article at Annex, on the growing importance of Central Asia, is relevant here. (10) It cites the unique experience of this exploratory trip, more than twenty years earlier, when I was sent as the US Ambassador to the Newly Independent States, perhaps the only Ambassador the United States will ever have to Russia's Near Abroad and Central Asia.

The entire region was in some confusion at that time, with uncertainty all around—about the future, about the new governments, about the outside world and its possible interest, or lack of interest in this vast "new" region. But I came to respect the orderliness of the cities, the developed infrastructure—this was not Western Europe, but everywhere we went the infrastructure was solid and the cities were well-organized, clean and attractive. So I came to understand that there were positive elements in the legacy of Russian and Soviet rule, which were evident in this vast Central Asian space.

As with any pioneers, we sometimes had to fend for ourselves. One day we were sitting in our plane at a Central Asian airport, unable to leave because we did not have enough fuel to get to our next destination. The small local airliner next to us loaded its passengers, and then inexplicably unloaded them about 20 minutes later. Soon afterward our pilot came on board and said we were ready to take off. This was puzzling, but I later learned what had happened. Our pilots were equipped with cash to buy fuel, which they carried in elaborate money belts, and they had just bought the last fuel available at the airport, paid for in cash.

Throughout the former Soviet Union there was confusion and disorientation—at a stroke the power and influence of the country, its long-time ideology, its currency and its huge Eurasian empire, all seemed to collapse at once, with values and the future put sharply into question. I was apprehensive that I would be received with hostility, but just the opposite was the case, and the visit seemed to be welcome by the local people. Everywhere I went I made sure that my "military attaché" went with me, in uniform. He would stand next to me, or just behind me, and this was my way of clearly and visibly announcing to anyone who saw us that we were a senior American delegation, that I was important enough to have a senior military officer as an aide, and that we were there to show the interest of the United States of America in the country we were visiting.

One senior government leader said I was the first American he had ever seen, and I was, indeed, the first senior American official to visit many of these places. And it was a useful trip; it was possible to see the problems which were looming, and I reported to Washington on some of these. I could foresee a broad range of issues developing, but also great positive potential, as the people in these vast regions became accustomed to the new situation.

But I was also aware that there was already a feeling growing in Moscow that Russia had special prerogatives in this vast "new" space. I wrote a book chapter, published in 1995 by the Center for OSCE Research ("CORE") at the University of Hamburg, warning about Russia's likely efforts to regain control of this "Near Abroad" region, or at least to keep the influence of other countries and cultures out, and to protect the interests of the ethnic Russians who were now outside of Russia itself. This chapter seemed eerily prophetic when Russian President Vladimir Putin seized the Crimea and supported separatists in Eastern Ukraine in 2014—15, almost twenty years later. It was called "Russia's Near Abroad—A Dilemma for the West," and is included as an Annex to this book. (5)

It is necessary to have some understanding of the shock and bewilderment which swept the whole Soviet space when the USSR broke up. No one could possibly have anticipated the sudden dissolution of the USSR; virtually everyone assumed that this vast amalgam of regions, previously independent areas and homelands for differing ethnic and national groups, which had formed one of the strongest countries in the world for half a century or longer, would continue forever.

And why would anyone think otherwise? But from one day to the next, and without any warning, this complex amalgam of peoples, nationalities and ethnic groups simply came apart. We who were outsiders, and who observed this sudden transition, needed to understand it and to convey the pervasive sense of shock which was felt throughout the former Soviet space. These new countries would take some time to adjust to their situations, and this adjustment would not always be easy, as we have been seeing recently in Ukraine.

Albania

At about this time the CSCE also received a communication from Albania, stating that—after more than twenty years—it wished to accept the original Finnish invitation and join the Conference. This communication was received by German Ambassador Wilhelm Hoeynck, who was at that time the Ambassador of the country which was Chairman in Office of the CSCE, and who later served as the first Secretary General of the OSCE. Hoeynck and I were friends, and he consulted with me privately as to how to respond to the Albanian government's communication.

When the CSCE Ambassadors learned of this approach, there was a feeling among them that there should be some step or qualifying judgment before we could just let Albania in as a full member. Many years had gone by, during which all the member states had been bound by the undertakings in the Helsinki Final Act, and Albania had not followed these obligations, or been committed to them, during this long period. In addition, Albania was known for its isolation and its harsh Communist dictatorship. While everyone recognized that Albania, as a European country, had the right to belong to the CSCE, we all thought that there should be some form of measurement as to whether Albania was conforming, or at least trying to conform, to the Helsinki provisions, since they had opted out of those obligations for so long.

I suggested to Hoeynck that the CSCE should carry out some sort of review of Albania's situation with respect to the obligations contained in the Helsinki Final Act and the Charter of Paris, as well as their intentions with respect to those obligations in the future. Hoeynck asked me how we could do that, and I replied, "Easy; we will send a mission to Albania and carry out a review of their policies and actions. It will be a kind of "snap-shot" of where they stand, so we can then judge their future progress." By that time I had gone on several CSCE missions, and had traveled to Central Asia, so it was easy for me to conceive of the CSCE carrying out a similar mission in Albania.

Hoeynck ran with this idea, and it was immediately implemented. An official Swedish history of the CSCE-OSCE, published by the Foreign Ministry in Stockholm during the Swedish Presidency of the OSCE, recounts this episode and identifies it as forming a key precedent for all of the OSCE's later missions, etc. to different problem areas in the OSCE region.

Following the CSCE mission, and an evaluation by the CSCE member states, Albania was admitted as a full member of the CSCE on June 19, 1991.

I went to Albania myself, on an official mission as part of the reopening of bilateral American relations with that country—a sort of extension of my mission to the Newly-Independent States. I was still based in Vienna, and still had the use of an Air Force plane for such missions, so I took a small delegation, including the General who was my chief military advisor, and flew from Vienna to Tirana. When our executive jet approached Tirana, we started a slow circling maneuver over the airport where we were to land. After a couple of such circles, the young Air Force pilot turned and shouted to me from the cockpit: "Hey, Mr. Ambassador, you want to see why we can't land?" After a moment of fleeting panic, which fortunately passed very quickly, I said yes, and he then turned the aircraft on its side so I could look down at the main landing strip of Tirana Airport. There we saw small boys shooing cows off the runway with sticks!

Driving from the airport into Tirana was a small challenge. There were virtually no cars on the country roads (there were very few cars anywhere in the country at that time) and so herders and others would use these flat, paved areas to sit, to play cards, take naps, etc., and we had to be careful, rounding the curves, that we did not hit anything, or anyone.

In Tirana I met with political leaders—political life was just getting started after more than forty years under the Communist dictatorship of Enver Hoxha. But it was already active and vigorous. It was obvious that Albania had been cut off from the world during this long period. There were few cars in the streets, and throughout the countryside small bunkers had been built—presumably to serve as defensive gun emplacements in case of an invasion. But they were so randomly scattered, and so numerous—I was told that there were more than 700,000 of them across the country—that they conveyed an impression of irrationality more than anything else.

These visits were necessary but did not lead to on-going activities. US Embassies were soon established, and they went about the normal work of developing political analyses and building relationships with the host country and its people. My visits proved to be purely symbolic. But Albania did join the CSCE, after many years of absence, and I believe that has been a positive influence in the subsequent development of the country.

Nagorno Karabakh

Following the admission into the OSCE of the newly-independent states from the former USSR, and the creation of a small group of states to prepare a peace conference in Minsk to try to settle the war over Nagorno Karabakh, I received a call from Washington at my office in Vienna. Secretary of State Baker wanted me to get the preparatory discussions for the Minsk Conference going, in order to begin some movement toward a settlement of the Nagorno-Karabakh conflict, and to permit the convening of the anticipated peace conference in Minsk.

I called Mario Rafaelli, the newly-designated Chairman of the Minsk Group, an Italian politician who had been a Deputy Minister of Foreign Affairs, and asked him to convene the first meeting. He did this at the sumptuous Villa Madama, a country house on a hill outside Rome which was designed originally by Raphael himself, and was used as the Ministry's luxury facility for senior-level conferences. The newly-created Minsk Group, which has ever since—for more than twenty years—been seeking (sadly without success) a settlement to the conflict over Nagorno Karabakh, was "kick-started" at the Villa Madama June 1-6, 1992.

That initial session of the Minsk Group was, well, complicated. There were a number of actual players present—the parties to the conflict, of course, the Russians, and the Turks, who had some key interests in the problem and the region. But the other participating countries were not very engaged, and sent whoever was available to observe what was going on. For example, one delegate, whose "day job" was as a diplomat stationed at his country's embassy in Rome, had to leave mid-way through the afternoon negotiations in order to walk his dog. Fortunately I was assisted by a fellow Foreign Service officer, Marie Yovanovich, who spoke fluent Russian and knew the region well—she later served as the US Ambassador in Kyrgyzstan and Armenia.

The first problem we faced echoed the similar problem which famously stymied the Paris negotiations to end the Vietnam War: the status of potential delegations and how they would be seated. The Armenian delegation insisted that there would be a delegation of Armenians from Nagorno Karabakh which would sit behind a placard with that name on it, and of course the delegation from Azerbaijan refused this option, which would have implied some sort of independent status for the region, and was thus unacceptable for them. Nagorno Karabakh was, and still is, legally an autonomous region within Azerbaijan. After a day of wrangling we found a solution by agreeing that the representatives of the two ethnic population groups from Nagorno Karabakh would be associated with the delegations of Armenia or Azerbaijan. But that was just the beginning of the sticky, rancorous, and sometimes very heated, arguments which followed. I tried to be inventive and to find a positive path forward, with only limited success. The wrangling seemed endless.

At one point there was a break in the negotiations and I took a walk outside to get some fresh air. It was an extraordinary place, with formal gardens and a view out over the surrounding countryside toward the distant hills of Rome. I was reminded of the W. H. Auden poem, "Embassy," which Pierre Morel had circulated to the Ambassadors at the end of our complicated negotiations leading up to the Summit Conference in Paris. We diplomats were indeed at that rural villa, wearing our pricey shoes, and poised in the distance were the opposing armies, "with all the instruments for causing pain," and with the possible prospect of "a land laid waste, its women weeping and all its young men slain." As in Auden's poem, much depended on whatever diplomatic "charm" we could bring to bear, but this element was not very evident in these tough, down-to-earth discussions about that bloody conflict in the mountains of Karabakh.

Amongst the long floral alleyways I ran into one of the interpreters, also getting some air. I did not know this distinguished lady, who had obviously interpreted at many negotiations over the years, but as I approached she looked me in the eye and said: "You have the patience of an angel."

And it was true that I put a lot of patient effort into finding at least some tiny basis of understanding among this rancorous group—at this first meeting and at many other such meetings, in many places, over the following several years. But in the end, that first meeting, and the many others which followed, adjourned with only an agreement to have another session at a later date. I could see that this would be a very long and difficult negotiating process, as indeed it has proved to be. More than twenty-two years later it is still stuck at more-or-less the same place.

This was the first time that it came home to me that in such situations the mediator is, more often than not, the only one in the room whose objective is to find a solution, and that without some strong, determined outside intervention or pressure, there is little incentive or possibility for reaching even a temporary peace after a bloody conflict. When there have been massacres and blood has soaked the earth it is just very difficult to bring peace. Hatreds and the need for revenge are too strong, and only the passage of time can make it possible to approach issues in a rational way. Today, the Minsk Group is still turning in circles, searching for the beginning of some sort of peace process.

"Full Metal Jack"

Shortly after this meeting I went on the first of my several trips to the Caucasus region, including to Nagorno Karabakh itself, where a temporary ceasefire had to be arranged to permit our delegation to enter. Each trip was an adventure in itself, but the first couple of them may be worth recording.

It is perhaps appropriate to say at the outset that this region, this Nagorno Karabakh, is indeed a justifiably fabled place, with green mountains and plunging valleys shrouded in morning mists. The people live in small villages or remote farmhouses where the rooster's morning call is often the only sound to disturb the peace, and the sun sets across ranges of green peaks and shadowed ravines. It is a land of milk and honey, that has inspired songs in different languages, and it is a hard place to forget.

Using my US Air Force plane, our OSCE group went first to Moscow, with Prince Karel Schwarzenberg of Czechoslavakia designated as the Chairman of the Delegation, representing the country which held the rotating Chairmanship of the OSCE at that time, and a number of other specially-named national representatives from "Minsk Group" countries. We met with senior officials of the Russian Foreign and Defense ministries, including the Minister of Defense, for discussions of the situation on the ground in the conflict areas of Armenia and Azerbaijan, and particularly in Nagorno Kharabakh itself. I noted that we were traveling on a US Air Force plane, which would take us to Baku, but that we did not have transportation to Kharabakh itself. The Minister immediately and very generously promised to provide helicopter transportation to take us from the big former Soviet airbase in Azerbaijan to Stepanakert/Khankendi, the chief city of Nagorno Kharabakh. We were of course very appreciative of this offer, which would save us the time and difficult challenges of making this trip by land.

When we got to Baku I sent the US General who was assigned to my delegation to Yerevan, the Capital of Armenia, using our plane, to arrange a cease-fire so that we could visit Nagorno Kharabakh. This was done without a problem, and when he returned to Baku we flew to the Russian airbase in Azerbaijan to take a helicopter to Nagorno Kharabakh itself, as had been arranged with the Russian Defense Minister in Moscow. As we landed at the huge Russian base we could see rows of aircraft, including many helicopters.

After some minutes of waiting, the Russian commander of the base came in a limousine to meet our plane. I explained the purpose of our visit, which was apparently unexpected, and we asked about the helicopter which was supposed to take us to Nagorno Kharabakh. But the General smoothly replied that there were no helicopters on the base. We had actually seen many helicopters, as we were landing, so we objected, and there followed a brief confrontation. Schwartzenberg was uncomfortable, so I took the lead in insisting on the helicopter which had been promised to us in Moscow. Finally, the Russian General said, without any explanation for the turn-about in his position, that our helicopter was waiting for us.

We were driven to the waiting helicopter, which was already warming up for take off. Our pilot looked like a character out of the old US comic strip "Smilin' Jack." He was handsome, blond, and wore a well-used brown leather flying jacket with a fur collar, a white silk scarf, and an officer's cap set way back on his head. We sat on the smooth steel floor of the helicopter, with the doors open, as it flew "nap of the earth" style, up through the narrow valleys and snow-capped mountains to the main city of Nagorno-Kharabakh. The flight was difficult, because of the defensive helicopter flying style, shifting and turning sharply to follow the gorges in the mountainous terrain, and the fact that there were no seats in the helicopter and we had to hold on to anything we could grab to avoid sliding across the slick floor and out through one of the open cargo doorways.

Just to convey the very contentious nature of everything in this region, it should be noted that the main town of Nagorno Karabakh, Stepanakert, was re-named after Stepan Shahumyan, a leader of the Armenian Communist Party, but has continued to be known as Khankendi by the Azerbaijanis. Stepanakert/Khankendi replaced the nearby, traditional Azerbaijani city of Shusha as the principal city of the region—officially called the Nagorno Karabakh Autonomous Oblast in Soviet times—and Shusha, with its picturesque minarets, has now been largely destroyed. We could see smoke rising from very recent shelling damage all around these neighboring cities as our helicopter circled to land—the artillery had clearly stopped only a few minutes before our arrival.

We set down in a football stadium, and as we exited the chopper the pilot said emphatically to me, with a broad grin—and in perfect English: "I'll be back at five o'clock ... and I'll wait for five minutes." He used the fingers of his right hand to show the "five" in each case. He then added, "Have a nice day," with a broad grin, and took off. We were immediately surrounded by a large number of bearded and heavily armed men.

After some back-and-forth with the leaders of this group, we were taken to an office building in the center of the city, where we held what appeared to be considered official discussions in a meeting room. We explained the meaning and purpose of our visit, and asked to see both of the towns, as well as some front-line areas. We were taken on a tour of both Stepanakert/Khankendi and Shusha, which I followed on the large-scale maps I had been given in the Pentagon. These maps were fascinating for our hosts, because they indicated every contour and every building—even single isolated houses. They were clearly much better maps of their region than these militiamen had ever seen before. The US Army had better maps of their country than they did!

Both of the main cities had suffered damage from artillery shelling, and numerous buildings had been destroyed or badly damaged, especially in Shusha. Roads were difficult to navigate in our Lada "Niva" jeeps, and at one point the leading Niva got stuck in a huge mud hole, with the mud completely covering its wheels. In a mountainous area we could observe the opposing lines of battle. We also saw numerous casualties, both dead and wounded, some in the field and some in makeshift morgues. But about the only thing we were able to conclude from the visit was that there was indeed some very vicious fighting going on in the area. To complicate matters, one of the Ambassadors in our group was excessively nervous, and calmed his nerves by taking frequent swigs from a flask of whiskey, which made his behavior strange, especially in the front-line situation we were in.

The stories we heard were shocking. There were numerous random atrocities on both sides, with both sides claiming the need for revenge. Hostages were taken routinely, and rape and killing of women and small children was common. It was a difficult situation to comprehend—we were diplomats, used to embassies in capital cities, and we could not easily digest what was happening here. Our hosts thought we were experts in conflict, or something like that; they even thought I was a military officer because of the olive drab hunting parka I was wearing. But in reality we were creatures of the urbane diplomatic life, in our polished shoes, accustomed to unhurried discussions in luxurious villas, and not to the rough life of the battlefield.

With my maps I could follow how far we had moved away from our landing point, and when half of our allotted time had expired I insisted that we return to our helicopter rendez-vous point. Since I had supplied the airplane for this excursion I claimed my responsibility for sticking to the program. And I did not want us to miss our helicopter ride. My hunting jacket gave me a military look, and our hosts thought I was the official military advisor, especially because I was following our movements on a military map, and timing our movements. But the plain truth was that I was the only one in the group with some military experience. We arrived at the rendez-vous point on time, and left on our helicopter as programmed. Shelling resumed, in both directions, as soon as we were airbourne. We could see the smoke from the guns.

On another occasion I went on a similar trip, this time led by Jiri Dienstbier, the Foreign Minister of Czechoslovakia under Vaclav Havel. The visit was much the same, except that we traveled up to Nagorno Karabakh in cars, and were handed over by the still-active officers of the KGB in Azerbaijan to officials they knew personally—and who I assumed were their recent KGB colleagues—on the other side of the line. There was a certain amount of friendly greeting between the officers on the two sides as our visiting group moved from one car to another. They were colleagues who had not seen each other in some time—and they laughed and slapped each other on the back. Another lesson in the many legacies of the former USSR.

This second visit was no more enlightening than the first, but there was a big difference—we were driving, and this made the trip much longer as we drove up to Stepanakert/Khankendi. We held "official" discussions of the situation in a government building, did a walking tour through the city, and took shelter in a makeshift morgue when there was a false alert about incoming shelling. We were about to start driving back to our cross-over point when our hosts indicated that dinner was waiting for us. Dienstbier immediately accepted and we drove to a shrouded restaurant which was filled with people, where we were served an elaborate dinner, complete with Armenian wines and after-dinner liquors. I think I was the only member of our group who was not drinking any alcohol, which annoyed Dienstbier, who felt we had to respond positively to the hospitality. These diplomats all regarded me as something like their military escort, and were annoyed when I kept insisting that we had to leave. They were all having a great time toasting and eating, and saw no reason to cut it short.

At a certain point I realized that it was getting very late, and that we would have difficulty getting back to the cross-over point on time. The restaurant windows were shrouded so as not to attract artillery shells, so it was not really possible to see whether it was light or dark outside. I had in mind the way shooting had started immediately when we took off, on the first visit, and did not want us to be caught in the battle zone after dark. I was the only holdover from that first trip. So I began urging Dienstbier to leave. But he was adamant that we could not insult the hospitality of our hosts, and continued eating and toasting.

Finally, we got into the cars and began to move, but it was very dark by that time, and we were, of course, driving through the darkness on a very rough road with no lights. There were no lights anywhere. The drive was painfully long. Finally we were down on the plain and moving fast across flat land toward the hand-over point. As we approached the rendez-vous location, shooting started, and we could see the tracers crossing just above the roofs of the cars. We passed several tanks and military vehicles. At a certain place, which the drivers seemed to know but which did not have any visible distinguishing characteristics, the cars stopped and we jumped out and began running, with our heads down, guided by our hosts. The tracers were crossing just above our heads.

We were handed over from one side to the other in the dark—one moment my arm was being held by one person, the next moment it was being held by someone else. Our escorts on both sides knew each other by their voices, and seemed sure we were in the right place. As our new escorts took us firmly by the arm we ran toward a ruined building, and down some steps into a basement room, which was equipped like a well-used living room. We were offered tea, or brandy, and most of us took both. I asked our host, one of the ex-KGB officers, if everyone was alright, but his answer was guarded. In this part of the world, as I have learned, you are best off in the hands of the KGB (or its equivalent)—they are the toughest, and the most professional, and they have their connections.

After about an hour of getting organized we moved carefully to another set of cars, and took off on the long drive to Baku. When I reported to the State Department on this episode, my colleagues there started calling me "Full Metal Jack," drawing on the name of a film which came out at about that time, called "Full Metal Jacket." So I became known in the corridors of the State Department as Full Metal Jack.

When I reflected on all this I realized that the physical dangers of moving between opposing sides in a military confrontation are similar to the bureaucratic dangers of trying to find a sensible path between opposing political factions in Washington. I actually survived the physical dangers in my career much better than I did the bureaucratic ones.

The next day we took off in my Air Force plane to take Dienstbier and his assistants back to Prague. As soon as we were airborne,

Dienstbier said he wanted to stop in Tbilisi to meet with Shevardnadze, who by then had returned from Moscow to his native Georgia, where he was later elected President. I told Dienstbier very firmly that this was a U.S. Air Force Plane, that it was operating under my orders, and that we were flying straight to Prague with no stops. But he insisted and seemed prepared to elevate the matter and send a message immediately to the US Secretary of State, who was, after all, his direct opposite number.

So, after consulting with the pilot—who just shrugged and said "It's your plane," and reflecting on the prospect of having the Foreign Minister of Czechoslovakia complain to my boss, the Secretary of State, about my hospitality, I agreed, and we adjusted our course to land in Tbilisi, where Shevardnadze had been notified somehow, and apparently was preparing to host a luncheon for Foreign Minister Dienstbier.

When we landed everything seemed to be in order. There were cars to take us away from the airport in a full diplomatic motorcade, and we were driven to the President's country house, where a very long table had been set out, with numerous Georgian diplomats and interpreters for the various languages spoken by our group. It was a very different setting from lunch/dinner the previous day in Nagorno Karabakh.

It should be noted here that Dienstbier and Shevardnadze came from very different backgrounds and very different life experiences. Shevardnadze was a conventional Communist party official, who had been close to Gorbachev and was rewarded by being appointed as Foreign Minister of the USSR. Following the breakup of the USSR he returned to his native Georgia and was elected President, but his life experience had been as a senior official in the Soviet communist governmental system, based in Moscow.

Dienstbier, on the other hand, had been crushed by the communist system in his country. He started as a journalist but was immediately pegged as a potential trouble-maker and was forced to take jobs for twenty years as a gardener and janitor. Even his friend Vaclav Havel was treated better, and was able to write some plays. So Dienstbier, who had been appointed Foreign Minister by Havel, had little in common with Shevardnadze, and there was no particular reason to expect them to get along well.

But they did, and the luncheon progressed through long humorous stories told by one or the other of them, and translated by the several interpreters who were stationed at intervals along the long, narrow lunch table. There were toasts, and much raucous laughter, and everyone was very jolly when we got back into our cars to return to the airport and continue our trip back to Prague.

I asked myself at the time what lesson I should draw from all this? And my answer, also to myself, was "none." Political people, of all persuasions, have a social side, and love to tell stories and to wonder, in public reflection, about their experiences. These two people had very different experiences of life under communism, but they were also prepared to share their experience, their impressions, and their jokes, when freed by the fact that each of them represented a sovereign country. Having a sense of humour can be a great asset in life, which permits a person to live through, and look back on, many of life's experiences, with irony and even amusement.

The Caucasus and A First Peace Proposal

Meanwhile, back at my base in Vienna, the Minsk Group negotiating process began to take more and more of my time—there were meetings and travel obligations to try to influence the thinking in Azerbaijan, Armenia, Turkey and of course Russia.

I also traveled around the USA to speak to local groups of Armenian-Americans about the Nagorno Karabakh conflict. These people were always very interested, but sometimes they were hostile when they realized that I was trying to find a compromise solution which would be stable and lasting. Many of them were not interested in compromise. On one occasion I was invited to speak at the Kennedy Center at Harvard, and my presentation was in a large stairwell used as a locus for lectures that would attract a large audience. I found myself being heckled by Armenian-Americans, and had to stop my presentation to remind them that I was not the enemy—I was the principal mediator, trying to find a solution. I found the attitude of these people very hostile to the basic idea of a peaceful solution to the conflict. Fortunately they were not typical, and I met with many Armenian-Americans who were very sincere in their support for peace.

The US Congress passed the Freedom Support Act, which was designed to provide assistance to the newly independent states of the former Soviet Union, and this was signed into law by President Bush on October 24, 1992. But Section 907 of the new law singled out Azerbaijan and prohibited any provision of assistance to that country. It was inserted into the law as a result of the strong efforts of the Armenian-American lobbying groups in Washington, and put the US in an unbalanced position with regard to the conflict over Nagorno Karabakh. While the effects of that law were subsequently reduced, in 2001, through a provision under which the President can waive its provisions (which has been done routinely since that time), the overall political effect of Section 907 of the Freedom Support Act has been to tilt the US position with respect to the conflict over Nagorno Karabakh, and to make it more difficult for Washington to take an impartial leading role in seeking an agreed solution to the conflict. It thus impedes a peaceful settlement rather than facilitating one—which I do not think is in the interests of anyone in the region.

As the designated US mediator for this conflict, this section of the law also put me in an awkward position, since it appeared to align the US with one of the parties to the conflict. I was scrupulously neutral during my work on this matter, and it was unhelpful to have this section of US law on display, because it created distrust on one side of the negotiation.

Another complicating factor was that an Armenian terrorist group, called ASALA (for "Armenian Secret Army for the Liberation of Armenia") was active during this period, in many places in Europe and North America, with bloody attacks and assassinations in France, Italy, Turkey, Greece, the Netherlands, Belgium, Lebanon and the USA. At one point ASALA assassinated the son of a former Turkish colleague and friend of mine, the highly respected Ambassador Ozdemir Benler, who had become the Ambassador of Turkey to the Netherlands, and there were even attacks in Los Angeles. Numerous people were killed in ASALA attacks, worldwide. This was an unacceptable aspect of the Armenian world community's activities, and I made my views on this known to responsible members of the American-Armenian community, who fully agreed that these activities brought shame on the Armenian diaspora. Later, some known ASALA operatives took leading positions with armed units fighting in Nagorno Karabakh, which only served to discredit that para-military effort.

During this period I was carrying out visits to both Armenia and Azerbaijan, trying to find ways to advance a peace process on Nagorno Kharabakh. I used my plane to fly to Yerevan, where I landed in the middle of the night and was driven directly (and discreetly) to the residence of Gerard Libaridian, the Armenian President's foreign affairs advisor. Libaridian, an Armenian-American academic from the Boston area, was a reasonable and likeable person, and we became friends. Later he became a professor at the University of

Michigan—the state of Michigan is one of the centers of the Armenian diaspora in the US, along with Boston and California.

Libaridian's official residence had a small passageway connecting it directly to the President's office suite, and so I would wind up having meetings in the small hours of the morning with Armenian President Levon Ter-Petrossian, before dashing back out to the airport and continuing on in the darkness to Baku. I followed this routine at least twice while I was in my "Minsk Group" role.

Yerevan was like a city under siege. Electricity was in very short supply, and at night the city was completely dark. On one occasion, after the US Embassy opened, I stayed at the very modest apartment of the American charge d'affaires—a personal friend who had previously been stationed in Baku and so understood both sides of the conflict. At night there was no electricity anywhere in Yerevan, and it was hazardous to go outside, since there were no streetlights, and a number of wandering packs of wild dogs added to the risks. Armenian life continued, of course, and one time I was invited to the main brandy distillery, where they do not let you leave until you have consumed at least one shot of every brandy they have ever made, going back at least 20 years.

The first time I arrived in Baku, things were in chaos there. I landed close to midnight and was driven through the dark streets of the city to what was then the Foreign Ministry. It was shortly after midnight by the time we got there, and I was hustled up a grand staircase to go to my meeting with the Minister, who was waiting for me.

My meetings were friendly, but the situation in Baku during my first visit there was troubling. There was no electricity, the buildings in the handsome older part of the city were badly damaged and had not been cleaned in ages, and the streets were full of rubble and fallen trees and branches. There was factional fighting going on and the regime of President Abulfaz Elchibey was under siege. Elchibey (this adopted name means "noble messenger" in Azerbaijani) was a nationalist historian and former dissident, elected in the post-independence nationalist enthusiasm, but he was not able to manage the complex situation of state-building while staving off civil war and assuring the necessary defenses around Nagorno Karabakh. My meeting with him, though warm, gave me the impression that he was not the master of the hard, practical elements which he needed to control. There was a full-scale war going on with the Armenians, and in the Azerbaijani countryside there were armed groups supporting different factions and threatening to take over the government in Baku. I stayed in the old Moscow Hotel, near the site of the Azerbaijani Majlis (Parliament), where the iconic "Flame Towers" now stand. There was a sign in the lobby requiring guests to check their weapons before going up to their rooms. Since I did not have a weapon, this rule did not apply to me.

In later visits to Baku things were better, and I stayed in the Presidential Guest House, just behind the official Presidential office building. This was after Heydar Aliyev took office, and started pulling the country out of disorder and onto a path toward positive development. In my meetings with him I was impressed by his determination and organized approach to the country's problems. It took years, but Azerbaijan under President Aliyev lifted itself out of the state of darkness and chaos it was in when I first visited it. The change, from dark streets to beautiful, clean, well-lighted avenues and promenades is nothing less than miraculous, and I never cease to admire the determination and societal organization which has produced this change.

Bill Clinton was inaugurated as President on January 20, 1993, but despite my apprehensions (after my previous experience—noted above—when a Democratic President succeeded a Republican one) this did not at first have any effect on my role. I was encouraged to continue in my Minsk Group activities—our objective of finding a solution to the Nagorno Karabakh conflict appeared to be just as important for the Clinton team as it had been for the Bush Administration, and since no one had any better idea for pursuing a settlement than continuation of an active US role in the Minsk Group, my activities continued.

I was even handed some prominent roles—for example I was a participant in a small working luncheon which President Clinton hosted at the White House for Turkish Prime Minister Tansu Ciller on October 15, 1993, during her first visit to Washington. Ciller was the only woman Prime Minister Turkey has ever had. When the time came, President Clinton said, "Jack, why don't you explain to the Prime Minister the complexities of this Nagorno Karabakh issue, and what we have been trying to do to resolve it." So I did that, as succinctly as possible. Prime Minister Ciller was very interested, and very well informed on the matter.

On March 8, 1993, I was invited to testify about the Nagorno Karabakh conflict before the Helsinki Commission at the US Congress. This was the same body which I had worked with when it was first created, and when they became part of our delegation to the first CSCE Review Meeting, in Belgrade in 1977. The Commission was presided for my session by Senator Dennis DeConcini, a Democrat from Arizona, and Congressman Steny Hoyer, Democrat from Maryland, the two Congressional Co-Chairs of the Commission. I appeared along with Ambassador Hafiz Pashayev, the first Ambassador of Azerbaijan to Washington, and two representatives of Armenian-American organizations. I was greeted with respect by the Co-Chairmen, and gave a candid report on the situation in the conflict and our on-going efforts to bring about some sort of interim solution. The text of my testimony, and the questions which followed, is included as an Annex to this book. (6) The questions were not "hard" questions; it was an informational hearing, as is a tradition in the US Congress.

Ambassador Pashayev gave a presentation after mine, and he faced some polite, but more serious and challenging questioning. I was impressed by the organization and effectiveness of the Armenian-American lobbyists, and concluded that it would be difficult for Washington to maintain a neutral position with respect to this conflict, because the Armenian-American lobby was so well-organized and supported, and it represented important groups of voters in a number of key states, including California, Michigan and Massachusetts. But I was convinced that the US role should be that of a neutral arbiter, helping to stabilize the situation, end the fighting on a fair basis, and over time to help to establish a balanced and lasting peace. I have always thought that this was the best way forward for everyone involved, and could lead to broad peace and shared prosperity for all the peoples of the Caucasus.

On June 8, 1993, at a press briefing in the State Department, I announced an initiative, jointly supported by all the member states of the Minsk Group except those that were parties to the conflict, to whom it was addressed. This proposal (a summary of my presentation is attached as an Annex (7)) was designed to push the negotiations forward, to implement UN Security Council Resolution 822, to create some pressure on the parties to the conflict to move in a positive direction, and to start some momentum to move toward at least an interim solution to the conflict. It brought together the Minsk Group with the backing of the UN Security Council. The states which were participating in the Minsk Group at that time (other than the parties to the conflict) were Belarus, the Czech Republic, France, Germany, Italy, Russia, Sweden, Turkey and the USA, and they all supported the proposal.

The initiative, which had been handed to the conflicting parties beforehand, asked them to accept its conditions by the end of that week. It was designed to implement Security Council Resolution 822 of April 30, 1993, which had recognized the role of the "Minsk Group" as the forum for negotiations between the belligerents, and requested immediate withdrawal of Armenian forces from the regions of Azerbaijan near Nagorno Karabakh.

There were some interesting points in my briefing of the press on this initiative. I said that the US was impartial in the dispute, but condemned the violence on both sides, that we were deliberately participating in a multi-lateral effort on this matter rather than trying to do something by ourselves, and that we had taken the decision not to have a US military presence on the ground in the area. I also stated that we viewed the heads of government of both of the countries which were parties to the conflict as moderate leaders, and wished to support them both. We anticipated a ceasefire, accompanied by international monitoring to stabilize it, with some accompanying measures such as lifting of the mutual blockades in the region. This initiative specifically excluded trying to decide in advance on the ultimate political solution to the Nagorno Karabakh problem, leaving that for further negotiation.

This was a sort of high point in the early work of the Minsk Group, and might have led to progress toward a more permanent solution. It energized the discussions at the time, but did not get very far; the incidents on the ground, which kept the conflict going, flared up again, as they had in the past, and prevented any progress in the negotiating process.

At that time there was still some hope that the Minsk Group format might lead to a resolution of the conflict, a hope which began to dwindle from that time onward. The Minsk Group has unfortunately been unsuccessful, in the more than two decades of activity which have followed, in advancing toward some solution to the conflict. It has not even been successful in stabilizing the situation and reducing the risks of military confrontation. Despite all our planning for introduction of peacekeeping forces, with the creation of a group of military advisors to plan for eventual peacekeeping, it has not even been possible to arrive at a situation where further steps, or further progress, would be possible, and peacekeeping forces have never been deployed. Young men on both sides of this long-stalemated war continue to die, as snipers do their work. It is one of the world's truly wasted regions, where all sides could prosper with even a minimum of restraint and mutual understanding.

Later, in 1996, when I visited Baku on other business, I was interviewed by Azerbaijan International Magazine about my views on the Nagorno Karabakh issue, and the text of that interview is included as an annex to this book. (10)

A Washington Farewell

Mario Rafaelli, the Italian politician who was the first Chairman of the Minsk Group, had to withdraw from that activity because of his obligations in Italy. After a brief period without an official Chairman, the Italians wanted to be relieved of their Chairmanship responsibilities, and concluded a private bilateral deal with the government in Stockholm under which the Chairmanship would be taken over by Sweden.
In private discussions with both the Italian and Swedish representatives I made known my indignation that such an arrangement had been worked out privately. The CSCE had established certain traditions of openness, and I felt that this was a back-room deal, which had no place in a CSCE forum. The Italians should have submitted to the CSCE, or at least to the full Minsk Group, their desire to be relieved of their Chairmanship responsibilities, so that candidates for the succession could have come forward. The US was not directly involved, since, in my opinion, we could not have taken the Chairmanship role, in view of our strong and very active Armenian-American community, and the fact that such a step would have appeared provocative to both the Russians and the Iranians.
More practically, I learned that the Swedes foresaw a radical change in the way the Minsk Group would operate, which was also to be simply imposed on the other Minsk Group participants. The Swedish Chairman-designate thought his approach would be one of personal "shuttle diplomacy" between Baku and Yerevan, without the involvement of the full membership of the Minsk Group, or even of the small leadership contingent which had emerged within that group. Here too, I did not believe it was up to any single person or member country to simply decide on the way the negotiation should be conducted.
When I heard this news I realized that such an approach would leave me (and thus the USA) out. I thought such a strategy would

guarantee that the Minsk Group and its views would have little effect on the parties to the conflict. The only voices they considered important were those of Russia (which still had significant forces, and influence, in the region) and the United States, which everyone regarded as the principal international arbiter, and which I had established as the leading element in the Minsk Group. The Russians operated on their own, often without even informing the Minsk Group, and the only country participating in the group which could offset Russia's presence in the region and its varied means for exerting influence was the United States.

I thought that without some visible US involvement, commitment and leadership, any effort on Nagorno Karabakh would be futile, and would therefore be a useless approach to the problem. It was not a question of logic, but rather one of influence. While I recognized Russian sensitivities about the Near Abroad, and wrote about them at the time (see, for example, my 1995 book chapter called "Russia's Near Abroad; A Dilemma for the West", at Annex 7), I also thought that it would be useful to show that we were not simply conceding the region to Moscow for influence and control. The Nagorno Karabakh conflict, with all its violence and complexity in the midst of the break-up of the USSR, offered us—the United States and the West—an opportunity to pursue a more assertive and constructive policy in the region, which could have at least partially offset traditional Russian influence. The Minsk Group gave us just such an opportunity, but it was deliberately reduced in importance and ultimately ignored by Washington.

Following the change in the Minsk Group chairmanship, and with the change in the Administration in Washington, I became increasingly convinced that progress would be very difficult in this negotiation. Any US activity would require considerable resolve and political courage, because the problem was inherently complex, and American-Armenian groups were very influential politically. One day when I was in Baku I read in the International Herald Tribune President Clinton's announcement that he was sending the Marines to Haiti to stabilize the situation there. His speech made it clear that the Administration made an important distinction between problems in America's "back yard," such as Haiti, where the US recognized that it had an important responsibility, and problems which were outside this "back yard," and where the US would not get involved.

I thought about the implications of this for some time. I was, of course, operating in a region which was clearly not in America's "back yard," and was of truly secondary importance for Washington. It was an area where no American Administration would want to get involved, and so my personal efforts were really at the limit of what Washington would do to help to resolve problems in the area. The only other power which could help to resolve the issue I was working on was Russia. But Russia, in my view, was a major part of the problem, and not a very desirable party to resolve or manage this particular issue—certainly not on its own. Moreover, without meaningful US leadership the problem was likely to go on for a very long time, with sporadic casualties and no possibility for people in the affected regions to return to their homes. I was operating in a region which was outside the area of strong US interest, in someone else's "back yard," and I made a mental note to raise this broad issue the next time I was in Washington.

When I was next in the State Department I asked for a meeting with the senior State Department official with oversight of US relations with Russia. I explained what I saw as my problem—the fact that the Russians were complicating the Nagorno Karabakh issue and making a stable resolution of the conflict—even a tentative one— very difficult, or even impossible. I had become the de facto leader of the negotiating process, and thought that without a strong US leadership role it would not be possible to reach an agreement among the parties in the Minsk Group process. At the same time I understood the limits on what Washington—under any Administration—would be prepared to do in this area. I also thought that the Russians were a part of the problem, and therefor should not be in the lead in finding a solution.

I recognized that there were limits on what the US could do—certainly it would not be a good idea to send US troops, or even advisors, to that part of the world, nor for the US to play a role in a possible peace-keeping operation; this would be too provocative for the Russians, as well as the Iranians, just across the borders to the north and south. But I thought the negotiating process depended largely on the US pushing and pulling the two sides to some reasonable agreement, or at least to an "interim agreement" which, optimistically, might remain in place for a very long time.

The response I received was perfectly rational and realistic. The issue I was dealing with was just too remote from Washington, too sensitive for Moscow, and it was clear that the Administration—almost certainly any US Administration—simply would not want to get involved in more than a superficial way. The fact was that Washington, under any President, would be content to have a symbolic US presence in the Minsk Group negotiating format, but would not get involved beyond that level.

As I left the office I wondered how I could continue in the role I had established for myself. I had worked to develop the Minsk Group into a serious negotiating body, but without visible US commitment and participation—as was planned by the new Swedish Chair—the Minsk Group process would have no real impact on the parties concerned, and would gradually become superfluous, even ridiculous.

I also thought the Russians were playing their own game in order to maintain leverage throughout the Caucasus, and that if the West showed indifference on the Nagorno-Karabakh issue, the Russians would continue to use it to maintain their presence and their central role in the region. This was the place where we could show our interest in the region, by leading an effort in favor of peace. But it was clear to me that was not going to happen.

After some reflection I asked the State Department to replace me as the US representative. I knew that without visible US participation and leadership, the Minsk Group would not be credible to the participants in this conflict, and since I had been the most active and creative member of the Minsk Group my departure would diminish its importance. But if the new Swedish Chairman acted alone I would have no role in the way these negotiations would be pursued, and without visible US involvement the whole Minsk Group operation would not be credible.

Asking to be moved from the Minsk Group position did not make me very popular with the personnel section of the State Department, which preferred that people just accept the assignments they were given. And finding an energetic and imaginative replacement for me, who would be willing to take such a risky and thankless job, took some time. But eventually I was relieved of this duty and was replaced in the position by Joe Presel, a fellow Foreign Service Officer. There have been a whole series of American successors in this position, as the Minsk Group has continued its work, over a period of more than 20 years, without reaching a real solution to the problem, even a temporary one.

Of course at some point I also had to leave the CSCE; I was a career diplomat, and I needed to move to another assignment. My longtime colleague and friend John Kornblum called me in Vienna and asked if I was interested in going to the next round of CSCE negotiations, which was to take place in Helsinki. I saw that next round as likely to be a continuation of the slow negotiating process on development of the CSCE institutions which had already opened in Vienna and elsewhere, which I thought would be pretty boring after my adventurous work in the Caucasus. So after some reflection I told him that I thought this would be an appropriate time for me to leave the CSCE. Kornblum was then assigned to replace me as head of the US delegation going to Helsinki, leaving me with only my role as the US mediator for the Cyprus dispute—which was more symbolic than anything else, since the negotiating process in Cyprus was inactive at that time.

I was transferred back to Washington, which reduced my standard of living considerably, and also made travel to the European region much more difficult. The US mediator for the Cyprus issue was a long-standing Ambassadorial position, but it was based in Washington, and the negotiating process was stymied, with little likelihood of progress for at least a couple of years—probably much more.

My one achievement in relation to the Cyprus issue was a small but important initiative: when the continuation of the mandate for the UN Force in Cyprus came up for a vote in the Security Council for the first time after the break-up of the USSR, Russia vetoed it. This seemed pointless; the Force was not controversial (though it cost some money every year), but it was a key element in maintaining peace and stability on the island. It was not, strictly speaking, a "Peacekeeping" force, since it was put in place to preclude further Turkish advances. But it served as a separation force between the two armies on the island, so it had the same purpose as a "Peacekeeping" force.

There seemed to be no major reason for the Russian veto, other than relatively small cost savings. So I took the first available plane to Moscow, got an appointment with a senior official in the Foreign Ministry, and appealed for the Russians to reverse this veto. I argued that Russia had as much interest in maintaining peace in Cyprus as anyone else, that this small military force did not threaten any Russian interests, and that its running costs were limited. My Russian interlocutor listened seriously and took ample notes. By that time I think I was viewed with some respect in the Russian Foreign Ministry; they knew me well. Some weeks later the matter came up for another vote in New York, and the Russians did, indeed, reverse their veto.

But the possibilities for me to do anything serious or creative with respect to the situation in Cyprus were very limited. So after looking over the various alternatives and not getting any encouragement from the leadership in the State Department, I applied for early retirement from the Foreign Service. I did not think I would be offered an attractive position in the circumstances—my policy-level service in two Republican Administrations had made me look, for the Democrats, at least, like a Republican supporter, even though I had no party affiliation whatsoever. I concluded that for this reason I was unlikely to get any significant assignment under the Administration of President Bill Clinton, even though he had always seemed personally friendly and appreciative of my views.

I was very tired of working frantically, sometimes in difficult and dangerous situations, without strong support in Washington or even, at times, without anyone in Washington even being aware of where I was or what I was doing. I was certain, for example, that my difficult and dangerous role in relation to Nagorno-Karabakh—and my trips to that area—were of no significance in Washington, which really just wanted the problem to go away. Key people in Washington did not even know I was there. And the personnel department viewed me as a maverick.

I was also quite bitter. I thought that with strong US leadership it would be possible to find at least an acceptable interim solution to the Nagorno-Karabakh dispute, and I knew better than anyone else that without US leadership nothing would be possible. In fact, I felt that leaving it to Russian leadership, which was the unspoken or implicit approach being followed, would be a guarantee that the problem would never be solved, because the Russians would keep the situation as it was, and use it forever as leverage against both Armenia and Azerbaijan, to keep them in line and to prevent them from straying too far away from Russia's national interests. I still believe this is the case, and my views have only been reinforced by what has happened recently in Crimea and the rest of Ukraine.

The annexation of Crimea was a flagrant violation of the provisions of the Helsinki Final Act—specifically of the key conditionality for changes in frontiers, which was carefully worked out at the highest level between the United States and the USSR—as well as all other norms of international behavior. It is certainly true that the history of Crimea being "given" by Russia to Ukraine, when both were parts of the Soviet Union, makes it a special case. No one anticipated at the time of the Helsinki agreement that Ukraine would become a separate country, and the Crimea is heavily Russian. But the Donbass has become Ukraine's Nagorno Karabakh, a permanent point of leverage for Russia to influence Kiev, with Crimea serving as an example of what can happen if Russia's interests are not heeded.

At the same time, it must be said that the triumphalism of the West at the conclusion of the Cold War left Russia in the role of a defeated—and later even a dismembered—major power, and was bound to lead to a revival of Russian nationalism, and to growing support for some sort of revanchism. The triumphal slogan of "a Europe whole and free" was unfortunately a grinding insult to Russia. For Moscow the half of Europe which had been under their domination, as well as the whole of their cherished "Near Abroad," had slipped away, leaving Russia diminished, isolated and without the discredited ideology which had sustained them, and their world leadership role, for most of the century.

It was only a matter of time before the bitterness and the perceived need to re-establish itself as a major power, would lead Russia to start to show its strength and independence once again. This is, in fact, what we have seen in the last few years, under a nationalist leader, Vladimir Putin, who is ideally suited to this role. Russia is a key world power, and Russians are a proud people who have always been the leaders in the vast regions where they have dominated, and they found themselves treated as a defeated and humbled nation when the Soviet Union, the heir to the vast geographic entity which was the Russian Empire, suddenly broke apart.

Long after the horrendous and bloody war with Germany, long after Soviet tanks had over-run Berlin, with huge human suffering on both sides, long after the flag of the USSR had been hoisted over the Reichstag, it was the USSR which broke apart, just one year after Germany had been re-united. From the viewpoint of many Russian patriots, this was a humiliating situation which needed to be revised.

It was possible, in the aftermath of the breakup of the USSR, to foresee the way Russia would come back, and many of us did. Russia will never accept that its "Near Abroad" is not somehow a special Russian space, where the interests of Russia and of Russians must be given respect, and which is a key to Russia's national security. That Russia now has a leader who is once again staking out Russia's national interests in these areas should be no surprise to us—it was bound to happen, just as it did in Germany, some years after World War I. Moving weapons systems closer to Russia, bringing some of Russia's nearest neighbors into NATO, heralding the idea of a "Europe whole and free," were all red flags for Russian patriots. And so they backed a leader who represented their national pride, and who was ready to re-assert Russia's national interests in the face of Western triumphalism.

This is by no means a justification for Vladimir Putin's behavior with respect to Ukraine—the annexation of Crimea and the support to separatists in the Eastern part of the country. It is simply to note that we need to understand the thinking of Russians with respect to these "near abroad" regions, and toward the Russian populations who live in them, if we are to find, and pursue, a peaceful way forward in our relations with that important, leading world power.

The OSCE as it is currently structured offers limited, but interesting and potentially useful possibilities for helping to ensure peace and stability throughout the vast space of the former USSR. This nascent OSCE function has been demonstrated most recently by the activities of OSCE Observers in Ukraine, and should be developed. The OSCE has to some extent been marginalized as a sort of official NGO, but it has a genuine role to play in conflicts, or potential conflicts, of this kind, in regions where outside powers are hesitant to engage, and where the entry of forces external to the region could be provocative. In such situations the concept and practice of introducing OSCE Observers can be very useful in separating combatants or potential combatants in certain circumstances. This emerging function of the OSCE merits encouragement and development, especially in regions of Europe where stabilization is needed.

I originally proposed the creation of an on-going group of OSCE "Helsinki Observers" in an article in 1988 which was published in English in the Atlantic Community Quarterly and in French in Politique Etrangere, and I repeated this proposal in the Bulletin of the OSCE's Office for Democratic Institutions and Human Rights in 1995. I still believe it would be a useful way for the OSCE to insert itself into regional issues such as that in Ukraine today. The text of this proposal is included as an Annex to this book. (11)

Europe today, showing areas of local conflict in this region.
© Derivative work of Europe countries map en.png by San Jose, based on the Generic Mapping. Tools (http://gmt.soest.hawaii.edu/) and ETOPO2 (http://dss.ucar.edu/datasets/ds759.3/). Source: Wikimedia Commons. Licensed under CC BY-SA 3.0 (s. https://creativecommons.org/licenses/by-sa/3.0/deed.en)

Reflecting on Russia and the Near Abroad

Following my departure from the State Department I looked for a place to carry out some reflective research as I tried to re-organize my life. Inevitably this research was focused on my recent experience, trying to mediate a peaceful settlement to a bitter war, under the auspices of the CSCE.

Through Jim Goodby, a friend from our days together at NATO, who later became Ambassador to Finland but was better known as an expert on nuclear weapons systems, and negotiated one of the CSCE's several agreements on CSBMs, I became a visiting scholar at the US Institute of Peace (USIP), where Goodby was a Visiting Fellow. USIP is a government think-tank in Washington, focused on issues of peace and conflict; I think they simply made up the title of "visiting scholar," in order to have some auspices under which to accommodate me.

I spent a very useful and positive year at USIP, developing ideas, participating in the many conferences and discussions around the Washington "think-tank" circuit, and issuing papers. I issued a peace plan proposal for the Nagorno Karabakh conflict, which is still available in the archives as a USIP "Occasional Paper." For the ceremonial issuance of this paper I invited the Ambassadors of both Armenia and Azerbaijan to my presentation, and they came. I still think that paper is a pretty good illustration of a balanced peace agreement which could stabilize the South Caucasus region, be of great benefit to both sides of the conflict, and open the way to prosperity for all concerned. But of course the conflict is driven and maintained by factors which have nothing to do with logic or the need to find a compromise solution. Rather, it is driven by long-standing memories, on both sides, of horrific and bloody past episodes of violence. And rational, balanced, concepts for compromising, in order to live side-by-side in peace, can make no headway in such a situation. In these circumstances it would be prudent to settle on a stable temporary arrangement which can last for a substantial period of time and permit some distance to develop between the present and the hate-filled past.

I was also invited to Stanford University—the Center for International Security and Cooperation (CISAC)—to give a few lectures, and these were captured in a small book called "The End of the Cold War is Also Over," by which I meant that it was time to put the euphoria of the end-of-the-cold-war era behind us and start preparing for the new world challenges which were then emerging.

Toward the end of my year of research I applied for a USIP grant to produce a book on the Minsk Group negotiating process. I became a participant in the broad research effort carried out by the Carnegie Foundation on the causes and possible prevention, or resolution, of the conflicts in the European region at the end of the 20th Century, under the leadership of the Carnegie Commission on Preventing Deadly Conflict. The result was published as a study in a USIP book on conflicts which arose in the aftermath of the Cold War, and which were either resolved or were "missed opportunies" for conflict resolution. (12)

Obviously, the Nagorno Karabakh problem was (and, unfortunately, remains) one of the key case studies under the "missed opportunities" heading. If we had been able to push through some kind of settlement to the problem at that time—even some sort of interim settlement accompanied by serious peacekeeping measures—it would have saved many lives, and much of the misery which has been experienced in the region over all these years might have been avoided. But the positions of the "parties to the conflict" were too raw, there were open wounds on both sides, and it was not even possible to discuss issues calmly and rationally. Without being able at least to have such a discussion it is virtually impossible to make progress toward an acceptable solution.

But the Nagorno Karabakh issue was part of a much broader picture, which I began to understand when I was on my unique mission of opening relations with the newly independent states from the former Soviet Union, and I wrote about this broader picture in my chapter called "Russia's Near Abroad; A Dilemma for the West." In it I foresaw the difficulties that would be faced in the regions of the "Near Abroad." This vast space also includes many other lands, and peoples, some more important and well recognized than others, but all with a place in the huge area which Russians consider their extended homeland.

The Russian presence is felt very strongly in some areas, like the Eastern part of Ukraine, or the trans-Dniester area of Moldova. In other regions it is less dominant, but the Russian culture is still very present, and history identifies some of these regions as Russian for specific reasons that of course vary from region to region. Throughout these areas there are ethnic Russians who still believe that their cultural, historical, ethnic and ideological center is Russia itself. These are the people who Vladimir Putin was referring to in his speech following Russia's annexation of Crimea, when he said that, "Millions of people went to bed in one country and awoke in different ones, overnight becoming ethnic minorities . . . . The Russian nation became . . . the biggest ethnic group in the world to be divided by borders."

Putin was not wrong in this analysis. He was reflecting an issue which has been dormant since the breakup of the Soviet Union, the territorial heir to the Russian Empire, but which is now back on the table. Russia claims a role with respect to the whole of the post-Soviet space, and it claims to speak for the Russian people, wherever they are. This is a looming issue, currently being manifested in the fighting in Ukraine, but which can, potentially, become active anywhere in the post-Soviet areas. There are large Russian minorities in the Baltic states and elsewhere, for example, which could pose problems if they are not treated with care.

Another aspect of this history and its affect on the situation today is the fact that Russia claims the leading role in settling disputes throughout its former lands. Russia is involved, in one way or another, in conflicts in Azerbaijan-Armenia, Georgia, the North Caucasus, Moldova and Ukraine. Other similar problems lie buried in the complex regions and borderline divisions throughout the spaces of the former USSR. None of these conflicts or issues looks like it will simply fade away, and the Russian presence is a factor for stability in most of these places. So the Russian presence appears justified—even essential—in many of these regions.

Over time, this may change, but Russian interest and possessiveness about these regions is unlikely to fade away any time soon. Fortunately the special history of Crimea is unique, and it is unlikely that Russia could reclaim another territory under the same logic.

But the broader issue of Russia's "near abroad," and the possibilities for confrontation and/or conflict in these areas is quite real. Most of these regions, though not all, are pretty remote from other countries, so it is useful that the OSCE has developed some experience and rationale for inserting itself, at least in an observer status, when this is clearly needed.

In the present circumstances, when NATO, the European Union, and many other international entities, are unable to play much of a role in responding to Russian problems, it would be wise to expand the OSCE's activities throughout this region, so that it will have a credible presence which is widely felt and is seen as relevant to local issues. The OSCE has a unique ability to operate with legitimacy in these areas; it is widely accepted as non-threatening, and it represents universal values that are fully supported by all the OSCE's member states. OSCE Observers have proven their value in Ukraine.

The US should also show more interest in this vast region than it has. With the growing Chinese involvement in Central Asia, as a neighboring region, as a source of raw materials, as a market, and as the most direct route to Europe, the region is likely to develop rapidly. Europe needs to have on-going stability in the vast post-Soviet space, which is its nearest neighbor and which can have important effects on Europe's future, both positive and negative. But in addition this space is of great potential interest for Europe, if only as the likely transit route for the forthcoming direct railroad line from China to the West. In particular there should be a special and concentrated effort to resolve the lingering conflicts in the area, which have the potential at any time for provoking broader confrontations.

Prague

While I was working on my book project related to the Nagorno-Kharabakh conflict, in 1995, I was asked to become the President of a new research institute, called the "Open Media Research Institute (OMRI)" in Prague. This was the privatized successor to the research institute of Radio Free Europe and Radio Liberty, which had been operating in Munich, with substantial US government funding, throughout the Cold War. This research institute had accumulated over the years a unique and far-reaching set of archives, "samizdat," and other original Cold War source materials, and it published a distinguished academic journal.

At the end of the Cold War Congress had decided to close the research institute, but George Soros, with his personal interest in Eastern Europe, intervened. Soros provided some funding for the institute, with its priceless archives, and moved everything to Prague. The idea at first was to continue supporting the radios through the research conducted by the same institute which had supported them throughout the Cold War. The new Open Media Research Institute (OMRI) published a daily summary of developments in the space of the former USSR and Eastern Europe, as well as a slick monthly magazine, called "Transition." I moved to Prague to run this new institute.

During my time as President of OMRI I published the main part of the memoirs of Anatoly Kovalev, the long-time Deputy Foreign Minister of the USSR responsible for relations with Europe (he held that position for 20 years), who had been the head of the Soviet delegation at the CSCE negotiations in Geneva in 1973-75, in "Transition" magazine. I was approached on Kovalev's behalf by my old friend, Vladimir Petrovsky, who had been the Secretary of the Soviet Delegation to the original CSCE, and who had become the overall Director General of UN institutions in Geneva.

I was of course very interested to see these memoirs, wondering what they might contain, so I responded enthusiastically, and duly received a very long fax scroll which was translated into English by our OMRI staff. I read thru it all, but only part of it was of general interest, and I published that part in "Transition".

I thought this was supremely ironic: who would have thought that the young diplomat in the US delegation with the reputation of being a hard-liner, would, almost twenty years later, publish the memoirs of the tough, disciplined Deputy Foreign Minister who was the leader of the Soviet delegation?

Life's turnabouts never cease to amaze me. Thanks to the efforts of my research assistant, who was from Moldova, and the cooperation of the Hungarian staff of the library at the Central European University in Budapest, the part of Kovalev's memoires which I published in Transition magazine in Prague, after receiving them from Moscow via Geneva, are included as an annex at the end of this book.

But OMRI turned out to be a short-lived institution, and when I finished my one-year contract in Prague I returned to Paris. One day I was sitting in my apartment, appreciating life on the Ile St. Louis, when I was called by John Imle, the President of Union Oil of California (Unocal), the well-established energy company which discovered oil in the Los Angeles area at the end of the nineteenth century. Unocal was headquartered in Manhattan Beach, California, and Houston, Texas, and was the fourth or fifth largest energy company in the US. I had originally met Imle in Baku when Unocal and other Western energy companies started visiting the region following the dissolution of the USSR.

Imle said that Unocal needed my political expertise and experience, especially in the Central Asia—Caucasus region, where they were deeply involved, and he invited me to join the company as Vice President for International Relations. I accepted, and left that very afternoon to join the Unocal plane enroute to Asia. They picked me up, ironically, at the airport in Moscow, flying in over the North Pole from Los Angeles. And after that I did not really look back. The energy business is absorbing and exhilarating—a great adventure in itself—and I plunged into it with enthusiasm. My days as a diplomat were over.

***

Epilogue

Some years after joining the Unocal Corporation I was in New York on company business, and completed my appointments early on a wintry afternoon. I decided to go out to the Brooklyn Museum to see an exhibition of Kajar court paintings from Iran, which were on temporary display. I caught a taxi in front of the Yale Club; it was snowing.
We moved slowly through Manhattan because of the thickening snowfall, and crossed the Brooklyn Bridge. I asked the driver, a woman with an accent who was not young, where she was from. Russia. Where? Near the Ural Mountains. When had she come to America? She left Russia in 1975.
1975! It was like a bell ringing, and waking me to a whole different world—one which I had all but forgotten! At that instant I knew that she was Jewish, and that she had been able to leave the USSR in the positive aftermath of the signing of the Helsinki Final Act.
I asked her how she had managed to get out, what was her story?
By this time it was snowing heavily, and we were driving slowly, painstakingly, inching our way through the center of Brooklyn. Thru several blocks the lettering on the walls and billboards was all in the Hebrew alphabet, then a few blocks later it was in Chinese, then Arabic, then Cyrillic. Something which, perhaps, can only be seen in Brooklyn.
And as we crept along, she told me her story: she was from a small village near the Ural Mountains. She had lived there with her family, a plain existence: growing vegetables for the winter, keeping chickens, cutting wood for the fire, drawing water. They had applied for visas to emigrate to Israel, but the visas never came. They had long ago given up hope.
And then, late one night, there was a knock on the door. It was an official from the village. He said their visas had been granted, they were free to emigrate. But they would have to leave immediately, on

the morning train, or they would lose the opportunity. They could take just one suitcase with them—one for each person.

The family stayed up all night discussing the situation. They would be leaving behind their home, their relatives and friends, all their possessions, everything they had ever known. But they decided to leave, and in the morning they took that train.

There followed a year or two when they were moved from one refugee center to another. They made choices, and, finally, they arrived in New York. At first, the mother was the only member of the family to find work, as a taxi driver. She had driven a taxi ever since. Twenty years as a taxi driver in New York City.

I was stunned. I knew that she and her family had received their visas to leave as a part of the USSR's limited efforts to show they were carrying out some of their obligations under the Final Act, in the aftermath of the Helsinki Summit. So I asked her whether she thought it was all worth it—leaving their country, and their lives, behind to come to America.

She stopped the car, in the snow, in the middle of the main avenue of Brooklyn, and turned around to face me. "Are you kidding," she asked? "My son is a doctor in Los Angeles, my daughter is a lawyer in Manhattan, my other son is a public relations executive in Philadelphia. It changed our lives!"

My driver deposited me by the gardens at the entrance to the Brooklyn Museum, and I stood for a few minutes in the heavily–falling snow. I reflected on this story, and on the way I too had arrived in the USA many years before, as a small child, with my mother and sister, coming down the ramp from an Italian ship during the Second World War, with nothing but the clothes on our backs. And then growing up as an American, just as this woman's children had done. Life had come full circle, and this was my Helsinki, revisited.

****

Annex

The following documents, press articles and book chapters are included here because they shed light on the events described in this book, as well as the thinking of the author as these events were unfolding. The text of the "Joint Declaration of Twenty-Two States" is included since it is rarely seen in the context of the CSCE/OSCE, because of its more limited list of signatures, but is very relevant to the history of the CSCE/OSCE and to the evolution of events in Europe at the time of the signature of the Charter of Paris for a New Europe.

Annex 1: Anatoly Kovalev: Looking Back on the Helsinki Final Act

Annex 2: John J. Maresca: The CSCE at Its Inception: 1975 in Myth and Reality

Annex 3: JOINT DECLARATION OF TWENTYTWO STATES
PARIS, 19 NOVEMBER 1990

Annex 4: Baltic States' Exclusion from Paris Summit of the CSCE. Excerpts from contemporary reports in the Estonian press

Annex 5: John J. Maresca: Russia's "Near Abroad"—A Dilemma for the West

Annex 6: IMPLEMENTATION OF THE HELSINKI ACCORDS

Annex 7: CSCE Negotiations On Nagorno-Karabakh. John J. Maresca, Joint Statement

Annex 8: Betty Blair: Forging a Lasting Peace. The Nagorno-Karabakh Conflict. An Interview with John J. Maresca

Annex 9: John J. Maresca: ENSURING CSCE PROMISES ARE KEPT

Annex 10: John J. Maresca: FOREIGN DEVILS ON THE SILK ROAD—TAKE TWO

Annex 1

Anatoly Kovalev: **Looking Back on the Helsinki Final Act**[1]

In this 20th anniversary year of the signing of the Helsinki Final Act, the chief Soviet negotiator of the 1975 agreement, Anatoly Kovalev, reveals some of the USSR's difficulties in making concessions on human rights and freedom of information. In these excerpts from a new, unpublished memoir, Kovalev lifts the veil on the Soviet delegation's discussions with Moscow and concludes that those who supported the act were 'renovationists' who helped to bring the concept of human rights to the former Soviet Union.

> "With the Helsinki Final Act, the people—all of us and each of us—became subjects of international law and acquired the status of active participants in interstate relations."

On trying to convince the KGB to accept Soviet concessions to the "Basket Three" section of the agreement, which covered human rights and free information and was the main problem area for the USSR:

Regarding the development of our instructions [Moscow's instructions to the Soviet negotiators]. I realized that it would be useless to begin [seeking Moscow's] agreement from a working level. "Cut the bottom out of this third basket" was the scathing phrase that [Foreign Minister Andrei] Gromyko uttered several times within the wide circle of Foreign Ministry officials—half-jokingly, but for the most part seriously.

At one of the meetings of the Foreign Ministry collegium, I proposed ratifying the UN pacts on human rights. Soon they were ratified. This gave

---

[1] "Anatoly Kovalev: Looking Back on the Helsinki Final Act," Excerpt from the memoirs of Ambassador Anatoly Kovalev, as published in *Transition* magazine by the Open Media Research Institute, Prague, 30 June 1995. © John J. Maresca.

our delegation [in Geneva] elbow room to conduct negotiations on human rights, at least regarding the conditions and formulations of the UN pacts.

In the process of working on our instructions, I called [KGB head Yury] Andropov. He asked the question point blank: What do you need? Of course, I did not go into details. First, I requested the opening of foreign cultural centers in Moscow. To my surprise, Andropov agreed to add it to our instructions, surrounding the opening of such centers with several conditions. Further, I began to convince Andropov of the need to stop jamming foreign radio programs. I raised the idea that it was better to do it on our own than under pressure. He promised to proceed in precisely this manner and fulfilled his promise.

On discussing the 1974 arrest of Alexander Solzhenitsyn with Andropov and the impact the decision to bring Solzhenitsyn to trial could have had on the Helsinki Final Act negotiations, which were then focused on human rights.

Andropov greeted me, as usual, amicably. Pivotal in the conversation was the question obviously disturbing him: what to do with Solzhenitsyn? I answered that Solzhenitsyn was a great Russian writer and that, in my opinion, he should not be brought to trial or touched in general.

This conversation continued. Alexander Shelepin, then the chairman of the Soviet trade unions, flew to Geneva. He told me that the Politburo had made a decision to bring Solzhenitsyn to trial. He asked me whether he could report that the head of the Soviet delegation in the Geneva negotiations was not against the court case. I answered categorically "no." I expressed my belief that this could derail the Geneva negotiations and the whole all-European process. I laid out this position in a telegram quickly dispatched to Moscow.

> *"As the Geneva negotiations drew to a close, it became obvious that without making concessions on several concrete issues in the section on information and contacts, a consensus on the final document would not be reached."*

[Solzhenitsyn was expelled from the country rather than brought to trial.]

On taking a personal stand in recommending the acceptance of the controversial "Basket Three":

As the Geneva negotiations drew to a close, it became obvious to me that without making concessions on several concrete issues in the section on information and contacts, a consensus as a whole on the final document would not be reached. But these were complicated issues requiring unusual changes in our existing practices and those of other Warsaw Pact countries—ideas that required the green light from Moscow.

Before making a final decision, I asked my wife to walk alone with me along the Geneva river. I told her that I planned to send Moscow a proposal that carried the risk of serious career difficulties that would also affect the situation of our family. Was she prepared for that? "I am prepared," she answered. And she added, "I consider it your duty."

> "Until the Helsinki Final Act, our ideological clichés were built on the idea that only socialist states or governments reflected the will of their peoples."

Late in the evening, the members of the delegation met in my office. I laid out for them a plan for finding mutually acceptable resolutions to the last remaining issues in the final document.

From the very beginning of the meeting, the reaction of my colleagues indicated that they were not psychologically or politically prepared for such a drastic change in several of the positions that they had maintained right up to that evening with such firmness and skill. They were also concerned that Moscow would not understand us. For the first time during the entire Geneva stage, the opinion of the head of the delegation did not find support from even one of the delegation members. Petrovsky was absent: he was somewhere, in the city. Dubinin and Kondrashov [the KGB representative in the delegation] spoke the most definitively against my ideas.

Ending the discussion, I said that I would submit to Moscow only my personal ideas and not the ideas of the delegation. Then, in front of my colleagues, I signed the telegram. In less than 24 hours, I received a telegram from Moscow [expressing] agreement to all my suggestions.

On the Soviet-era "renovationists" who "loosened the soil" for advocates of human rights by supporting the Helsinki Final Act:

We ... met our partners [in the CSCE negotiations] halfway for several concrete items filling the "third basket." In particular, we accepted a formulation—which for those times was very liberal—that member states would examine in a positive and humane spirit requests from people who wished to reunite with members of their families: they would also lower fees levied in connection with these requests in order to ensure their moderate level. They would try gradually to simplify exit and entry procedures for personal and business travel.

There were also concrete items in the sphere of increasing access to and exchange of information. The stipulated measures included: gradually increasing the quantity and number of titles of newspapers and printed publications imported from other member states and augmenting the number of points where such publications would be sold. A significant improvement in the working conditions of journalists was also envisioned.

In particular, accredited journalists from the member states would be granted multiple-entry and -exit visas on the basis of the agreement; opportunities for journalists to meet personally with their information sources would be increased; and journalists would be allowed to pass on to their agencies all the information that they had gathered from their professional activities, including tape recordings and undeveloped film.

These were not minor or technical details. In the stagnant atmosphere of the mid-1970s, and even now, facilitating the work of journalism fraternities is the daily bread for publishing agencies, radio, and television. ...

Until the Helsinki Final Act, our ideological clichés were built on the idea that only socialist states or governments reflected the will of their peoples. This postulate left many loopholes for the interpretation of any international document, however majestic it sounded, and however democratic its facade appeared. This facade hid ideological irreconcilability and incompatible ideas. In the Helsinki Final Act, the people—all of us and each of us—became subjects of international law and acquired the status of active participants in interstate relations.

Despite the conceptual concreteness of the formulations, the spirit of humanism and democracy permeating the Final Act loosened the soil for the emergence of human rights movements and Helsinki groups.

Already in the 1940s, a group of people with unorthodox views about the surrounding world began to grow and take shape in our country and in many others. Seeking to define them, I would say "a breed of reformers." In one word, they are not time-servers but "renovationists." They are people of different professions, nationalities, and ages who, some sooner and some later, arrived in general at similar conclusions and estimations. These people are the veterans and volunteers comprising the backbone of the Helsinki process.

Anatoly Kovalev was the Soviet deputy foreign minister (responsible for Western Europe) from 1971-1986 and the first deputy minister of foreign affairs (responsible for the CSCE and Western Europe) from 1986-1991. He was head of the Soviet delegation to the Helsinki Final Act negotiations, and in 1990 he accepted the Nobel Peace Prize on behalf of Mikhail Gorbachev.

Annex 2

John J. Maresca: **The CSCE at Its Inception: 1975 in Myth and Reality**[1]

I confess to having had a thirty-year love-hate relationship with the CSCE. Perhaps I am unique among those who were responsible for the negotiation of the Final Act of 1975 because of my long association with the CSCE in the years that followed. After the Final Act was signed in Helsinki, I returned to Washington to head the State Department office responsible for the CSCE. In that capacity, I pursued the commitments of the Final Act by establishing an annual report on their implementation and pressing NATO to commission a similar report. I then returned to the first follow-up meeting of the CSCE in Belgrade in 1979. I published a book entitled "To Helsinki"[2] on the negotiation of the Final Act. And I returned once again to the CSCE as head of the US Delegation when the Conference reconvened in Vienna in 1989. In Vienna, we negotiated the "Charter of Paris for a New Europe", signed at the Summit in 1990 to symbolically close the Cold War.

On the one hand, my involvement in the CSCE was clearly one of the dominant experiences of my diplomatic career. But the ambiguity of American views towards this sprawling negotiating process, the political battles related to it in Washington, and the effects of all this on me personally, left scars each time I worked directly with the CSCE. And the ups and downs of successes and dead-end failures in the CSCE process itself have been difficult not only to judge, but also to live through.

It was always professionally and psychologically dangerous – a kind of high-wire act – because the American negotiators had virtually no instructions, no real communication with the political leadership in Washington and no back-up. If you made a misstep, there would be no one there to

---

[1] First published in: OSCE Yearbook 2005. Institute for Peace Research and Security Policy at the University of Hamburg (IFSH), p. 29-38. © Nomos Verlagsgesellschaft, Baden-Baden. Reprinted with kind permission.
[2] John J. Maresca, *To Helsinki: The Conference on Security and Cooperation in Europe, 1973-1975*, Durham, NC 1985.

catch you. And in the end it became physically dangerous too, at least for me.

In the early 1990s I flew "nap of the earth" style into war zones in the Caucasus in rickety old Russian Army helicopters. "I'll be back at five o'clock", my Russian Army pilot said to me once, as I disembarked on a CSCE mission in the middle of God-only-knew-where. "And I'll wait for five minutes." Few people in Washington knew what I was doing, and even fewer cared. The result for me has been that, while sharing the fascination that other Helsinki hands have felt for this sporadic negotiating process, I have also tried to distance myself from it.

***

It was August 1975 in Helsinki and I was indeed "the only American who understood what was going on in the negotiations", as the Assistant Secretary of State for European Affairs, Arthur Hartman, put it to Henry Kissinger at the time of the Summit. And Hartman was right – I understood it all: the complex relationships between the different issues, the key personalities involved, what was at stake and how to resolve the various Gordian knots so that the result would be acceptable. The Final Act was acceptable, it was done and Gerry Ford and Leonid Brezhnev and all the others signed it.

Unfortunately for me, the CSCE was always something of a political football in Washington – the Republicans embarrassedly disowning it despite the fact that the main events happened on their watches; the Democrats trying hard to blame the Republicans for ignoring the CSCE's potential, while also trying desperately to take the credit for making it work, particularly with respect to Russian Jewish emigration and East European hopes for independence, issues that resonated among the American electorate. Looking back over the thirty years that have passed since the Final Act was signed, during many of which I was deeply involved in CSCE negotiations and activities, I ask myself again that question we all posed in Helsinki in the summer of 1975: What is the real significance of the Final Act? This remains the central question for those of us who participated in the negotiations, who observed them and measured the results against the historical forces at work in Europe at the time. The heart of the matter is the extent to which this negotiation, this event, this document, this historical episode, had something to do with the unraveling of the Communist system in the USSR and its satellite governments in what was then called Eastern Europe.

The specifics of what was negotiated were modest, especially to the experienced analytical reader. In the autumn of 1975, I was invited to speak on the Helsinki Final Act to an assembly of interested professors at the Harvard Faculty Club. The first question after my presentation was from an indignant professor who had only heard of our negotiations when President Ford announced that he would participate in the signing: "Why were we not informed that these negotiations were going on?" In reply, I said that everything we were doing was public and that at least two American professors I knew had followed the negotiations closely, out of personal interest. The real question, I threw back, was why American academics in general, so focused on nuclear negotiations and other strategic matters, were not interested in our conference.

A second, only slightly more respectful question was this: "With all this paper, all this complex language, was this two-year negotiation really worth it?" As it happened, just the week before the State Department had arranged for the reunification of two Czechoslovak children with their parents, on the basis of the family reunification provisions of the Final Act. I told the story, and then added: "If one child is reunited with his or her parents because of our effort, then it was worth it."

But such reunifications were rare, sporadic successes in a much broader situation, which had not changed, and did not change in any fundamental way for another dozen years.

It is tempting, now that the Cold War is over and Europe has evolved into such a different place, to exaggerate the importance of the Final Act and its role in bringing about the historical changes that took place towards the end of the century. I have heard many people do this, especially those who were involved in the CSCE negotiations of that period. It is also tempting to exaggerate the importance of the roles played by oneself or one's group. I have also observed this recently, at so-called "oral history" sessions, and in myself, too. But is it correct?

Certainly the CSCE had its place in the historical evolution of that time, but was it a force for change or a reflection of it?

The content of the Final Act is, in fact, rather thin. Taking a look at what was vaunted by the Western group at the time as the Basket Three "Family Package" of freer travel, marriages between nationals of different states, family contacts, and reunification, one wonders why these modest points should have been considered so threatening by the Communist countries that they resisted accepting them at the negotiating table for two years. And the Final Act's simple allusion to human rights must be contrasted with the fact that human rights were already laid out very fully in the Universal Declaration of Human rights of 1948, which is legally binding for all signatories of the United Nations Charter, unlike the commitments of the CSCE, which were purely political. The CSCE really added very little to the existing obligations in this field.

And yet the Soviet Union did indeed ferociously resist every positive adjective, every clarifying comma, and carefully sought to add qualifiers and weaken the verb forms to avoid any sense of real obligation in the "freer movement" sections of the document. The Soviets, so it appeared, deeply feared those adjectives and verb forms. The reality was that the low priority attached to these initiatives by Western governments, particularly the administration in Washington, had led the Soviets to conclude that they did not need to accept them and could get to Helsinki without doing so. These "freer movement" ideas had been dreamed up and drafted on paper at the working level, primarily in the Political Committee at NATO, in Brussels. While they had been officially endorsed by Western governments, no senior Western political personality was in a position to argue them out with the Soviet leadership.

The Soviet Basket Three negotiator took advantage of this situation. He was a master of the techniques of bullying, ridiculing, and humiliating his Western counterparts and did so whenever possible. He held the line against all those threatening stronger adjectives and verb forms right up to the last moment. He even resisted the urging of his fellow delegation members, even the chief of his own delegation. This was recounted to us regularly by his colleagues in the corridors of the negotiation and afterwards. And it was also noted in an article I published in 1996, in the now-defunct magazine "Transition", by the chief Soviet negotiator, Anatoly Kovalev, shortly before his death. The Soviet Basket Three negotiator resisted those adjectives until he was overruled by the Kremlin and the Politburo of the Communist Party itself, at the very last moment, in order to make way for the Summit Meeting in Helsinki that Leonid Brezhnev so ardently wanted. Why such fierce resistance? It seems absurd today. Ironically, though, it almost did not matter what we put into the Final Act. All of our efforts on specific proposals and airtight wording were irrelevant. What mattered — perhaps the only thing that mattered — was that there *was* a Final Act and that it seemed to represent some sort of consensus agreement on human rights and "freer movement of people and ideas". As we learned in the months and years that followed, the dissidents in the USSR and Eastern Europe would have agitated on the basis of almost any CSCE document. And it was, finally, the agitation of the dissidents and the yearnings of ordinary people that brought down the Communist system.

This real impact of the Final Act was only revealed later, and it was both dramatic and singular, as well as complex, multi-faceted, subtle, and unexpected. What we found as the Cold War drew to a close was that the Final Act had created a new dynamic, based on a newly universalized set of values. And, perhaps most importantly, it had created a new dimension, a new space, in which to pursue these values.

The Final Act created a new space, a space in which new kinds of events were possible. And we did not realize this until history demanded such a space, because the events that took place later were unthinkable in 1975.

***

The drama came in Central Europe in the sultry summer days of 1989. At that time, a number of East Germans, on vacation in Hungary, sought exit visas to cross the border into Austria. They knew that if they could reach the West German Embassy in Vienna, a short distance from the Austro-Hungarian frontier, they would immediately be issued West German passports, and be free. Free.

The Hungarian government, itself evolving in response to popular demands, was caught in a dilemma. A bilateral treaty with the German Democratic Republic (GDR) precluded it from issuing such exit visas to GDR citizens without the prior consent of the GDR government. But Bucapest's reading of the Helsinki Final Act was that the Hungarian government was required to allow persons to leave the country if they wished to do so. For whatever combination of reason and rationale, the Hungarian government decided that it was more important in 1989 to respect their commitments under the Final Act than it was to respect their bilateral obligations to the GDR. The result was that thousands of East German vacationers joyously crossed the border into Austria and made their way, as fast as they could, to Vienna and the West German Embassy. At the time, I was the American ambassador to the CSCE meeting in Vienna, and I well recall the astonishment and pleasure we all felt at seeing those tiny East German "Trabant" cars left by the side of the road. The East German families that had been driving them simply abandoned them when they ran out of gas, and hitchhiked the rest of the way to Vienna and the West German Embassy, where the queues of passport applicants stretched around the corner.

But those East Germans abandoned more than just their cars. They were so anxious to reach freedom that they left behind all of their possessions, their apartments, and their relatives, without any real hope of ever seeing them again. It was a moving historical moment. One could sense that this was indeed the tiny trickle coming through the dyke and that the dyke itself would collapse very soon.

Events rushed ahead that year as East Germans clambered over the walls of the West German Embassy in Prague, leading to the collapse of East Germany, of Soviet domination of Eastern (now again called Central) Europe, and even the disintegration of the USSR itself. My Austrian colleague sent me a section of the demolished barbed wire fence that had sealed the frontier with Hungary. I still have it, twisted and rusty, in my office. Farmers once again began ploughing long-unused fields that crossed the border.

In 1989, I participated in a meeting of American ambassadors in Europe, held in Berlin, where the discussion was on the implications of these events. Most of the ambassadors present thought that Moscow would crack down and suppress this latest round of agitation for freedom, as it had in the past. But three of us, Henry Grunwald, Dick Walters, and I, argued that there was something different at work here and that it would be very difficult for the Soviets to walk this cat back.

Even more surprising developments began to take place in this new space. One day, Albania, isolated from the rest of Europe since the 1940s, asked to become a member of the CSCE. In Vienna the Conference was caught by surprise by this unexpected *démarche*. Albania had been invited to join the original CSCE negotiations in 1973, but had never responded; no one doubted that they were eligible to join. But how to admit them to the CSCE space after so much had happened on the basis of commitments taken years before?

The key ambassadors conferred at the Hofburg Palace, where the CSCE met. We decided we needed a "snapshot", meaning a report, of conditions in Albania at that moment, to be able to judge how the country would implement its commitments after becoming a member. But how to do this on behalf of the CSCE? Easy, I told my German colleague, since Germany held the rotating CSCE Chairmanship at the time: We will send a CSCE mission to Albania to report on conditions there. How can we do that, he responded; the CSCE has never had a mission. If we decide to do it, I said, we can do it. That was the first CSCE mission. Since that time CSCE missions (now sometimes called "centres" of "offices") have multiplied all over Europe and Central Asia, with different mandates and wide-ranging specialist staffing, giving the CSCE an entirely new dimension for encouraging respect for its values. I was sent to Albania and the Newly Independent States as a special envoy, to evaluate the situation on behalf of the United States and to explain the basis for our bilateral relations. I met with the leaders of these governments, most of them quite surprised to find an American ambassador in their midst. In Tirana, the defence minister, a sophisticated engineer in his fifties, told me I was the first American he had ever seen.

The Charter of Paris for a New Europe, signed in 1990, established the CSCE's Office for Democratic Institutions and Human Rights (ODIHR) in Warsaw, an important institution in its own right, which now helps to ensure, through election monitoring and other devices, that the democratic and human rights standards optimistically referred to in the Final Act of 1975, and in later CSCE agreements, are respected in practice.

Another example of what was made possible by the creation of this new dimension through the Helsinki Final Act was an obscure but important document called the "Joint Declaration of Twenty-Two States". This document, negotiated in the lead-up to the Paris Summit of 1990, was signed at the Elysee Palace by all the members of NATO and the Warsaw Pact. It declared that the Cold War was over, and that there was no longer any reason for hostility among them. If there is a document that confirms that the Cold War was over, this "Joint Declaration" is it. Such a document could perhaps only have been negotiated in the unique CSCE space.

The Final Act had also held the door open for the reunification of Germany, through its language on possible peaceful changes of borders: "They [the participating States] consider that their frontiers can be changed, in accordance with international law, by peaceful means and by agreement." This sentence was negotiated personally by Andrei Gromyko and Henry Kissinger on behalf of the West German government, for this specific purpose. As one striking example of the low esteem in which Washington held the CSCE, the negotiation of this key clause of the Final Act was ridiculed publicly by Kissinger as a negotiation over the "placement of commas", though it was the placement of the two commas in this phrase that gave it its full significance: changes in frontiers *are* in accordance with international law if they are brought about by peaceful means and mutual agreement.

When the Cold War ended, there were indeed many changes in European frontiers, some peaceful, some convulsive, as history caught up with the evolutions that had taken place between 1945 and 1990. In Germany, in the USSR, in Yugoslavia, and in Czechoslovakia, borders were changed. Some established states disappeared, some new ones appeared, and some old ones reappeared. Of course, the Final Act was not used as the basis or the rationale for the actions that led to these national changes, but the Final Act nonetheless did foreclose many questions, or even possible obstacles, that might have been raised against them. One day, my East German colleague, whose place at the conference table, in alphabetical order, was right next to mine, told me he was saying goodbye. He was an engaging man, to whom I had once tried to explain what "market forces" are. We wished each other well, as ambassadors do when one is transferred. But the next day there was no longer an East German at our conference table.

And the CSCE had not yet reached the limits of how it could surprise and respond to new developments. When the USSR dissolved into independent republics, the first issue posed for the CSCE was how to treat the Newly Independent States that had been parts of the USSR. The answer was clear for those new states that were physically within geographic Europe – Lithuania, Latvia, Estonia, Belarus, Ukraine, and Moldova, plus of course Russia. They were indisputably eligible for CSCE membership. But what attitude should the CSCE adopt towards the new states of the Caucasus and Central Asia – Georgia, Armenia, Azerbaijan, Kazakhstan, Turkmenistan, Uzbekistan, Tajikistan, and Kyrgyzstan?

Many Europeans argued that these new countries were "not European" and therefore could not rightly belong to a European conference. But my view was that these countries had been members of the CSCE from the beginning as parts of the USSR, which was one of the Conference's original participating States. They had thus already accepted and were bound by the commitments of the Final Act, unless they chose to renounce them as independent countries. So not receiving them as CSCE participating States would be tantamount to throwing them out, an action for which there was no justification.

Moreover, I argued that if these countries had the vocation to adhere to the Final Act's commitments, we should welcome that and seek to ensure that these commitments were respected after independence. In the end, these new countries were all invited to join the CSCE in their own right, and today the OSCE and its missions (or centres or offices) are active throughout these states, and in former Yugoslavia, giving the new states important ties with Europe and the West.

It can be argued, I believe, that the evolution of these states since their independence has been influenced by their membership of what is now the OSCE. OSCE observers from ODIHR in Warsaw have watched over and commented on their elections (as they have also done in the most recent American presidential election), and OSCE Centres and Offices in many of these states offer a glimpse of the system of values recognized in the Final Act. That these Newly Independent States should be linked – even by so fragile a thread as the OSCE – with transnational standards of human rights and democratic governance is a positive element for their development. Indeed, we have heard echoes of Helsinki in events in the Baltic states, in the Caucasus, and most recently in Ukraine, as these countries have pursued their destinies. Even the much ridiculed "arms control junk food" of CSCE military security commitments, the so-called Confidence and Security-Building Measures (first called Confidence Building Measures, CBMs, which later evolved into CSBMs), have had a certain underappreciated importance. This family of modest gestures towards military *détente* first appeared in the Final Act and was developed and expanded in later CSCE negotiations. It was in one of those later negotiations that agreement was first reached on a no-notice military inspection regime between NATO and the USSR, opening the door to other such inspection regimes in relation to nuclear missiles and conventional forces.

The CSCE has had its failures, too, but that is to be expected. The Final Act contained hopeful language on the peaceful settlement of disputes, later developed into a "mechanism" for resolving interstate disagreements. But this has remained on paper only, and the CSCE mechanism has never been used for specific dispute resolution.

It is true that the CSCE has sometimes been able to enter situations in a "good offices" role, when other organizations could not. This was true, for example, of its missions to Chechnya. But it has not done well at conflict mediation thus far. I can bear witness personally to this, since I was a part of the CSCE's first mediation effort – between Armenians and Azerbaijanis in relation to the conflict over Nagorno-Karabakh. That initiative, oddly called the "Minsk Group", is still going on, still without any real success. This mediation, which was politically – and also physically – dangerous at a time when the vicious conflict in the area was still raging, has been a failure, at least thus far. Or is this failure actually because the United States government has not really pressed for a settlement, in view of its own conflicting political interests in the region?

When Yugoslavia began its descent into the inferno of ethnic cleansing and ruthless civil conflict, the CSCE was unable to muster an adequate response. There were discussions in CSCE meetings, and resolutions were passed. But in those early days, the United States thought this should be a "European problem", and pushed the European Union to take the lead in dealing with it. And the Europeans, who could not even agree on a general approach, were slow, inept, and lacking in the essential political will. Under the circumstances, the CSCE was reduced to adding some symbolic CSCE representatives to the EU's all-but-useless "observer force".

But perhaps the CSCE and its varied emanations have avoided conflicts, which have not surfaced because of the efforts of its institutions. This was the intent of the CSCE in establishing a position called the High Commissioner on National Minorities. The two persons who have held this position, former Dutch Foreign Minister Max van der Stoel and, currently, Rolf Ekéus, a Swedish diplomat, have concentrated their work in countries where there is potential for internal conflict, and their interventions have apparently had positive effects. While it is of course impossible to know what might have happened without these efforts, even if only one conflict has been avoided this would be no small achievement in view of the number of wars that have broken out in Europe after the close of the Cold War.

***

How should we understand this vast panorama of events in the CSCE's "space", which opened in August of 1975 and has not yet closed, though shifting priorities may yet sideline it? In my book about the negotiation of the Final Act, I suggested that the Final Act was a kind of ersatz peace treaty, substituting for the formal peace treaty, which would most likely never be signed, to close the Second World War. Now, many years later, I realize that I was at least partly wrong. My analysis at that time was too simple, too instantaneous, and perforce did not take account of the evolution that has taken place in the thirty years that followed.

The way I would summarize it now is this: The Final Act opened a vast political and historical dimension of opportunity, in which it became possible to settle the remaining issues from World War II. The Cold War, it now appears, was a lingering and long-unresolved final battle of that war. Only when the Cold War battle ended was it possible to say that the Second World War had truly been closed.

The "peace treaty" ending the Second World War is, in fact, a complex of documents that includes the Final Act, the Charter of Paris, the Joint Declaration of Twenty-Two States, the agreements on German reunification, and many other less central instruments. And now, when one can move freely across the German plains through Poland into Ukraine and even Russia, Europe is indeed whole again, free of the legacies of the war.

Much of this history took place within the new "space" created by the Final Act. Perhaps it would be an exaggeration to say it could *only* have taken place after the Final Act. The peoples of Europe are really the force that changed the situation from that of the Cold War to what Europe has now become. But I believe it is fair to say that the progression was eased thanks to the effects of the CSCE.

***

From the time in 1973 when George Vest called me to ask if I would join him in the US Delegation to the negotiations in Helsinki, I was fascinated by the CSCE. I have always had a great admiration for Vest, a truly talented and original multilateral negotiator, with a folksy style all his own. "If you just sit there, and are prepared to listen to people," Vest used to say, "people will come and talk to you." I can see him now, straddling a backless leather bench in the lobby of the CSCE Conference Centre, with other ambassadors circling about, waiting to have a word with him. And perhaps, after all, this is the main strength – and the legacy – of the CSCE: a place where people will listen, and therefore a place where people can talk. Is this a modest achievement, or is it the key to finding solutions?

Annex 3

JOINT DECLARATION OF TWENTYTWO STATES
PARIS, 19 NOVEMBER 1990

The Heads of State or Government of Belgium, Bulgaria, Canada, the Czech and Slovak Federal Republic, Denmark, France, Germany, Greece, Hungary, Iceland, Italy, Luxembourg, the Netherlands, Norway, Poland, Portugal, Romania, Spain, Turkey, the Union of Soviet Socialist Republics, the United Kingdom and the United States of America

greatly welcoming the historic changes in Europe,

gratified by the growing implementation throughout Europe of a common commitment to pluralist democracy, the rule of law and human rights, which are essential to lasting security on the continent,

affirming the end of the era of division and confrontation which has lasted for more than four decades, the improvement in relations among their countries and the contribution this makes to the security of all,

confident that the signature of the Treaty on Conventional Armed Forces in Europe represents a major contribution to the common objective of increased security and stability in Europe, and

convinced that these developments must form part of a continuing process of cooperation in building the structures of a more united continent,

Issue the following Declaration:
1. The signatories solemnly declare that, in the new era of European relations which is beginning, they are no longer adversaries, will build new partnerships and extend to each other the hand of friendship.
2. They recall their obligations under the Charter of the United Nations and reaffirm all of their commitments under the Helsinki

Final Act. They stress that all of the ten Helsinki Principles are of primary significance and that, accordingly, they will be equally and unreservedly applied, each of them being interpreted taking into account the others. In that context, they affirm their obligations and commitment to refrain from the threat or use of force against the territorial integrity or the political independence of any State, from seeking to change existing borders by threat or use of force, and from acting in any other manner inconsistent with the principles and purposes of those documents. None of their weapons will ever be used except in selfdefense or otherwise in accordance with the Charter of the United Nations.

3. They recognize that security is indivisible and that the security of each of their countries is inextricably linked to the security of all the States participating in the Conference on Security and Cooperation in Europe.

4. They undertake to maintain only such military capabilities as are necessary to prevent war and provide for effective defense. They will bear in mind the relationship between military capabilities and doctrines.

5. They reaffirm that every State has the right to be or not to be a party to a treaty of alliance.

6. They note with approval the intensification of political and military contacts among them to promote mutual understanding and confidence. They welcome in this context the positive responses made to recent proposals for new regular diplomatic liaison.

7. They declare their determination to contribute actively to conventional, nuclear and chemical arms control and disarmament agreements which enhance security and stability for all. In particular, they call for the early entry into force of the Treaty on Conventional Armed Forces in Europe and commit themselves to continue the process of strengthening peace in Europe through conventional arms control within the framework of the CSCE. They welcome the prospect of new negotiations between the United States and the Soviet Union on the reduction of their shortrange nuclear forces.

8. They welcome the contribution that confidence and security-building measures have made to lessening tensions and fully support the further development of such measures. They reaffirm the importance of the "Open Skies" initiative and their determination to bring the negotiations to a successful conclusion as soon as possible.
9. They pledge to work together with the other CSCE participating States to strengthen the CSCE process so that it can make an even greater contribution to security and stability in Europe. They recognize in particular the need to enhance political consultations among CSCE participants and to develop other CSCE mechanisms. They are convinced that the Treaty on Conventional Armed Forces in Europe and agreement on a substantial new set of CSBM's, together with new patterns of cooperation in the framework of the CSCE, will lead to increased security and thus to enduring peace and stability in Europe.
10. They believe that the preceding points reflect the deep longing of their peoples for close cooperation and mutual understanding and declare that they will work steadily for the further development of their relations in accordance with the present Declaration as well as with the principles set forth in the Helsinki Final Act.

Annex 4

Baltic States' Exclusion from Paris Summit of the CSCE
Excerpts from contemporary reports in the Estonian press

"Ševardnadze viskas Balti välisministrid Pariisi konverentsilt välja," (Shevardnadze threw Baltic foreign ministers out of the Paris conference), *Päevaleht*, Tallinn, 20 November, 1990.

The Baltic foreign ministers were invited to the conference by France as "distinguished guests", with conference badges where there was " ... " in place of a country name. Before the start of plenary, the Baltic delegations were asked to leave Room 2, to go to the French foreign ministry. Minister Roland Dumas explained that he was forced to withdraw his invitation. The reason was a protest submitted by the Soviet Union the previous night. A formal pretext was an article published in "Le Monde" on Sunday, where there had been an ambiguous interpretation of the status of the Baltic states. Mr. Dumas explained that the conference site is international territory and he had been forced to concede to demands made as uncompromising. The Baltic delegations tried after that to organize a press conference. The Conference secretariat removed the announcements from the conference premises.

"Balti küsimus Pariisis jäi lahtiseks," (Baltic question remains open in Paris). *Päevaleht*, Tallin, 21 November, 1990. The same headline appeared in *Edasi* on the same day.

The Prime ministers of Denmark and Iceland organized a press conference for the Baltic delegations. Originally they had considered including the Baltic representatives in their Delegations. Mr Meri admitted that the Baltic states were "pretty much in isolation." The Danish Prime Minister Poul Schluter told the Danish press: "We understand Gorbachev's problems, but the Baltic states are not part of the Soviet Union." Most clear support to the Baltic states came from Denmark, Iceland and Sweden.

Prime Minister Ingvar Carlsson: "The Swedish government fully supports the right of the Baltic states to self-determination in the spirit of the Helsinki accord." Czechoslovakia, UK, Poland, Hungary and Holy See also expressed support. Indirectly also Finland. In the evening of November 19 the Baltic states held their informal reception, which was visited by representatives of several countries. Some observers note that the countries supporting the Baltic states have to pay a price. According to the information agency CTK, Gorbachev cancelled his meeting with Vaclav Havel, without giving a reason.

"Vaidlused Balti riikide staatuse üle jätkuvad." (Debate over the status of the Baltic states continues), *Päevaleht*, November 21, 1990.

Although the Baltic foreign ministers met with Secretary of State Baker on Sunday, the U.S did not express its public support for the observer status of Baltic states. The representative of Soviet delegation: The Baltic states have no right to participate until they have achieved independence according to the Soviet Union constitution and legislation.

"Pariisi lugu," by Riina Kionka, *Edasi*, December 30, 1990.

The confusion in Paris proves the need for institutional and procedural reforms in the OSCE. It also indicates that the Baltic states will not achieve their goals solely on the basis of legal arguments. There is also a need for political will among the participating states.
There is a need for an independent secretariat for the CSCE. Currently the hosting country foreign ministry provides the secretariat. This secretariat has to refrain from participating in the political process of the conference and from acting on behalf of the host country foreign ministry. France was in breach of both requirements. The secretariat attempted to cancel the press conference for the Baltic States. And Minister Dumas failed to stand up to his right to invite any guests he likes to the event. He referred to his obligations as the CSCE host. But the right to invite guests is a different matter and has nothing to do with the role of the hosts.
Gorbachev threatened to leave if any Soviet republics participated in the conference. But the Baltic States are not legally Soviet republics, so they should have been allowed to participate, and this would not have been

against Gorbachev's demands. One lesson of Paris is that the consensus rule has to be reformed or relaxed. If consensus is required, it will be difficult to admit any new members to the CSCE, as in many cases some sensitivities of existing members are involved.

The head of Soviet delegation Yuri Deryabin had previously considered admitting the Baltic states as special guests as an "elegant solution". Suddenly in Paris it turned out not to be so elegant any more.

Annex 5

John J. Maresca: **Russia's "Near Abroad"—A Dilemma for the West**[1]

1. The Breakup of an Empire

Years ago, I met a French civil servant in a small port city on the West coast of Africa. He told me he had been in a town in the interior when the country had gained its independence, As he passed the railroad station, he noticed a festive crowd patiently waiting in the hot midday sun, and asked the station master why so many people were there. The answer was this: "They know Freedom is coming today, and they know it is important, so they assume it will arrive by train."

When the rotting structure of an empire ultimately begins to crumble, the process of breakup is always pretty much the same. Neither the colonial populations nor the people of the mother country are prepared, politically or psychologically, for the separation, and the result is a protracted period of struggle. There is violence in the colonial areas and a mass exodus back to the mother country. Economic chaos is pervasive, and bitterness in the mother country leads to nationalistic rear-guard actions aimed at preventing or reversing the colonies' progress toward independence. In the colonized areas the struggle is often fratricidal as a new national identity is forged; political alliances are formed or broken, and minority groups within a colony sometimes try to capitalize on the moment to seize their own freedom.

In most cases, this period of struggle has preceded the independence of the colonies, although some aspects have tended to continue into the post-independence period as well. The Russian/Soviet empire was not immune to these symptoms. But instead of experiencing this period of struggle primarily before the independence of the colonies, in the Russian

---

[1] First published in: "Crisis Management in the CIS: Whither Russia?" Hans-Georg Ehrhart, Anna Kreikemeyer and Andrei V. Zagorski, eds. © Nomos Verlagsgesellschaft, Baden-Baden, 1995. Reprinted with kind permission.

case it is happening largely after their nominal independence. In fact, Russia and its former empire—the area which Russians like to call their "near abroad,"—is going through this period of struggle now, and will probably take years, possibly decades, to complete the transition. All of the features of exodus, bitterness, economic chaos, rear-guard actions and fratricidal competition have already appeared in some areas, and will surely emerge elsewhere before the process has run its course.

In Moscow political leaders are wrestling with the problems posed by this period of struggle. Ironically, the situation parallels in many ways the circumstances which followed the Bolshevik revolution, when many of the areas which had been colonized by the Czars also broke away from Russia and enjoyed brief periods of independence. The Bolsheviks used a variety of techniques then to regain control over the breakaway republics, just as Moscow is doing now in a classic effort to resist further movement toward real independence for the former Russian colonies.

2. The Russian Concept of Peacekeeping

There is little agreement in Moscow as to how this should be done, or even whether it is a good idea. Although millions of Russians believe it was a mistake to let the "near abroad" go, there are also many Russians who are aware that recovering Russia's dominance of these former colonies will mean that Russia will once again have responsibility for them too, at a time when each one of them is frought with complex problems and the Russian government is having enough trouble just keeping Russia itself united and economically viable. But as often happens in periods of difficulty, aggressive nationalism appears to be winning the debate over the proper role for Russia in the so-called near abroad. As a consequence, there has been no objection to the fact that the defense ministry has taken the lead, ostensibly with the purpose of restoring order and ensuring security on Russia's frontiers.

The Russian defense establishment, badly demoralized by its humiliating withdrawal from Eastern Europe at the end of the Cold War, has been an armed force without a mission since the collapse of communism, which formed its ideological justification and gave it a purpose. Now it is being positioned, politically and psychologically, to be the defender of the ethnic Russian populations in the newly-independent states and the imposer of stability everywhere on the territory of the former Soviet Union. This has given the Russian army a palpable new sense of purpose.

The world's image of the Russian armed forces is of an underfunded, ill-housed and unprepared military organization which is no longer a threat to international security. This may be the case on the strategic level, with an important caveat for Russia's nuclear arsenal. But within the former USSR the Russian army still looms larger than life. Russia's armed forces have 2 million men under arms, the full range of equipment, and a tough approach to problem-solving which is often reflected in the comments of their leader, defense minister Pavel Grachev.[2] This is a military force which is capable of intervening anywhere in the former USSR, and has already done so with relative success in Tajikistan, Georgia and Moldova. The Russian army has interlinked bases, command, control and communications channels, and supply routes throughout ex-Soviet territory. It controls mountains of weapons and ammunition supplies, plus "volunteers" and cheap mercenaries of every technical specialty. Its officer corps is a far-flung fraternity (which always had very few members from the distrusted Asian and moslem ethnic groups) that still has enormous influence in every defense ministry among the newly-independent states. Furthermore, the old KGB intelligence networks are still largely intact, and very little can happen in the vast ex-Soviet space without it being known in the defense and internal security ministries in Moscow.

The military and its backers like to think of all their operations in the so-called "near abroad" as peacekeeping, and apparently believe that they should be backed and even paid for by the international community at large. But the Russians have developed their own concept of peacekeeping which is quite different from the classic definition, and which contrasts sharply, not only with the longstanding practices of the United Nations in this field, but also with normal relations among independent states.

The Russian concept of peacekeeping is really more like forceful suppression of violence than it is like the impartial and pacific approach of international organizations. Even the expression, when used in Russian,

---

[2] See, for example, Grachev's statement before a negotiating session on Nagorno-Karabakh that "Whatever I propose, that's what we're going to agree on," cited in Elizabeth Fuller, The Karabakh Mediation Process: Grachev versus the CSCE?, RFE/RL Research Report, Vol. 3, No. 23, June 10, 1994.

means something different.[3] Concretely, Russian troops engaged in such operations are authorized to use force not only to defend themselves if they are attacked, but also to suppress violations of the peace, whatever the cause. UN peacekeeping missions are only authorized to use force in self-defense. Russian peacekeeping also does not put the same stress on the negotiation of stable political solutions as is the case in international operations. Suppression of violence is itself a goal. For the international community peacekeeping is only an unavoidable expedient which may help to make it possible to organize a rational political negotiation to find a resolution to the underlying dispute. In this approach the goal is clearly the achievement of a negotiated political solution, not just the suppression of violence.

The Russian approach grows naturally out of the historical experience of the Russian and Soviet armed forces with respect to security problems within the USSR. When such problems arose, the army was sent to impose order. They often accomplished this objective brutally, and in some cases the legacy they left behind only complicated and embittered the underlying dispute. Many historians contend that in fact the deliberate policy of Stalin was to keep local hostilities alive, or even to create or fuel them, in order to ensure that distant parts of the Soviet Union would always be dependent on the Center for their security.[4] A part of the dilemma for the West is the possibility that Russian peacekeeping troops would use intimidation or force to suppress elements they considered unfavorable to Moscow's interests, just as Soviet forces did before them. Coupled with the Russian interpretation of their peacekeeping role is a strongly-held view that maintaining peace and stability on the territory of the former USSR is the exclusive prerogative of Russia. This view, too, resembles the possessive attitudes of virtually all colonial powers with respect to their former colonies, but is perhaps felt even more strongly in the case of Russia because of the country's historic xenophobia, particularly toward the West. Many Russians see their country as having a

---

[3] See, for example, Therese Raphael, Russia: The New Imperialism, The Wall Street Journal, June 22, 1994.

[4] For a detailed analysis of the Russian approach to peacekeeping, in contrast to that of the West, see Pavel K. Baev, Peacekeeping as a Challenge to European Borders, Security Dialogue, Volume 24(2), pp. 137-150.

unique role across Eurasia, and do not believe outsiders have any place in this area.

Current Russian suspicions of outside attempts to settle problems in the former USSR have come out most strongly in the behavior of Russian representatives with regard to the conflict over the mountain enclave of Nagorno-Karabakh, in the Trans-Caucasus. This is because this is the one conflict on former Soviet territory in which an international body—the "Minsk Group"—has been mandated to find a solution. Here the Russians, led by defense minister Grachev, have made a concerted effort to undercut international initiatives, to keep the international community out, and to resolve the problem themselves, using their own troops, as a way of ensuring their domination of the region. The Russians have appeared prepared to accept accusations of bad faith in this instance, as the price of ensuring exclusive Russian predominance.[5]

The development of the Commonwealth of Independent States (CIS) has helped to provide a facade of international cooperation in dealing with conflicts within the former USSR. In cases where there has been international interest, such as Georgia, Azerbaijan and Tajikistan, the Russians have made a point of calling their proposed peacekeeping interventions CIS operations, even when participation by non-Russian CIS members was no more than symbolic. Russia has tried to establish the CIS as a recognized international organization equivalent to, say, the European Union. Their effort has been to obtain international acceptance that the CIS has exclusive competence for dealing with conflicts on the territory of the former USSR. All CIS operations would, of course, be dominated or possibly even exclusively manned, by Russia.

Russia's tendency toward keeping the international community out of the former USSR appears to date from late 1992 or the beginning of 1993, and was perhaps signaled to the world by foreign minister Andrei Kozyrev's "mock speech" at the Ministerial session of the CSCE in Stockholm in December of 1992. Kozyrev gave such an aggressive, hard-line speech that his listeners were shocked. It closely resembled Soviet speeches of the sixties or seventies. With respect to the "near abroad,"

---

[5] For background on the Nagorno-Karabakh dispute see "War in the Caucasus: A Proposal for Settlement of the Nagorno-Karabakh Conflict," Special Report, United States Institute of Peace. 1994.

Kozyrev said that "The space of the former Soviet Union cannot be viewed as a zone where the CSCE norms can be applied in full. This is in effect a post-imperial space where Russia has to defend its interests by all available means, including military and economic ones. We shall firmly insist that the former republics of the USSR immediately join the new federation or confederation, and this will be discussed in no uncertain terms."[6] An hour later, possibly because journalists were sending off dramatic reports of the event, Kozyrev took the floor again to explain that it was all a hoax; he just wanted to show his colleagues what Russia's policies might be like if hard-line nationalists gained power.

Yet the policies of the Yeltsin government began to evolve rapidly from that time, especially on a few leading edge issues such as the role of the international community in resolving the Nagorno-Karabakh war. Before 1993 was over Kozyrev's "real" policies closely resembled the hard-line nationalist policies of his "mock" Stockholm speech. In particular, Russia's determination to regain control over the whole of the former USSR had become obvious to all but the most naive Western observers.[7]

The world became conscious of the evolution of Russia toward an aggressive nationalism only when Vladimir Zhirinovski made a strong showing in the Russian parliamentary elections in the autumn of 1993. Some analysis have suggested that the Yeltsin government adjusted its policies because of the electoral strength Zhirinovski showed at that time. But in fact the evolution of policy began much earlier, and what the appearance of Zhirinovski really revealed was the growing depth and breadth of nationalist feeling in Russia as it progressed through a period of economic and political retrenchment.

The general state of disarray in Moscow makes it difficult to find any really credible, authoritative and complete statement of Russian policy toward the newly-independent states of the former USSR. It may be that there simply is no centrally-developed or approved policy concept or list of policy objectives. Rather there may be an accumulation of separate actions by different ministries, all seeking to reflect and anticipate what

---

[6] Moscow News, December 16, 1992.
[7] For another view of Russia's expanding efforts to regain control of the see Bruce D. Porter and Carol Saivetz, The Once and Future Empire: Russa and the 'Near Abroad,' The Washington Quarterly, Summer, 1994

they see as the tendency of political opinion. And all receiving at least the tacit approval of president Yeltsin.

But by observing Russian actions and the aims which Russian negotiators have pursued in their dealings with the new states, it is possible to draw up a representative list of policy directions. Based on this crude revival of Kremlinology, the Russians appear to want to:

- Control the outer frontiers of the whole of the former USSR. The Russians point out that there were no marked or even surveyed internal borders in the former USSR, and to establish them now would be very costly.[8] By their logic, a better solution is simply to re-establish the old frontiers, and man them with Russian border forces. Current exceptions to this general rule include the Baltic States and Azerbaijan, but in the latter case the Russians are actively pressing for re-introduction of their border guards along the frontier with Iran.
- Maintain military bases throughout the former USSR. After the Russians forced Eduard Shevardnadze to capitulate and invite Russian forces into Georgia, the only areas where Russian basing is in question are, once again, the Baltic States, where Estonia and Latvia are still struggling to get the Russians out, and Azerbaijan, where the government clearly does not want the Russians to come back. Russia is currently exerting strong pressure on the government of Azerbaijan to agree to the reopening of their large base in Gandzha. The other new states never managed to get rid of the Russians.
- Exercise economic and financial control. This is being accomplished in most places through the CIS economic and financial agreements, under which each newly-independent state yields to Russia key decision-making powers. But this process could also be dangerous for the Russian economy, since loading the failing economies of the new states onto the economic disaster of Russia itself could bring even greater problems.
- Control natural resources throughout the former USSR, particularly energy resources. Not only does Russia itself need these resources, it also knows that they are a prime source of hard currency, and could emancipate some former colonies from Russian control. The

---

[8] Raphael, op cit.

Russian technique for gaining control over resources is not very subtle; Russia simply demands a share, and is also insisting that pipeline routes from the Caucasus and Central Asia should cross Russia.

- Keep the international community out. For Russia the international community means the United States and its surrogates, and Russian xenophobes are determined to exclude American influence, as well as Turkish or islamic influences, to which Russia is particularly sensitive along its southern frontier.

- Finally, the Russians are determined to preclude a breakup of the Russian Federation itself, the 'empire within an empire,' which includes many colonized peoples. Some peoples within the Russian Federation have already demanded, and received, greater degrees of autonomy for their regions, drawing inspiration from the actions of minority peoples in the "near abroad." The favored technique for ensuring control over Russia is to re-establish control over the whole of the former USSR through consolidation of the Russian-dominated CIS. This would re-establish the traditional buffer zones and theoretically insulate the Russian Federation from such potential instabilities.

As part of their effort to obtain recognition of their special role in the former USSR, the Russians have attempted to equate their activities there with US activities in the countries of America's 'backyard,' such as Haiti, and French activities in countries of special interest to France, such as Rwanda. Russia's linkage of these issues in negotiations within the UN Security Council resulted in American agreement to an ambiguous UN acceptance of a Russian/CIS peacekeeping force for Georgia, in return for a Russian non-veto on the Security Council resolution approving a US-led invasion of Haiti.[9]

It should be noted that the Russians have few qualms about interpreting any international community statement relating to their "peacekeeping" roles as something of a mandate. Their troops in Tajikistan have worn the familiar sky-blue colors of the UN, even though they have never been given a UN mandate to do so. Thus, even an ambiguously-worded UN decision on the force in Georgia will be used by the Russians as a full UN endorsement.

---

[9] There has been little reporting in the press on this incident. One of the few articles to appear at the time was Lally Weymouth, Yalta II. The Washington Post. July 24, 1994.

3. The Western Dilemma

Russia's deliberate juxtaposition of the Russian role in Georgia against the US role in Haiti and the French role in Rwanda has posed more starkly than ever before the dilemma of the appropriate Western attitude toward Russia's activities in the so-called near abroad. This attitude has been equivocal up to now.

The reasons for this Western ambiguity seem to be, first, that the West is not prepared to undertake peacekeeping in much of the former USSR. Westerners therefore do not consider themselves in a position to criticize the only country—Russia—which is ready to step in, regardless of the Russians' methods or motivation. Second, many in the West have been hopeful that an emerging democratic Russia would not revert to an imperialist policy. These people have believed that giving Yeltsin the benefit of the doubt in the 'near abroad' would encourage him to show a greater sense of responsibility. The facade of the CIS, as thin as it may be, has also confused many westerners who may not have perceived the very real differences between this emerging mechanism for a new Russian domination and the European Union's democratic structures.

In addition, Western countries have become more reluctant to intervene in post-Communist disputes after their experience in ex-Yugoslavia. Their priorities currently include the maintenance of stability in nearby regions and the avoidance of conflicts which are likely to send further waves of refugees as immigrants toward their shores. For America this refugee-phobia is focussed on Asia, Latin America and the Caribbean. But for Europe it is concentrated on Africa, the Middle East and South Asia. Instability in the former USSR can only add to these problems. Islamic immigrants are viewed with a particularly wary eye in Europe, although this aspect is seldom highlighted.

At the same time, Russia's effort to obtain recognition as the mandated peacekeeper for the 'near abroad' tends to force the issue, especially when the Russians compare their role with Western peacekeeping practices, as in Haiti or Rwanda. The first question is whether or not Russia's justification for its interventions, and its actions in carrying them out, differ from those of Western countries in similar circumstances. If there are such differences, the question then becomes whether or not Russia's actions in the so-called "near abroad" are acceptable, and if they are not, what might be an appropriate Western response.

The issue is a broad one, posing moral, political and practical issues. Perhaps the key factor to bear in mind is that the whole of the former USSR, as noted above, is engaged in a colonial struggle associated with the breakup of the

Russian/Soviet empire. With this aspect in mind, the differences between Russian peacekeeping in the 'near abroad' and Western-sponsored peacekeeping operations is clearer.

The Russian relationship with the new states of the former Soviet Union is still in the very sensitive phase of anti-colonial struggle and separation of a colonial mother country from a set of colonies. Russian interventions in this area cannot be distinguished from attempts to simply prevent or forestall independence. Such interventions touch all the sensitivities which dominate a period of decolonization, and are as likely to exacerbate problems as they are to resolve them. Even if violence is stopped through the threat of Russian force, this will only prolong the suppression of nationalist feelings which caused the problem in the first place. While the US relationship with Haiti, and the French relationship with Rwanda do have similarities with post-colonial relations, neither is in the immediate period of anti-colonial struggle.

Also, neither the US nor France seeks a permanent place in these countries; indeed, much of the debate in both Washington and Paris has concentrated on the problem of how to get out once an intervention has been undertaken. Issues relating to how to conclude an intervention and withdraw are among the key criteria for intervening at all in the US Administration's policy on peacekeeping interventions. In contrast, the Russians seek a permanent military presence.

Nor have the U.S. or France sought to integrate the countries in which they intervene into a state-like structure controlled by them, especially against the will of the country concerned. But that is precisely what Russia has been doing in pressing Georgia and Azerbaijan to accept Russian troops and join the CIS. This extraordinary behavior resembles forcible conquest more than it does the peacekeeping concepts of the end of the twentieth century.

Moscow has pressured Georgia (and Azerbaijan) for a variety of permanent concessions such as bases, border guards and agreement to Russian dominance of economic policies, while refusing to put its intervention forces under the discipline and control of an international organization, such as the UN or the CSCE, which would then be able to decide the eventual date of departure of the Russian contingents. These factors make it difficult to accept that the Russian peacekeeping operations are comparable in any way to international operations, and it was certainly a mistake to allow Russia to equate them, even tacitly, during the UN Security Council negotiations.

4. A 'New Yalta Line' for Europe

Nonetheless, the ambiguity of the Western attitude remains. Does the West, in fact, feel more comfortable with a new Yalta-style division of spheres of influence and responsibility, especially if it is only implicit and is not overtly stated? Perhaps. Of course no Western country could agree to a formally-recognized division. But, sadly, the evidence to date is that, provided the 'new Yalta line' is pushed Eastward from the line which divided Cold War Europe, an implicit division is being quietly accepted.

The reason is simple realpolitik: no Western country is prepared to undertake interventions of any kind in Central Asia or the Caucasus; they do not want to see conflicts in those areas go unended; and all would prefer to give Russia the benefit of the doubt (or turn a blind eye) and let the Russians handle the complex problems of these regions by themselves. Thus there is indeed an implicit 'new Yalta line' beyond which stabilizing responsibilities are seen as belonging to Russia.

Where then does the new dividing line fall, differentiating those areas which are sufficiently interesting to the West to warrant its intervention when needed, and those areas which are not that interesting? This is not yet entirely clear, and may take some time to be pinned down. There are three possibilities, under which:

- Central and Eastern Europe outside the territory of the former USSR are of interest to the West, but the countries on the territory of the former USSR are not;
- Central and Eastern Europe including the Baltic States are of interest to the West, but the other countries of the former USSR are not; or
- Central and Eastern Europe including the Baltic States, Ukraine and Moldova (and possibly Armenia and Azerbaijan) are of interest to the West, but the other countries of the former USSR are not.

It is not yet clear which one of the above descriptions will best define the emerging Western consensus about a 'new Yalta line' for Europe. While it may sound cynical to discuss the issue in these terms, that is unfortunately the practical implication of recent Western policies.

The key Western policy decision thus far has been NATO's adoption of the "Partnership for Peace" program. This program ostensibly equates all the countries of Europe and the former USSR in terms of their potential relationship with NATO. Austria or Poland theoretically has the same potential for developing a close relationship with, or joining, NATO as Kyrgyzstan or Tajikistan. This is clearly absurd, and the net effect of the Partnership for Peace program has therefore been to postpone the difficult decisions about which countries would be close to, or join, NATO, and fall on the Western side of the new line, and which countries would not develop such close relations, and would find themselves on the Eastern side of the line. Since Russia itself cannot join NATO without destroying it or at least rendering it meaningless, the Eastern side of the new line will obviously be a Russian-dominated area.

The Partnership for Peace thus reinforced the security vacuum in which the countries of Central and Eastern Europe have been left. The resulting sense of doubt and uncertainty, far from its stated purpose of creating a Europe without dividing lines, actually adds to the instability of the pre sent equation and multiplies the temptations to Russian nationalists to re assert themselves in these areas too.

Of the states of the former USSR, the Baltic Slates have been clearest in stating that they want to become a part of the West. The likelihood is that, given their special history and Western outlook, they will continue to receive moderate Western support. Even the Russians, by agreeing to withdraw their forces from the area, appear to have accepted this as inevitable. But beyond the Baltic States the picture is much more doubtful.

The big question mark, of course, is Ukraine. No doubt events in that country itself will, more than anything else, determine whether the "new Yalta line" falls to the East or to the West of Ukraine. If the political evolution in Ukraine follows a pattern similar to that in Belarus, few Western countries will contest the development of closer Russo-Ukrainian ties, and Ukraine would then have moved itself behind the 'new Yalta line'.

The Trans-Caucasus area may already be partly behind the new line. Only Azerbaijan is still holding out against Russian pressure to permit basing of forces and control of frontiers and oil. But thus far there has been little interest in the West in giving real support to Azerbaijan, because that would appear to take the Azerbaijani side in the country's bitter dispute with Armenia over the enclave of Nagorno-Karabakh.

The states of Central Asia are already doomed by Western indifference and impotence to be in Russia's new orbit. While technically all these countries can develop relations with the West, there is virtually no chance for them to truly break away from Russia. Western countries have simply been too slow in realizing the significance for the world's economy of the resources of the Caspian basin and Central Asia, which could provide the industrialized nations with fossil fuels well into the next century.

As the Partnership for Peace relationships with NATO are sorted out, they will formalize the 'new Yalta line.' This will not exclude further opportunistic Russian pressures on selected countries, such as Bulgaria or Serbia, which may be more sympathetic and interesting to Russia. It is even possible that, if the ambiguity of the Partnership for Peace period lasts long enough, Russia will succeed in bringing some of the countries of Central and Eastern Europe back under its influence and into its security space. Unfortunately the Partnership for Peace included no barriers to guard against such a possibility.

5. The State of Independence of the Newly Independent States

The situation of each newly-independent state from the former USSR, and the West's response to it, is different. The following brief analysis summarizes the status on a case-by-case basis.

The Baltic States. These three small countries have a history which gives them special consideration, and they have expressed the clearest Western vocation. They have received significant encouragement and assistance from the West, particularly from the Scandinavian countries with which they have a special affinity. Their economies are making progress. Once Russian troops have left Estonia and Latvia, as they are committed to do, independence will be more of a reality. The one remaining problem will be that of the large ethnic Russian minorities, which are resented by the indigenous peoples and could spark difficulties and provide an excuse for Russian intervention later.

Kaliningrad. This area is something of an anomaly because its native population has largely disappeared and it has been made into a huge Russian military base. But it is also clearly a colony and a potentially destabilizing factor. The West has been reluctant to raise the issue, but it has been raised by both Poland and Lithuania and will not go away.

Belarus appears to be headed back toward close association or merger with Russia, and no Western country will contest this.

Moldova is ethnically close to Romania and so has special support from Bucharest. But it also has a complex dispute with ethnic Russians in the

Trans-Dniestr region, where a Russian army, with Moscow's encouragement, is defending a breakaway 'republic.' The West has shown little interest in getting involved in this problem.

Ukraine, as mentioned above, is the principal question mark in the area. It is under strong pressure from Russia over debt repayment, fuel supply arrangements, the division of the Black Sea fleet, and perhaps most ominously, the dominant Russian population of Crimea which is seeking a closer relationship with Russia. The West has been keenly interested in Ukraine and its many problems, but has given only half-hearted support. Most Westerners do not want to offend Russia on this issue, and the Ukrainians themselves have been reluctant to follow Western advice on their economy and their nuclear weapons. This is why the question of where Ukraine fits in relation to the 'new Yalta line' will depend primarily on Ukraine itself.

The Trans-Caucasus. Armenia has continued to be heavily dependent on Russia even after its nominal independence, mainly because it needs Russia to offset Turkish support for Azerbaijan in the war over Nagorno-Karabakh. Despite the largely misdirected support of the Armenian diaspora, Armenia appears unlikely to escape the Russian orbit, unless the Karabakh war can be ended very soon. Neither is Georgia after Russia forced its government to accept CIS membership and Russian bases. In a potentially important precedent the UN agreed to monitor the Russian peacekeeping force in Georgia and to set up a fund for voluntary contributions to help pay for it, thus giving it some UN coloration. Since the West was unwilling to provide peacekeepers, this decision sealed Georgia's fate and condemned it to the Russian orbit.

Azerbaijan remains a test case for both Russian intentions and the Western response. It is the one country in the former USSR where there is a valid international offer to monitor a ceasefire in the local conflict. But Russian pressures to accept bases, border guards and oil sharing have been strong, and Azerbaijan has received very little support from the West. It gets better support from Turkey and other Islamic countries, which compounds both Azerbaijan's bitterness and Russia's suspicions.

Central Asia. The key test case in this area thus far has been Tajikistan, where no Western country has been willing to become involved, and where the Russians have installed their troops in support of a friendly regime. Apart from commercial possibilities, such as oil and gas resources, the West is clearly not interested in this area. In fact, many otherwise generous and well-informed Westerners complain that the newly-independent states of this area were improperly admitted to the Conference on Security and Cooperation in Europe (CSCE), since they are not European. A recent European initiative to look at minority problems went 110 far as to leave this area, as well as the Trans-Caucasus, out entirely, thus signaling that the region is too distant, and its problems too intractible, for Europe to be bothered.

The Russian Federation. The 'empire within an empire' should not be overlooked, despite the West's reluctance to mention it as a potential problem. Within Russia's borders are many colonized areas and people., such as the Tatars, some of which have already raised their voices seeking, and obtaining, greater autonomy. There is of course very little that the West can do in real terms to affect the course of events within the former USSR. At the same time the W oil does have a moral and political responsibility to recognize the situation. there for what they are, and to consider ways in which it can be helpful, even if it is unwilling to become involved on the ground in areas which arc: distant from its central concerns.

6. The Role of the CSCE

But the role of the international community can go beyond just the identification of what is acceptable and what is not. Fortunately, all the new slates of the former USSR are members of the CSCE, and so it is possible to use the CSCE in various ways in this area. The CSCE has an excellent record of innovation in the field of preventive diplomacy. Its missions, with mandates tailored to the local circumstances, can be useful and are non-provocative. Such missions could usefully be dispatched for visits, or in some cases, for longer periods, to help to understand problems or ease tensions. The CSCE's High Commissioner for National Minorities and its Office for Democratic Institutions and Human Rights (ODIHR) can also be helpful in these areas. The CSCE is the West's best vehicle for demonstrating concern for these new states, and for providing help in non-provocative ways.

Another worthwhile effort would be to press Russia to negotiate an acceptable basis on which Russian units can participate in UN or CSCE-sponsored and controlled peacekeeping or monitoring/observing operations on the territory of the former USSR. This will admittedly not be easy, since Russia holds that it has the prerogative to carry out such operations itself, or under the guise of the CIS. Up to now Russia has refused all reasonable proposals for playing such a role under the control of an international organization.

The challenge will be to demonstrate to the Russians, particularly the Russian military, that it is in their interest to share the burdens and responsibilities of these operations with the international community. The Russians do want their operations to be recognized as legitimate by the World Community, and this offers some leverage to international negotiators. More fundamentally, Russia must be brought to understand that if it wishes to be accepted as a responsible member of the World community, it must play by the same rules as apply to other countries. President Boris Yeltsin has a direct responsibility for ensuring that Russia's military leaders, including defense minister Grachev, adhere to these rules.

Up to now, the Western response to Russian policies has been ambiguous, largely because Russia's aims themselves have been ambiguous. But Russia's actions make it increasingly clear that Moscow is determined to regain control over all of the former USSR, with the possible exception of the Baltic States, and that its interventions in the 'near abroad' are important tools for accomplishing this objective. Ultimately the West will have to decide what its attitude will be if and when Russia simply ignores established international standards and pursues its own interests on the territory of the former USSR. And as a part of this process the West will also have to decide whether simply abandoning the new states of this region is compatible with its interests, and its principles.

Annex 6

IMPLEMENTATION OF THE HELSINKI ACCORDS

HEARING BEFORE THE COMMISSION ON SECURITY AND COOPERATION IN EUROPE. ONE HUNDRED THIRD CONGRESS. FIRST SESSION. ETHNIC VIOLENCE IN TRANS-CAUCASIA

Co-Chairman Representative Steny Hoyer.

MARCH 8, 1993

There will, hopefully, come a time in the history of mankind when prejudice, ethnic divisions and national differences will not lead us to kill one another. Unfortunately, thousands of years of history do not give us much sense of hope. But if there is to be a new world order, it will be based upon the commitment of the international community to exercise all of the resources at its command, to ensure respect for international borders and the peaceful resolution of disputes.
I look forward, as I said, Mr. Chairman, to hearing Ambassador Maresca. Few people in the world are more knowledgeable about the CSCE process, or have contributed more to its success than Ambassador Maresca. Those of you who have perhaps not read his book outlining the genesis of CSCE would be advantaged by doing so. And we are advantaged by having him present here today.

Ambassador, we know you finagled your schedule around and we appreciate it very much.

Ambassador Maresca. Thank you very much, Mr. Chairman.

Chairman DeConcini. Thank you, Chairman Hoyer.
We're very pleased to welcome Senator Grassley to the Commission on Security and Cooperation in Europe. I know he's taken an active interest

in this region throughout his entire career. He's travelled with the Commission on a number of missions overseas and I'll yield to the Senator from Iowa for any opening statement.

Senator Grassley. Mr. Chairman, I'm not going to make an opening statement. I just want to say that I appreciate very much being appointed to the Helsinki Commission and to work with you.
I had you and Congressman Hoyer invite me to participate in other ways in the past. I look forward to working in a more formal way with you and feel that you've done a great deal of good under your leadership. I look forward to continuing this work as we try to work for the cause of peace in the post-Cold War world. Thank you.

Chairman DeConcini. Thank you, Senator Grassley. Ambassador Maresca is no foreigner here to this Commission. He's participated in, and headed delegations. He's held numerous posts in security and European Affairs, including Deputy Assistant Secretary of Defense for Europe and NATO policy. The Ambassador is also an expert on CSCE. He is currently the U.S. Special Negotiator in the CSCE Conference on Nagorno-Karabakh as well as special coordinator for Cyprus. Ambassador, thank you for adjusting your schedule to be with us. Your testimony is extremely important for this Commission's record and for our own knowledge.

TESTIMONY OF AMBASSADOR JOHN MARESCA, U.S. DEPARTMENT OF STATE

Ambassador Maresca. Thank you, Mr. Chairman. And thank you very much for those very kind, generous words about my own work in the CSCE. I do have a formal statement which I will submit for the record.

Chairman DeConcini. It will be so printed in the record.

Ambassador Maresca. Thank you, sir. I thought what I would do, if you permit me, is to summarize a bit of that statement and to add some thoughts of my own.

Chairman DeConcini. If you would, please.

Ambassador Maresca. First of all, let me say that this is a cruel and little-known war, and I very much welcome this opportunity to discuss it with you and to discuss what the United States has been doing and hopes to do to try to help to bring this conflict to an end.

The United States' objectives from the very beginning of our efforts have been directed solely toward trying to find a peaceful solution to the conflict, and that continues, I think, to be our number one objective.

Let me say that this is a conflict on which there are two mutually exclusive views of exactly what it consists of. For one side, it is a question of self determination, and the people of Nagorno-Karabakh have expressed themselves and have the right to that self determination. For the other side, it is a question of the territorial integrity of the state of Azerbaijan and Nagorno-Karabakh is simply a region within that state, which has full sovereignty. And there is no question of some internal self determination within that state. These conflicting views of the conflict underlie all of the problems that we've had in the negotiating process and still are what lies between us and a peaceful settlement.

The CSCE negotiating process started about a year ago when the CSCE foreign ministers decided to create the conference on Nagorno-Karabakh. The conference had a much more limited membership, including the United States, Russia, Turkey, and some other countries who had decided to participate. Those include, of course, Azerbaijan and Armenia. The term Minsk Conference refers to the Conference on Nagorno-Karabakh. The reason is because Belarus volunteered to host the conference in its capital, Minsk. But in fact, the conference on Nagorno-Karabakh has never convened in Minsk because we have never succeeded in overcoming the preliminary conditions of the parties which would permit us to open the conference in Minsk.

In place of that, we have been negotiating in what has come to be known as the Minsk Group. These are preparatory negotiations and they have lasted since last spring, and have just concluded a session in Rome where we have tended to meet because of the fact that our chairman is an Italian politician. So, the terms Minsk Conference and Minsk Group, which are used throughout, refer to this group of the CSCE that has been conducting this negotiation.

We have been working on a package of agreements which are the key elements in a solution. They include, of course, a cease-fire, provision for international monitoring of the cease-fire, which would be provided by the CSCE, removal of barriers to normal trade and communications, and the opening of a negotiating process which would ultimately lead to a political solution on Nagorno-Karabakh itself. That is the package of agreements that we have been working on since last spring.

Over the summer, we conducted intensive negotiations in the Minsk Group, but these negotiations were stymied in September because of pre-conditions and our inability to find agreements which would bridge these pre-conditions. At that point, we began, and this was largely at the United States' initiative, we began a series of informal consultations, trying to reach agreement on the elements of a package which would permit us to continue the negotiating process and bring us to a solution.

We have come close to agreement several times. We've been closest in December and in January, and on each occasion, I was convinced, I must say, that we had actually reached an agreement. But in each case, it has immediately unraveled, on one occasion because of military events on the ground, and on the other occasion because of one side or the other being unable to join in the final compromises. Nevertheless, we are persisting.

I just returned from a session, another session of the Minsk Group in Rome last week, when we actually found again the beginning of an agreement. What we agreed on in Rome on this occasion was part of one important element in the package which I described, which is the terms of reference for a monitoring mission which would actually monitor a cease-fire. Now, the reason this is important is because it will, of course, take a lot of activity, a lot of work, in order to gain and to organize this monitoring mission so that it is ready to deploy. It will have to be financed by the full CSCE and approved by the full CSCE and it is the first time that the CSCE will ever have sponsored a cease-fire monitoring mission.

This agreement on the terms of reference permits us to move ahead in organizing a monitoring mission for the cease-fire. But obviously, it is just one element of the package. And in order to give it real meaning, we will have to meet again and continue negotiations on the calendar, which would lead to a cease-fire and the removal of barriers to trade in the beginning of the Minsk conference and many other individual steps, without which this first step will have no meaning. We hope to continue these negotiations later this month and in April. And I hope that this first success will lead to other successes and make it possible to put together the whole package that I described.

There are, I think, a number of assets in this negotiating process which we need to preserve and to use. The first asset is that everyone concerned is at the negotiating table. We have developed procedures which permit even the participation in the discussions of representatives from Nagorno-Karabakh. This has not been easy but we have that now in hand, and it worked well in Rome last week and I hope that will continue. We also have a link through the CSCE to a monitoring operation. Now, there have been many initiatives on Nagorno-Karabakh sponsored by one country or another, but they have failed because of the inability to immediately introduce a monitoring or observing force for the cease-fire.

Through this linkage with the CSCE we hope to be able to rectify that so that when a cease-fire is agreed, an international monitoring group can immediately take up positions.

Another advantage is that this negotiation is now linked to the CSCE and to the UN. It has been backed by the United Nations Security Council in two statements, and is now recognized as the negotiating process which really has the lead in finding a solution.

And finally, we have reached an agreement, and this is an asset. Anytime a negotiating process succeeds in reaching a single agreement, it is a big plus in its credibility and its ability to find the other necessary agreements.

Before I close, Mr. Chairman, and respond to questions or comments, I'd like to say a word about the implications of this conflict. Of course, it is a tragedy for the area, for the countries involved, for the people involved. And anyone who has visited the area, and I've been there myself several times, knows just how cruel, just how violent this conflict has been. But the implications are much broader than that.

For Russia, it is one of those conflicts on its southern border that threatens stability and which is either a negative, or hopefully, a positive model for resolving such disputes. For the region, I believe there is a very serious risk of escalation and spread of this conflict because of the interests of neighboring states and because of the escalation that we've already seen. For the CSCE, of course, it is a real challenge. The CSCE has not succeeded in bringing one of these conflicts under control up until now. If the CSCE can do that in this case, then of course, it suggests that it can do it in other similar circumstances. If it fails, then of course, many other conflicts of this kind might go unanswered too.

And I think for the United States, it is also a challenge. We are, in this instance, trying to play a role in a legitimate international effort which is trying to eliminate the risk of conflict before it gets started, without getting ourselves involved on the ground in a military way. We have played a leading role in this process from the beginning, and I think that it is appreciated by all sides. As I said earlier, our one objective has been to find a solution and I believe that that has given us credibility with all of the parties to the negotiation. That, I think, is a tremendous asset for the negotiating process and for our country. I sincerely hope that these negotiations can be successful because of the risks which I've alluded to, in case we fail.

Now, having given those few words of introduction, Mr. Chairman, I would be happy to respond to your questions or comments about any phase of this conflict or our role in trying to find a solution to it. Thank you, sir.

Chairman DeConcini. Ambassador, thank you very much.

I want to welcome one of the House Members, Ms. Eshoo from California. We welcome you here and I know you have a deep interest in this. You'll find this Commission to be extremely interesting, and maybe you can help us with some new directions in this effort.

I'd be glad to yield to you if you want to make any opening statement.

Ms. Eshoo. Thank you, Senator. I appreciate your warm welcome and it's a privilege to be seated near you and next to my colleague from the House, Congressman Steny Hoyer.

There are some that may wonder what brings me over here today. I see many faces in this audience that look exactly like my own family because you are. I am very proud of being half-Armenian, half-high, and I represent many Armenians from the Bay Area community as well as within my own congressional district.

So, this is not just a matter of the heart and the family, but obviously, something that we as human beings, recognizing the suffering that is taking place, that we do all that we can to bring that to an end but also, a policy that would ensure that lasting. So, as we turn our attention beyond our own borders and all of the domestic issues that plague our nation, I am very pleased to be here today.

I am going to withhold making anymore comments. I just wanted to make those as introductory comments for those that may wonder what brought this new House Member over. And I look forward to working with you and the people from the community. I want to thank those that have come forward today to give their expert testimony. I believe that I might have some questions of those that are here as well. Thank you very, very much.

Chairman DeConcini. Thank you very much.

Ambassador, you mentioned some pre-conditions that you were able to resolve, or at least thought you had, and then things fell apart. Did they fall apart because those pre-conditions were not adhered to, including the cease-fire which was one of those you mentioned? What other pre-conditions were necessary and where do they stand today?

Ambassador Maresca. Well, there have been very many pre-conditions put forward by both sides, or by all sides.

Chairman DeConcini. Have you been able to put them aside for the most part or what?

Ambassador Maresca. I would say some have been put aside in our last negotiating round. But the reason, the real reason why the solutions have fallen apart have been because of events on the ground. My own view is that

Chairman DeConcini. But you mean military events by that?

Ambassador Maresca [continuing]. Like military events, yes.

Chairman DeConcini. Which means the condition of cease-fire has never been met.

Ambassador Maresca. That's right, or restraint, I would say.

The point here is that both sides have to see beyond individual military events to their longer range interest in finding a solution and so far, they haven't been able to do that.

Chairman DeConcini. Well, I know you're an optimist or you wouldn't be here today or be in Rome last week, and go back again and again. What is your best judgment today? Do you think they're going to get a cease-fire? Has there been enough killing and devastation and everything else there to bring at least a cease-fire in time to talk? Or do you think this is just going to keep going on?

Ambassador Maresca. A very difficult question to answer.
You're right that one must be hopeful and continue to try. But I think we also must bear in mind that this is a region which, when it was a part of the Soviet Union, was filled with weapons and ammunition of all kinds because of what the Soviets saw as a security threat in that area. The Caucasus was simply chock-a-block with weapons of all kinds.
So, the supply of weapons is there. The animosity is very strong.
Feelings on this issue on both sides are very, very strong and I think that that will probably mean some fighting for some time to come. Even if we reach a cease-fire, I assume that there will be incidents for some time to come. On the other side, I think one has to see that the economic situation is disastrous. Of course, it's worse in Armenia than anywhere else, but in Azerbaijan too, economic possibilities are blocked by the conflict and in both countries—they know this full well—that creates a pressure to find some solution. But I wouldn't want to be overly optimistic about it. I think that it is a very difficult problem and because of the deep animosity and the availability of weapons, the likelihood is that at least some fighting will continue.

Chairman DeConcini. Congressman Hoyer?

Co-Chairman Hoyer. I'm just going to ask two questions. We, unfortunately, have a time problem and I wanted my other colleagues to have an opportunity to ask questions and then get to our other guests. How would you describe the role of Moscow in the CSCE talks?

Ambassador Maresca. There are several roles of Moscow. Unfortunately these days, I think one can not very simply ascribe one policy to Russia. But the foreign ministry's policy, I think, is a straightforward one of trying to find a solution and we have worked very closely with them to do that. The military, on the other hand, is very cautious about the Caucasus. They've had their own experiences there. I have spoken with the Deputy Chief of Staff in Moscow and he described to me with great bitterness, the experience of their soldiers going in there and being blamed for all the difficulties. There is also another feeling which is that Moscow is the former colonial master and that therefore, they should have nothing to do with the area, that they're not welcome there.

So, there are varying roles but what I can tell you is that we have, from the beginning, sought Russian cooperation as well as Turkish, because these are the two regional powers who have great influence there. And we have sought to find a middle path which would gather support not only from Russia, but also from Turkey and the two countries involved. This is not an easy thing to do because there is confusion in the area. Governments are new and it's rather a labyrinthine course that we have to follow, but that has been our effort from the very beginning.

So, basically, I would say that Russia has a lot of influence, can play a positive role, and as far as the negotiating process is concerned, they have definitely played a positive role.

Co-Chairman Hoyer. What are the implications, Mr. Ambassador, of President Yeltsin's suggestion or request that Russia play the role of guarantor of sort of pax Russica in the region?

Ambassador Maresca. Well, I personally don't much like the idea of guarantor powers in this area at all. We've had experience with guarantor powers and of course, when you give a guarantee, you have to be prepared to enforce it later. I think it would be a mistake to have any outside power have that prerogative in this area, whether it would be Russia or for that matter, ourselves, or any other country. I just think that's a bad idea. The situation is dangerous enough as it is. If outside powers were involved, I think it would be that much more dangerous and that's, I think, what the notion of a guarantor power leads you to.

Now, what I can conceive of is some kind of political guarantee by the international community of a given status, if one is eventually agreed. For example, the CSCE could approve of a final result, which would give a kind of international community guarantee of whatever the final result was. But that's a different notion from the one that we've heard so far of a kind of guarantor power or powers, which implies, as I say, some enforcement prerogative.

Co-Chairman Hoyer. Last question. I said two, but let me ask one more. You mentioned Turkey and Russia. What about Iran? Does Iran have any role? Would it be useful? Are they inclined to be useful or positive? Do they see themselves benefitting from continued conflict?

Ambassador Maresca. Well, certainly, Iran is interested. It is a power in the region. It's just over the hill, so-to-speak, from this area and has relations with both of the states involved. They have been interested in playing a role, in finding some kind of a solution, for some time and have sponsored at least one cease-fire agreement. I might say, like all the other cease-fire agreements, it fell apart immediately. But nonetheless, they have sponsored one and have constantly shown an interest.
They are not a member of the CSCE and therefore, they have had nothing to do with our negotiating process. But I think one has to recognize that they have an interest and influence in the area. And as it happens, the Italian chairman of the Minsk Group has occasionally kept them informed of the process and how it's developing, on the grounds that it's better that they understand it and are aware of whatever success we're making. I would also add that Iran is not viewed as a wholly impartial, disinterested state by the states in the region. There is a considerable amount of suspicion of their motivation by the states in the region and for that reason, I think, direct involvement by Iran, at this point, would not be a beneficial addition.

Co-Chairman Hoyer. Thank you, Mr. Ambassador. Thank you, Mr. Chairman.

Chairman DeConcini. Senator Grassley?

Senator Grassley. If a monitoring mission would be set up by the CSCE, how would the command and control of the mission be determined? I assume that we don't have any precedent for this, and has the thinking gone far enough so you can answer the question?

Ambassador Maresca. Yes, Senator, you're right that we have no precedent. On the other hand, we have a certain number of parallels and a lot of thinking has gone into this. And in addition to that, there is an agreement from last summer which sketches out how a CSCE monitoring operation would be run. And essentially, it puts any such operation under the control of the CSCE Chairman in office. The Chairman in office rotates and at the present time it is Sweden. So, we assume that our monitoring operation will be under the control of Sweden.

Now, how that chain of command will run exactly has not been worked out, but it will be an international group. The commanding officer in the field has already been chosen. He is Finnish, a Finnish military officer, and I assume that he will be reporting to a more senior military officer who will be Swedish, who will be responsible to the CSCE Chairman.

Senator Grassley. Would the mission be set up for an indefinite period of time or would it have certain timetables established, or maybe this is too early to tell?

Ambassador Maresca. We've done advanced thinking on this. It's not agreed but here again, our working assumption has been that we would send a group out there for a six month period, but under the assumption that they probably would have six month renewals. Six months is a kind of a minimum period below which, it's not economically sensible to send a group out and set them up.

So, our assumption has been that there would be a six month period and that the likelihood is that it would be renewed again at six month intervals, for as long as it was needed, which might be for some years.

Senator Grassley. Thank you, Ambassador.

Chairman DeConcini. Ms. Eshoo?

Ms. Eshoo. Yes, thank you, Mr. Chairman.

Mr. Ambassador, there may be, built into this question, the mark of the newcomer, but I am going to ask the question anyway. It is my understanding that the Minsk Group agreed on draft terms of a reference for a monitor mission and that the terms need formal Helsinki Commission approval which might come at the April meeting of the committee of senior officials.

Can you tell me what the draft terms of reference are?

Ambassador Maresca. Yes. The draft terms of reference describe the tasks of a monitoring mission and this is why they have been so difficult to negotiate between the parties to the conflict. Each one of the tasks that they would have to accomplish is loaded with advantages or disadvantages for one side or the other.

For example, one of the tasks would be that they would bring under control heavy weapons systems, such as artillery, tanks, APCs, aircraft, helicopters. And the sides have different advantages depending on which weapons systems you're talking about. Azerbaijan has more airplanes, for example. Both sides have helicopters. There are also advantages in terms of geography. Nagorno-Karabakh is up in the mountains, surrounded by a fairly flat hinterland controlled by Azerbaijan.

So, each side, of course, is looking at its advantages when discussing the control of heavy weapons. So, each one of these tasks as it was negotiated was a loaded political question. But basically, the tasks for this group would be to monitor movements and activities of heavy weapons to see that they were under control and not being used, to supervise the delivery of humanitarian assistance, to ensure that the barriers to normal trade and communications were being lifted, that sort of thing. This is what we're talking about and that would be what they would monitor, but not accomplish themselves. The states themselves would accomplish these things and the monitors would just watch to ensure that it was taking place.

Ms. Eshoo. Thank you. In terms of your being at the table and part of all of this, I think that maybe this is a little awkward to ask but it really, I think, goes to the heart of the issue. And that is, we're not talking about setting up trade relations between two nations. We're talking about a people that are literally freezing to death. So, as we talk about monitoring weapons, as important as it is, it seems to me that when people are suffering the monitoring of weapons almost becomes secondary. Freezing people and dead people can't use the weapons that are going to be monitored.

So, my question to you is, how can we separate out the issues that you have been eloquent in describing, but also raise the issue of humanitarian aid which is difficult to provide for people that have been blockaded and shut off. I mean, that's really what brings me here. I think that that's really what's at the heart of the issue.

What is it that you would recommend to the Helsinki Commission, to members of Congress, and to the President of the United States, that presents itself as an opportunity to do what I just described? And I understand that it is a difficult and complex issue because the underlying problems have endured for generations and that is what brings us to such a crossroads here today.

Ambassador Maresca. Well, this is, I must say, one of the most fundamental questions in this whole complex of issues, no question about it. And it has been a primary concern for myself and I think for the U.S. government from the very beginning.

We have been very active in an aid program which I don't have all the details on here since it is something that is handled in another section of the Department of State. But it has been very active, and especially when energy sources were cut back. The U.S. government went into a major effort to try to get energy into the area. As you know, in the case of Armenia, it's very difficult because it's land-locked. We have had high level discussions with Turkey and also with Azerbaijan about opening up possibilities for energy to come into the area.

We have had some success. As you may know, Turkey agreed before Christmas to deliver electricity, and then problems arose also from a military situation, because of the military situation.

But we have not relaxed because of that; we have continued. And I think that Armenia itself would tell you that the aid program has been very ample and effective. Unfortunately, energy is very difficult to supply by air. This is one of the primary problems that we have faced. And so, we have to find other ways to do it, but we have continued to do.

I think though that in spite of the problem, which has been a desperate one and I've been there and I know how desperate it is.
In spite of that, one has to continue working on a long-term solution. And in this, I'll say that President Ter-Petrossyan has been very astute in his long-range view of what needs to be accomplished. Armenia must have normal relations with its neighbors because of its situation. And while an emergency program must be carried out when they face such a desperate situation, nonetheless, the long-term solution must also be sought and that means an end to the war.
Believe me, I have as much of a feeling for this issue, I think, as you do. And I have been, myself, affected very deeply by what I've seen. But I do think that the United States has worked very hard on this issue and continues to work hard on it. And I think people in the area who are knowledgeable about this would agree with that.

Ms. Eshoo. Thank you.

Chairman DeConcini. Mr. Moran?

Mr. Moran. Thank you, Senator. Let me follow-up on my colleague's question and ask you to look into the future, based upon your current observations.
Five years from now, how do you think the situation might have stabilized, or what is necessary to have stabilized in the long run? I missed some of your testimony, so I don't want you to be repetitive of what you've already shared with the Commission. But I suspect, because my conversations with other people who have intimately involved, is generally what we can do currently to avert more bloodshed.
But over the next five years, what would you see as—where do you think we will be? And where do you think we ought to be and how could we get there?

Ambassador Maresca. Well, five years from now, I would certainly hope there was a political solution, which would mean also a resolution of the question of the status of Nagorno-Karabakh. I won't speculate on what

that would be because I think that must be a part of the negotiating process, and that outsiders are in a difficult position to suggest what it should be.
But I would hope that it would be settled in a way that would be satisfactory to all the parties and would ensure that the rights of the peoples were respected.

Mr. Moran. Well, Mr. Ambassador, that's a very idealistic statement, but that doesn't any new insight. Anyone would have answered that, but you have some first-hand knowledge. Give us a more realistic appraisal of what you think might happen, if you wouldn't mind?

Ambassador Maresca. Well, I'm sorry I have to duck on this one.
I really am. But I think I can not go into what might be the result of a negotiating process on this issue.
What I can say is this, that all the countries in that region, all the peoples in that region, have an interest in settling this conflict.
Because without a settlement, economic development, the development of free systems won't happen. We have the good fortune of having freely elected governments both in Azerbaijan and in Armenia. Both countries are trying to move toward free economic systems. Both have enormous potential, Azerbaijan because of the oil and gas resources that they have; Armenia because its geographic position just puts it at the crossroads of all the pipelines and supplies that may cross from the Caucasus to the West.
They all have an interest in finding a solution. I would hope that five years from now, a solution will have come about that will permit all of this to take place. That is to say, democracies and economic development, but exactly what it would be, I'm not in a position to say.

Mr. Moran. Let me take one more stab, if you don't mind. Do you think that there could ever be a stable peace in Nagorno-Karabakh, for example, without a physical lifeline connected to Armenia? Is that possible?

Ambassador Maresca. Yes, I think there will have to be some internationally monitored supply routes. That's for sure. This is a purely practical issue. I don't believe that the people in Nagorno-Karabakh will agree to a final settlement unless they have some assurances in this respect. And so, what they would be exactly, I don't know, whether they would be roads that were monitored, whatever. I just don't know. But whatever solution it would be would have to entail something in that line, otherwise, it won't work.

Mr. Moran. But it's feasible to have a transportation network and a utility network that would connect Nagorno-Karabakh with Armenia and not be unacceptably violative of Azerbaijan's territory and sovereignty as well?

Ambassador Maresca. Well, it's certainly feasible to have such links. I would hope though that given that amount of time, that it would be more feasible to get energy supplies, to get the normal supplies directly from the hinterland around them, which is Azerbaijan, rather than be totally dependent on Armenia. I think that's the normal situation. It always was the normal situation. This is an area which supplies farm products, for example, to the rest of Azerbaijan. This has been their economic livelihood. And I would hope that that kind of a normal situation would be restored and not just isolated routes to Armenia. I don't think it should depend on that, ultimately.

Mr. Moran. Well, that's what I was getting at. Whether you think it's possible to establish that again. That's the answer I was looking for. Thank you, Mr. Ambassador.
Thank you, Mr. Chairman.

Ambassador Maresca. Thank you.

Annex 7

CSCE Negotiations On Nagorno-Karabakh
John J. Maresca, Joint Statement

Excerpts from opening statement by Ambassador John J. Maresca, U.S. negotiator for Nagorno-Karabakh, at a briefing in Washington, DC, June 8, 1993.

We announced today... a joint proposal, an initiative, to get our negotiations back on the track again. This proposal is jointly sponsored by all the members of the so-called Minsk Group that are not directly parties to the conflict. We are hoping that it will be accepted by the parties to the conflict by the end of the week.
It's for that reason that I thought it would be a good idea to provide you with some background information on how we got where we are, what we're doing, and what the prospects are.
We have agreed with the other co-sponsors of this initiative not to go into the details of it prior to acceptance by all the parties to the conflict. However, I can tell you some of the general things about it.
Moreover, it is designed to implement Security Council Resolution 822, which I also have available if you don't have it on your own.
The points which are in the proposal are largely those points that are in the Security Council resolution. Just to give you some of the background, the U.S. approach on this from the beginning of the negotiating process has included a number of points. We have deliberately decided to be impartial in this dispute—to condemn violence on both sides, but to be impartial. We are essentially a mediator in this dispute.
We have decided to play a part in an international effort rather than trying to do something our own, and that international effort is represented by the so-called Minsk Group of the CSCE, which is the recognized negotiating body on this effort—recognized by the UN and by the CSCE, of course.

We've decided that we won't have a U.S. military presence on the ground in this area, and we've decided that the two democratically chosen leaders in the two countries—Armenia and Azerbaijan, both moderates who are interested in converting their countries to democratic systems and free market economies—are both deserving of support, and we have been supporting both of them.

Our effort has been to bring about, first of all, a cease-fire with international monitoring in order to stabilize it and some other stabilizing measures like lifting of what are called "blockades" in the region in order to permit a sensible, rational political negotiation to go forward. We are not trying to decide in advance what the solution, ultimately, on this problem will be. This is something that will have to be negotiated.

There have been a number of visits to the region. I've been there myself several times. Reports have been written about the problem. Last spring, the CSCE set up a thing called the Conference on Nagorno-Karabakh to be held in Minsk. That's where the name comes from. It's called the Minsk Conference, and the group which has been preparing for this conference is called the Minsk Group for that reason.

It has, I think, become a credible negotiating process, to the extent that it is recognized in Security Council resolutions, and it has brought all of the parties to the conflict to the table, which, of course, is the first step in any negotiation. It's produced one agreement already—that is, the Terms of Reference for an international monitoring operation as soon as a cease-fire has been agreed and stabilized.

These Terms of Reference include a lot of political points. It was agreed not just by the two states involved but also by representatives from Nagorno-Karabakh. So, it does represent a serious negotiating effort, and the CSCE is ready to send this monitoring team as soon as the cease-fire holds.

The Minsk Group negotiations also now, in the latest Security Council resolution, do have the direct backing of the Security Council. So, I think, there is no question now where the negotiation process should take place.

As happens in any dispute like this, the events on the ground are very volatile. There are events going on right now, too. And throughout the negotiating process, we've had ups and downs based on skirmishes of one kind or another—an attack, a seizure of a village, or whatever. This is part of this kind of conflict and part of the negotiating process that goes with it.

What we're doing right now is trying to get back to the negotiating table after one such military operation—which was a seizure by the Armenian side of a valley area called Kelbajar, which is not specifically shown on your map but which is to the north and west of the Nagorno-Karabakh outline on that map—which was seized about a month ago by the Armenian side.

Since that time, we've been trying to get back to the negotiations. We have made proposals—first of all, along with Russia and Turkey—to try to accomplish this. For one reason or another, those proposals were not accepted right away. But we have, as of last week, revised this proposal in certain ways, clarified certain points about it, filled in some details, and acquired the backing of all the other members of the Minsk Group. That is what constitutes the proposal that we put forward and which we announced today.

The last thing I'd mention, before I take questions, is that, essentially, what the Minsk Group is doing with this proposal is implementing—attempting to implement—the Security Council resolution. I think this is kind of an interesting new feature of the way this arrangement has worked, where a CSCE group is actually trying to implement a Security Council resolution. That's where we stand today.

Annex 8

Forging a Lasting Peace
The Nagorno-Karabakh Conflict

An Interview with John J. Maresca
Former US Ambassador to the OSCE[1]

by Betty Blair

In 1992, the Conference for Security and Cooperation in Europe (CSCE, now renamed OSCE) was given the responsibility of facilitating a resolution to the Nagorno-Karabakh conflict between Azerbaijanis and Armenians, now going into its eighth year. John Maresca, former US Ambassador to the OSCE, recounts those early days when he helped to set up the 10-member negotiating body, which came to be known as the "Minsk Group". Today, though not involved with diplomacy, he still takes a keen interest in the development of the region. In January, Ambassador Maresca revisited Baku on behalf of the Open Media Research Institute (OMRI) and in February he responded to our questions about his role in the negotiations over Nagorno Karabakh.

How did you personally got involved with the Caucasus?
My involvement in the Caucasus happened quite by chance. When the Soviet Union disintegrated, suddenly there were 15 Newly Independent States (NIS). At the time, I was the US Ambassador to what is now the Organization on the Security and Cooperation in Europe (OSCE). I argued that these countries should be offered immediate membership. As part of the USSR, they had already been members for 20 years. To refuse them would have been to have expelled them just when they were exercising one of their basic rights under the Helsinki Final Act-the right to self-de-

---

[1] First published in: Azerbaijan International (4.1) Spring 1996. © Azerbaijan International 1996. Reprinted with kind permission.

termination. Twenty years earlier, I had been involved as one of the negotiators of the Helsinki Final Act, and I believe my views were critical in shaping the US position on admitting the NIS to this European Conference.

But consensus did not come easily. Concerns were voiced, especially from the Europeans, who felt that not all the Republics were really European. Some people are still not happy with the decision but, in my opinion, membership in the OSCE has been an important lifeline, providing an alternative to Russian domination. In any event, we prevailed, and all 15 Republics were admitted. Afterwards, I was sent as a Special Envoy to open US relations with most of these states, and gradually became identified as the "Point Man" for the US on the Caucasus.

What has been your own role in helping to set up a forum for peace negotiations in this region?
During 1992-1994, I put a great amount of energy into trying to find a solution to the Nagorno-Karabakh problem. I ran many risks, both physical and professional, undoubtedly, more than I should have. They started calling me "Full Metal Jack" at the State Department, referring to my frequent trips to war zones. However, I believe my efforts were a major factor in the creation of what came to be known as the "Minsk Group" as a valid negotiating forum for the conflict.

About a year and a half ago, after leaving the US diplomatic service, I published some of my ideas on what might be the basic elements of a political solution on Nagorno-Karabakh, convinced that unless someone advanced a rational plan for compromise which might be acceptable to all the parties, the discussions could drag on forever. As an impartial outsider who had been dealing extensively with all parties and had come to understand everyone's "bottom line," I felt I could suggest ways in which all the demands could fit together to everyone's advantage.

I had helped to formulate the US' role in helping to resolve the problem, but I felt the US should have taken a much more active role than the Administration agreed upon in order to counteract Russian efforts to control the process. I did not think then, nor do I now, that Russia alone can, or even should, resolve this problem. On the contrary, I believe it requires international commitment.

What are the issues that must be resolved for both sides-Azerbaijanis and Armenians-in order to establish peace in the region? In other words, what do you believe is the "bottom line" for both sides?

The main elements for a peaceful settlement have already been accepted by all sides. In no particular order, they are:

1 A status of broad autonomy for Nagorno-Karabakh, under the continuing sovereignty of Azerbaijan;

2 Some form of guarantee for the security of Nagorno Karabakh;

3 Armenian withdrawal from Azerbaijan's occupied territories;

4 Special arrangements for the Lachin corridor and Shusha which would permit the Nagorno-Karabakh Armenians access to Armenia (possibly coupled with similar arrangements between Azerbaijan and Nakhchevan);

5 Arrangements which will permit at least the major portion of the refugees on both sides to return to their homes; and

6 A major international reconstruction effort.

Of course there are many details under each of these headings which must be carefully defined and which require difficult negotiations. For example, "autonomy" can mean many things-from education in one's own language to the choice of one's own police forces. So these points only represent a point of departure.

Only the parties themselves can work out the details which should be done through direct negotiations, and reported to the Minsk Group. This is not only the best way to resolve the conflict, but it also best guarantees each country's independence. The last thing Azerbaijan wants is an imposed settlement, either through military force, or outside intervention, or the growing "de facto" acceptance of the situation as it currently exists. The government of Azerbaijan, I believe, should initiate direct contacts with the leadership of the Armenian community in Nagorno-Karabakh. After all, these people are also citizens of Azerbaijan, and there would be nothing more natural than for the government to try to hear them out and reach a settlement. Ultimately, they too must be satisfied with the agreement.

What pressures do the Armenian and Azerbaijani governments face in trying to resolve the conflict?
Political pressures inside countries often make it difficult for national leaders to move toward compromise unless they are pressured from outside. So outsiders have an essential role to play in encouraging a peaceful settlement. Domestic pressures usually tend toward more extreme positions-such as trying to "win" a conflict by military means-and there is sometimes little political incentive to take the difficult steps required to arrive at a settlement.

There are political figures on both sides who continue to press for some form of "victory." These people do their countries no good, for they merely prolong the suffering. In Azerbaijan, those who would like to use oil profits to build a greater military capacity and then seek a military victory in the conflict would lead the country toward national disaster.

Why has the negotiation process been so slow?
Negotiations have been dragging on for four years, which is particularly tragic for the refugees. Blame for the delay must lie with the parties in conflict, who have been unwilling, up to now, to accept the need for some kind of compromise. As both sides have held out for some form of victory, the result is that everyone loses.

The problem is not in the structure of the negotiations, which are just a way of offering the opposing sides a place to talk to each other; rather, it is one of political will to reach an agreement. No outsider can impose a peaceful settlement; sovereign countries are responsible for their own affairs.

We hear so little in the Western media about what is happening in Nagorno-Karabakh. Why has the West seemingly been so hesitant to get involved?
Azerbaijanis have a point when they compare the West's willingness to go to war to defend Kuwait with the seeming indifference toward the Caucasus. Most lists of America's so-called "vital interests" include some language about "access to energy resources." Yet the Caspian Basin has not yet been identified in public perceptions as an important source for the world's energy. Western leaders are uncertain how they should treat

this region. It is a "new" region in the geopolitical sense, because until recently it was simply viewed as part of the USSR.

When I first became interested in the Caucasus and Central Asia, very few people in the West were even thinking about this region. This is gradually changing as more academics begin to study the area and more institutions initiate relevant study programs. I would like to think that I helped generate some of this interest. But it will take some time before Western publics equate the Caspian with the Persian Gulf.

There has been a gradual process of realization in the US and in the West in general, that the Caucasus and the Caspian Basin are important for Western interests, largely, though not entirely, due to the energy resources in the region. This has led to an increased interest in the various conflicts in the region-Nagorno-Karabakh, Georgia, and Chechnya.

What has been the effect of US Congressional legislation in regard to the "Freedom Support Act" (Section #907 passed in 1992) which denies all assistance to the Azerbaijani government, including humanitarian aid?

I think Azerbaijanis have a valid point when they complain about the American law which prohibits the US Government from giving direct assistance to the Government of Azerbaijan. I have written about this and testified before Congress, arguing that it is unfair. I do not believe such a provision would be approved by Congress were it voted upon these days; but to repeal such a law is quite difficult now. Hopefully, progress in negotiations will permit the President to confirm to Congress that the conditions of this law have been fulfilled, so that the restriction can be removed.

What else can be done to encourage the peace settlement?

Foreign oil companies and their countries have a special duty to encourage a peaceful settlement in Nagorno-Karabakh. I'm not convinced that they have carried out these responsibilities particularly well. Such companies are strictly commercial enterprises, true, but they have every reason to push for a peaceful, stable, democratic and free-market Azerbaijan so as to carry their own important work forward. Until now, they have generally acted as if the conflict was none of their business.

Perhaps they do not understand the enormous influence they could wield over the situation, or perhaps they've been afraid that the governments of Azerbaijan or Russia would resent their encouragement and turn to rival companies. This is short-sighted. For Azerbaijan, the way West is essential, both for prosperity and for real independence. That means working out some "modus vivendi" with Armenia. The sooner this occurs, the better for every Azerbaijani and for everyone with interests there.

How do you see Russia's role in the Caucasus?
Russia will always play a significant role in the Caucasus. They have always been involved historically, and they play too important a role in the balance of power for it to be otherwise. The Russian language and culture, economic and security interests, as well as Russia's own perception of their role on the Eurasian continent meaning that they will always have a key presence in the Caspian region.

However, the October 1995 decision by SOCAR (State Oil Company of Azerbaijan) and the AIOC (Azerbaijan International Operating Company) announcing dual pipeline routes (through Russia and Georgia) for "early oil" reflected the consensus that a single pipeline route through Russia would make energy supplies from the Caspian Basin too dependent upon Moscow. Chechnya certainly had a decisive impact on this decision to make multiple routes available.

Such a decision leaves future choices open. Commitments are being made by various players all the time, but until the actual construction of the major oil pipeline begins, all plans are subject to revision. Routes through Iran or Armenia certainly look impossible under the present circumstances, but the situation could change. Don't forget, the route through Chechnya looked relatively problem-free until a year ago.

Right now Russia is going through a complex period of adjustment resulting from the triple losses: (1) disintegration of their empire with its ideology and superpower status, (2) incredibly difficult economic times, and (3) political confusion. Some elements in Russia are not yet reconciled to the notion that the countries of the "Transcaucasus" are now independent. Nor have they realized that Russia's principal interest in this region is not to control it, but that it be stable so that it can be independent of outside domination and become prosperous. Such conditions, if they can be achieved, will best guarantee Russian interests in this region.

The Caucasus will need a lot of help, much of which Russia simply cannot provide. I'm very sympathetic to Russian problems, both in general and with respect to the changed role they are facing in the region, but realistically, it will probably take several years before Russia fully adjusts to its changed role.

The Russian attack on Chechnya demonstrated just how difficult the process of democratization is for Russia. The use of brute force to suppress a people with aspirations for independence or, at least, autonomy, is no longer acceptable to the world community. The modern way, the democratic way, if you prefer, is to treat such problems with dialogue, reconciliation, and efforts to adjust national policies to meet the genuine needs of minority peoples. One can only hope that Russia will learn some lessons from its experience with Chechnya. Russia is simply too important to allow its fate and its future to be determined by a war in Chechnya.

What about Azerbaijan? How well are they faring during this transition?
Azerbaijan is going through a difficult transition from a backwater of the Soviet Union to an independent democracy based on free market principles. This evolution will undoubtedly take many years. Along the way, there will be difficulties, and I hope Azerbaijan will be able to work through them and become a true democracy.

I have read the reports of the international observers who monitored the most recent elections, and it's evident that those elections were not perfect. There has been a tendency to suppress political opposition and even imprison some political figures. My friend and former negotiating partner, Tofig Kasimov, who as Foreign Minister was a tenacious defender of Azerbaijan's national interests, is in jail. While I'm in no position to judge the validity of the charges against him, I find it tragic that such a person, with all his ability to contribute to the construction of a modern society, is imprisoned. The same holds true for former President Abulfaz Elchibey, who lives in exile in his village in Nakhchivan. These are people Azerbaijan needs. I hope President Aliyev will find a way to bring them back not only to freedom but to a constructive role in the life of the country. Azerbaijan should be seen in the world as a mature and free society.

How did you find Baku on your last trip? Were there a lot of changes since your last visit?
On my latest trip to Baku in January, it was very satisfying to see how Baku has developed these past two years since I was there last. Economic progress is visible all over the city. Some of the beautiful older buildings are being renovated. There are new shops and restaurants and many new cars. The foreign community is much larger than before.

Baku feels cosmopolitan. I know all the other capitals of the Caucasus and Central Asia, and I believe Baku is destined to be the principal city of the region and a hub for economic, cultural and tourist activities. Underneath all the neglect of the Soviet period is a distinguished and historic city with the potential to be a real tourist attraction as well as a major center of the oil and gas industry. I hope the Azerbaijani government will continue to bring the city back to life.

What do you sense is the attitude towards peace in Armenia? Have you been there lately?
I visited Armenia last autumn where I found the economic situation, though difficult, much improved since my earlier visits. Electricity and hot water are limited, for example, although there is more of both than before. I've heard stories of children fainting in school from malnutrition. I'm told that the economic situation is marginally better in Nagorno-Karabakh, but I haven't been there recently.

Nonetheless, I believe there is a growing realization among Armenians, both in the Caucasus and among the Diaspora, which is just as important, that Armenia must find a way to resolve the conflict over Nagorno-Karabakh soon or lose whatever possibilities it has to establish itself as a free and prosperous country.

Lately, there has been serious debate over re-starting the nuclear reactor at Metzamor. This Chernobyl-type reactor sits atop a great earthquake fault line. An earthquake under that reactor could be disastrous for the whole region. Fallout could extend from the Black Sea to the Caspian, just as fallout from Chernobyl reached as far as northern Scandinavia. But the Armenians have no choice, since they do not have alternative energy resources of their own. So the situation is very difficult. And this is another reason why I believe the time is right to move toward a peaceful settlement to the war. Both sides need it.

I believe the time is relatively favorable for a peaceful settlement. A cease-fire has been in place for nearly two years, allowing passions to cool. The governments on both sides, including the Armenian authorities in Nagorno-Karabakh, are relatively stable and confident, which makes reaching agreements easier. Both sides are increasingly aware that they need an agreement-Armenia for economic reasons and Azerbaijan because of its refugee problems, its ability to attract investment and its necessity in maintaining independence. Critical to the whole process is that the publics on both sides want peace.

What are you doing professionally since you've left your diplomatic post with the OSCE?
Today, I'm a private citizen and do not represent any government, nor am I involved in the negotiating process. I preside over the Open Media Research Institute (OMRI) which is the privatized successor to the Research Institute of Radio Free Europe and Radio Liberty (RFE/RL), now located in Prague.

We have a staff of about 100 specialists and analysts who receive daily publications from the region and transcripts of radio and TV news broadcasts. We are intensively watching the evolution of the post-Communist states and publishing news and analyses in a Daily Digest, a weekly Economic Digest, and a bi-weekly journal called "Transition." We're becoming known as the most comprehensive private center in the world for study in this vast region. A large part of our funding comes from the Soros Foundation in New York.

Though my work extends far beyond the Caucasus, I don't suppose I will ever lose my fascination with this region and all its many peoples, nor my sense of the tragic waste and loss that have resulted from conflicts in this area.

What is your personal assessment of the peace process? Do you think that there is still hope for peace between the Armenians and Azerbaijanis, given the historical context of the conflict, or will the present "status quo" arrangement of a tenuous cease-fire continue indefinitely?
I'm still committed to this region and if there is anything I can meaningfully contribute to this process, I'll gladly do it. Personally, I've been harshly criticized at one time or another by both sides of the conflict. I guess that's the fate of people like me who try to find a middle ground of

compromise. It has sometimes been very discouraging and I've often asked myself if it wouldn't be better just to leave these people "to stew in their own juice." But somehow interest and hope manage to outweigh discouragement, leaving me convinced that a peaceful solution to this difficult situation will be found soon.

Annex 9

John J. Maresca: **ENSURING CSCE PROMISES ARE KEPT**[1]

When the Helsinki Final Act was signed in August of 1975 it represented a significant achievement; agreement between East and West on rules which set new standards for the behavior of states. But as hard as it was to bridge the gap on the sensitive issues covered in the Helsinki Accord, the most difficult task lay ahead. This was the effort to ensure that the commitments in the Final Act would actually be respected by the States that had undertaken them. For as President Ford said at the signing ceremony in Helsinki, history would judge the CSCE "not by the promises we make, but by the promises we keep."

But how would it be possible to ensure that the "promises" of the Final Act—the many commitments contained in its 30 thousand words—would actually be carried out? Virtually all Western observers were skeptical that the Soviets would respect human rights any more after the signing of the Final Act than they had done before. In the United States, in fact, the Accord was unpopular; it was unfairly caricatured as a Western giveaway, recognizing the legitimacy of the governments and frontiers in Central and Eastern Europe in exchange for empty promises unlikely to be fulfilled.

Since the Final Act was not a treaty, nor even an "agreement," and its clauses therefore did not represent legal obligations, it was thought that there was no way to "enforce" compliance. Even words like "obligations" or "compliance" were considered by legal specialists to be inappropriate in connection with the Final Act. The Act was referred to as an "Accord," because it did not qualify as a treaty or an agreement[2]. This was not just

---

[1] First published in: Bulletin of the OSCE Office for Democratic Institutions and Human Rights, Vol. 3, No. 3, Warsaw, Fall, 1995. The OSCE Office for Democratic Institutions (ODIHR) grants permission to use for educational and other non-commercial purposes.

[2] The agreed letter transmitting the Helsinki Final Act to the Secretary General of the United Nations specifically states that the Final Act "is not eligible, in whole or in part, for registration with the Secretariat under Article 102 of the Charter of the United Nations, as would be the case were it a matter of a treaty or international agreement..."

because the Soviets feared being pressed for compliance. The US was also unwilling to characterise the Final Act as a treaty or an international agreement because that would have required it to be sent for review to the Senate, where the Administration feared sharp criticism. Other Western countries had similar concerns. The fact that the Final Act represented a unique political and moral commitment did not alter the general skepticism with which it was seen.

Also, the officials responsible for America's bilateral relations with the USSR, taking their cue from the leaders of the Administration, did not want to upset what was viewed as a generally positive relationship with Moscow; they saw the multilateral Helsinki Accord as nothing more than a high-minded declaration, having little to do with the hard realities of US-Soviet relations. The same was true to a lesser degree of officials dealing with the countries of what was then called Eastern Europe. While these officials were interested in using the Final Act, because America's bilateral relations with these countries were still very limited, they all realized that the Communist governments would take their cue on implementation from Moscow.

Even American academia was at first indifferent or even hostile to the Helsinki Accord; no more than one or two American professors had shown any interest at all in the rather open negotiating process while it was going on. American professors were skeptical that the Accord would yield any results. The focus of scholars interested in relations with the USSR was on arms control, particularly the negotiations to limit nuclear weapons. Human rights specialists had taken up the cause of Jewish emigration from the USSR, but their strategy was to use bilateral leverage to force Moscow to permit more jews to leave. This approach was epitomized in the famous "Jackson-Vanik Amendment" which made "most-favored nation" trade status for the USSR dependent on freer Jewish emigration. The Helsinki venture was seen as largely irrelevant to both these areas of interest.

But the Final Act could not just be allowed to disappear. When the Helsinki negotiations concluded I was transferred from my position as Deputy Head of the U.S. Delegation back to the State Department as head of the small section which watched over CSCE-related matters. It so happened that my office was also responsible for sending instructions to the

US representative in the NATO Political Committee, amid-level coordination body at NATO Headquarters in Brussels, where representatives of all the allied states met once a week to exchange views on political issues. The Political Committee was the forum in which the NATO Allies had developed many of the Western proposals advanced in the CSCE. We proposed in the Political Committee that the Allies develop a system of joint monitoring of the implementation of the provisions of the Final Act. My small section sent instructions to our representative in the Political Committee to pursue this concept. After two months of negotiations there was an allied agreement to pool information on implementation and to produce periodic joint reports. This in turn permitted us to instruct our bilateral embassies to monitor and report on implementation, so that we could contribute to the NATO report.

Later, the law establishing the CSCE Commission of the US Congress required the President to submit periodic public reports on implementation, thus putting the implementation record into the public domain. The CSCE Commission's active interest helped to reverse the common American perception that Helsinki was a giveaway. It gradually became apparent that the contrary was true: the Final Act was destined to be an important tool for opening up the closed Communist societies.

This activity of "monitoring" the "implementation" of the Final Act's provisions was a key part of what came to be known as the "Helsinki Process," a kind of soft pressure encouraging the governments in the East to move toward human rights reforms and greater freedom of information. The Soviets objected to the idea that other countries had a right to "monitor" events in the USSR; they argued that in Russian the word for "monitoring" actually meant something closer to "controlling." But once the Western approach had been agreed, it stuck. In fact, it was the only way the West had to press for the "promises" of Helsinki to be kept.

The role of the media in this process was perhaps even more important. The 1970s and 80s saw an explosion in the availability of information through the international media, and there was no way that the societies in the East could be isolated from this process. The closed Communist systems were untenable in an age of massive availability of information through the telephone, fax, computers and copying machines, television and radio.

Public attention to the issues of the Final Act and the growing interest of the media multiplied the impact of the Accord in unexpected ways. It encouraged dissidents and democrats in the Eastern countries to press, within their own systems, for reforms that would match the Helsinki commitments. These courageous people developed substantial opposition movements, with historic implications. They were the principal force which ultimately brought about the collapse of the Communist systems.

One major issue which had been left unresolved at the time the Helsinki Final Act was signed was whether the CSCE would have regular meetings in the future to review the implementation of the Final Act. There were differing views on this, even among the Western countries; some were wary of creating an on-going all-European institution where the USSR would have a major voice. As a compromise it was agreed that there would be one Follow-up Meeting in Belgrade in 1977, and that a Preparatory Meeting would work out its agenda and procedures.

By the time the Preparatory Meeting convened it was clear to all the Western countries that periodic follow-up meetings would be indispensable to press for "implementation." The primary Western objective was to achieve agreement on regular follow-up meetings to review how the Final Act was being carried out. The Soviets resisted this concept, but in the end agreement was reached that the Belgrade follow-up meeting would not end without agreement on the date and place of the next similar meeting. This precedent was used for subsequent review meetings, thus establishing a regular pattern of conferences to review implementation.

The Follow-up meetings turned the West's public spotlight on the human rights records of the Communist countries in a new and more dramatic way than had ever been possible before. Criticism was thoroughly documented and supported by most Western countries. The practice of naming individual cases publicly, while it appeared undiplomatic and was resisted by the West Europeans, helped to personalize cases of human rights abuse, and make them more real. Through the attention of the media the names of dissident leaders became well-known in the West, giving them stature and even some measure of protection. The resulting pressures for reform were real and effective.

But there was much more which could be done. In 1988 I published an article simultaneously in English in the Atlantic Community Quarterly and in French in Politique Etrangere. The piece was called simply "A Proposal for Helsinki Observers." My idea was that the CSCE should name distinguished senior-level persons as free-roving observers. Their responsibility would be to watch over the implementation of the Helsinki commitments, and to report their findings. I suggested that the Observers be named by the member states in rotation for specified periods of time, so that there would always be several active observers and that some would always be from Western states. But this idea was not picked up; the CSCE was not in a dynamic period.

Later, as the Cold War was ending and the blocs were breaking up, I had a chance to bring this idea to reality. By an extraordinary coincidence I was named US Ambassador to the CSCE, fifteen years after I had been the Deputy Head of the US Delegation which negotiated the Helsinki Final Act and the Belgrade arrangement for regular review meetings. I became one of the principal drafters of the Charter of Paris[3], which sought to convert the CSCE to a post-Cold War operational role. The Charter of Paris established the first CSCE institutions, with a view toward ensuring that CSCE commitments would be carried out. Each of the new institutions—the Conflict Prevention Center (CPC), regular meetings of a Committee of Senior Officials (CSO), the Office for Democratic Institutions and Human Rights (ODIHR), and the Secretariat - has played a role in this broad and essential effort.

Albania, the one European country which had refused CSCE membership at Helsinki, asked to join. All the member states wanted to bring Albania in; the reasoning was that Albania had been invited to join in 1972, and the invitation was still open. But Western governments were concerned that Albania's human rights record was far below the CSCE's standards. I argued that CSCE membership would permit us to press Albania more effectively for human rights reforms, just as the West had done after the Final Act was signed. What we needed to do was to establish a "snapshot" of the human rights situation in Albania as a benchmark for its progress. To do this I suggested sending a CSCE Mission, consisting of several human rights observer-experts, to Albania with a mandate to report on the

---

[3] The Charter of Paris for a New Europe, was signed at the Paris Summit of the CSCE, November 19-21,1990. It established the first regular CSCE institutions and identified the area of conflict prevention and resolution as a primary mission for the organization in the new period.

human rights situation in that country. This was agreed and became the first CSCE Mission[4]. The device of sending observer missions to establish "snapshots" of the status of respect for key Helsinki commitments was repeated for each of the newly independent states of the former USSR, when they later joined the CSCE[5].

CSCE Missions became the device of choice for the CSCE's activities in the field. Missions were sent to former Yugoslavia and the former USSR, and are present now in a number of CSCE member States[6]. Soon a true 'Helsinki Observer" position was established as the High Commissioner for National Minorities[7]. The utility of this position is now generally recognized. All of these devices have helped to reinforce the overall interest of the member states in the good-faith implementation of the many commitments which have been undertaken in the 20 years since the Final Act was signed. The current phraseology is that these are "preventive diplomacy" efforts, simply because conflicts will be prevented if the Helsinki principles are fully respected.

The role of the CSCE has, of course, evolved, especially since the end of the Cold War. The challenge in 1975 was to press for evolutionary change in Eastern Europe and the former Soviet Union in a Cold War situation. Now the focus has shifted to pressing for the CSCE's values in areas of local conflict as well as throughout the newly-independent states. Fortunately all of these states are members of the CSCE, so that it is possible to press them to respect the undertakings in the CSCE documents they have accepted. The CSCE is virtually the only Western framework where these countries' problems get regular attention. But much remains to be done; these areas are unfamiliar to the West, and the names of victims of human rights violations there are often unknown outside their region. The CSCE can change this, just as it did in Central and Eastern Europe after the Final Act was signed.

---

[4] See CSCE Secretary General Wilhelm Höeynck episode in The Challenges of Preventive Diplomacy: The Experience of the CSCE Ministry of Foreign Affairs, Stockholm, 1994, pp.56-57.

[5] The newly-independent States from the former USSR were admitted to the CSCE at the meeting of CSCE Foreign Ministers in Prague, January 30-31, 1992.

[6] There are currently CSCE Missions either permanently or periodically present in Estonia, Latvia, Moldova, Georgia, former Yugoslavia, Azerbaijan, Tajikistan and Chechnya.

[7] The position of CSCE High Commissioner for National Minorities was established at the meeting of CSCE Foreign Ministers in Stockholm, December 14-15, 1992.

Ironically, an important question relating to future CSCE meetings designed to ensure respect for commitments was also left unresolved when the Charter of Paris was signed in 1990. This time it was the issue of how many member countries needed to agree before an emergency meeting could be convened. This issue was not settled until six months later, at the Berlin Meeting of the CSCE Foreign Ministers[8]. By that time Yugoslavia was already beginning to disintegrate, and the CSCE badly needed the possibility of convening emergency meetings. The first emergency meeting of the CSCE was held just two weeks later on Yugoslavia, but by that time the Yugoslav crisis had already spun beyond the control of international organizations, and the CSCE was not able to stabilize it. Had the possibility of convening urgent meetings existed earlier, the CSCE might have had a better chance of playing a useful role in staving off the looming conflict.

The concept of Helsinki Observers is still valid because the need to ensure respect for the commitments of Helsinki is just as great today as it was in 1975. The war in Chechnya, and the renamed OSCE's ability to respond to it by dispatching a group of human rights observers, demonstrates both the continuing need for OSCE missions and the type of response which the OSCE, perhaps uniquely, can provide in certain types of conflict.

The High Commissioner approach has also shown itself to be useful; perhaps there should be high commissioners with other mandates, on human rights, for example, or on freedom of the media. Commissioners could be attached to the ODIHR, travel to troubled regions, and report their findings to the OSCE's Senior Committee. From its beginning the CSCE has benefitted from ideas and innovation and an unusual ability to adjust and respond to current needs. This tradition must be maintained and expanded; if we believe in the values represented by the Helsinki Final Act, we must continue to work for their advancement and full respect.

---

[8] The Berlin Meeting of CSCE Foreign Ministers was held June 19-20, 1991.

Annex 10

John J. Maresca: **FOREIGN DEVILS ON THE SILK ROAD—TAKE TWO**[1]

There is a wonderful book, written in 1980 by Peter Hopkirk, which describes the fierce competition among international archeologists in the early 20th century, to find and claim credit for discovering the ancient cities of the historic "Silk Road" in the deserts of Xinkiang, China's vast and remote Western domain[2]. The effort brought distinguished academic figures into an energetic and creative race, in which some participants won big by hauling away caravan-loads of artifacts and were inscribed in archeological history, while others came home empty-handed and were forgotten. Their stories, and the artifacts they took home, are exhibited in some of the world's most distinguished museums, far from the Central Asian sand-dunes where they were found. Some of those long-abandoned desert cities have become tantalizing, barely-accessible attractions for the rare visitors to the remote regions where they are located.
With the break-up of the Soviet Union in 1991, vast areas of the ancient Silk Road region were once again open to "foreign devils" and their competition. But this time the exploration efforts have been in other domains—for political influence, trade opportunities, investments in potentially rich energy and mineral deposits, tourism, and the authorizations needed to develop the oil and gas resources which abound here, and to deliver them to world markets. The region has gradually become one of competition among outside players, with substantial prizes for the winners, in a new "Great Game" with unknown rules.
In 1991 I was asked by then-Secretary of State James Baker to visit each of the capitals of the newly-independent states from the former Soviet Union, with the mission of explaining to the leadership in each country how the United States would see its relationship with them as sovereign countries. The exceptions to this general mission were the three Baltic

---

[1] First published in: Baku Dialogues, ADA University, Baku 2015. Reprint with kind permission.
[2] "Foreign Devils on the Silk Road," by Peter Hopkirk, Oxford University Press, 1984.

States—Washington never recognized their forced incorporation into the USSR, so these were not "new" relationships for the US. But Central Asia was indeed a new region for America; in one Central Asian capital the Prime Minister noted that I was the first American he had ever seen. The region had effectively been closed to foreigners, certainly to foreign investors, for about 70 years, and before that its general remoteness discouraged all but the most intrepid visitors. In 1991 the countries of this area were under-populated and underdeveloped—even tourism was unknown. In the languid squares of the historic cities there were timeless scenes of older men lounging in shady tea stations, playing backgammon. But now, just twenty-three years later, these areas have changed. A sort of race is on, between American, Russian, European, Chinese and other Asian investors, as more and more business people, and governmental leaders, realize the enormous potential of the region. There are a number of factors which have brought about this dramatic change of status for Central Asia, from Soviet backwater to potential bonanza.

The first is simply the gradual awakening of outsiders to this region, its history, its peoples, its varied landscapes, access routes, languages, and cultures. A new book by Professor Fred Starr of Johns Hopkins University[3] positions Central Asia as the most advanced region of the world, more than a thousand years ago. At the same time there has been a learning process, about the resources which lie under the soil, and the fact that these newly independent peoples have their own identities, cultural attractions, and issues. One key milestone was the decision by the Organization for Security and Cooperation in Europe (OSCE), which includes the US and Canada, to offer these new states membership, on the grounds that they had already been OSCE members as part of the USSR. This brought OSCE missions of various kinds to the region, as well as contacts, assistance programs, and possibilities for involvement in regional undertakings. Mongolia has also now joined the OSCE. Tourism has grown dramatically, especially to historical sites like Samarkand and Bukhara. And the war in Afghanistan opened a whole new episode for the region, as the US scrambled to supply its army in what is perhaps the remotest region in the inhabited world.

---

[3] "Lost Enlightenment; Central Asia's Golden Age," by Professor Fred Starr, Princeton University Press, 2013.

There was also a rush to exploit the oil and gas resources in the area, particularly in Azerbaijan, Kazakhstan, Turkmenistan and Uzbekistan. The oil industry is particularly accustomed to risk, and so was immediately prepared to consider new resource prospects in these regions, even if they were remote. Companies of all nationalities entered the competition, from the US, Europe, China, Japan, and even Argentina. The so-called "Contract of the Century," signed in Baku, in the Caucasus, in 1994 between a consortium of Western and other companies and the government of Azerbaijan, showed what was going on: basically, major companies were buying or leasing the rights to exploit energy resources in these new areas, and the governments were planning to use the new wealth from commercial development to improve their own national situations. China also bought unilateral rights to oil and gas resources—in Kazakhstan and Turkmenistan—to supply its rapidly growing economy through pipelines so lengthy that they might be considered uneconomical by Western companies. The recent announcement of a huge deal to supply natural gas from Russia to China over the next several decades shows the dimensions of what is at stake. The gas will likely come from Russia's vast arctic resources, and can only be developed in partnership with western companies such as Exxon Mobil, which have the required technologies and know-how to exploit them.

At the same time there were political and strategic factors at work. Russia, through its giant gas monopoly Gasprom, which still controls about ninety percent of all gas pipelines in the former Soviet space, kept all local gas producers in line through their control of gas exports from their countries. Without the use of Russian pipelines, gas could not be exported, at least not in major quantities. By entering into a number of local conflicts, in various roles, Russia gained leverage on some other former Soviet republics, with the overall objective of retaining control throughout the "near abroad," the Russian term for its former adjacent colonies. Control of the "near abroad" space is an on-going general priority for Russia. Al Qaeda appeared in Afghanistan, sheltered by the hierarchy of the Taliban movement, making it impossible for foreign companies to work there. China began a two-pronged effort to assert its presence in the Eastern part of Central Asia by maintaining stability in the minority Uighur autonomous region in its West, while encouraging migration from Eastern to Western China. It is worth noting that Iran's 1979 revolution effectively took that country, an essential regional player, out of the Central Asian game, at least until things change and normal international relations are restored.

And then, suddenly, the overall Central Asian equation changed, as the 9/11 attacks on the World Trade Towers in Manhattan in 2001 obliged the United States to go to war in Afghanistan, in pursuit of the leaders of Al Qaeda who had organized the attack. This was about as remote from the US as it is possible to be, both culturally and physically, and also in terms of supplying an army in full combat in the field. An American army is very heavy, logistically speaking; it needs everything from flack jackets, night-vision glasses and ammunition to TV sets and beer. Very early it became clear that transiting Pakistan was not the ideal route for supplying the troops in Afghanistan, so the US Army developed another route, called the "Northern Route," through Russia, Khazakhstan and Uzbekistan to northern Afghanistan. Bases were developed across Central Asia to support this new supply route. It was an up-dated version of the Silk Road, although it was largely one-way—there may now be a million or so empty cargo containers lying about in the vacant spaces of Afghanistan.

In the aftermath of the Afghan war, many new opportunities emerged, such as the "TAPI" (Turkmenistan-Afghanistan-Pakistan-India) gas pipeline project now being advanced by the Asian Development Bank. This project, previously canceled when Al Qaeda bombed two American Embassies in East Africa, is now being developed again, reflecting the growing need for energy of the rapidly expanding economies of South Asia. The prospect that India and Pakistan will cooperate to construct this pipeline reflects its importance for both countries. The message here is that Central Asian resources are being sought not only by players to the East and West, but also by the dynamic economies to the South.

Iran, which is currently edging cautiously back into the commercial world, will, at some point, be an additional—and very big—player in this vast new game, both as a supplier and as a consumer of resources and products, as an investor and as a target for investments, and as a regional leader with political and cultural influence throughout the region.

These and other factors have called the attention of many Western business and national interests to the potential of the ancient Silk Road trade route. The growing map of pipelines for gas and oil, which currently extend from Azerbaijan to the Turkish Mediterranean coast, as well as from

Turkmenistan and Kazakhstan to China, and are now planned to reach across the Adriatic Sea to Italy, has inspired conventional traders and transporters to think in terms of road and rail transport from Europe through Turkey, Georgia and Azerbaijan, transiting across the Caspian Sea, and on through Turkmenistan and/or Kazakhstan to China's Central Asian border. A modern rail line is, in fact, being built which will cross Turkey and Georgia to Azerbaijan. Baku is preparing itself to be a dynamic hub for air, land and cross-Caspian Sea transportation—from Europe to Asia and vice versa. After all, would it not be cheaper, and more reliable, to ship Chinese manufactured goods across such a mythical rail line to Europe than it would be to transport them by sea around Vietnam, Myanmar, and India, to transit the Suez Canal? In addition, Central Asia is rapidly becoming a market itself, a destination for consumer goods and heavy equipment, in states with rapidly increasing buying power.

There are potential future issues which pose difficult questions. China and Russia are thought to have the largest potential shale oil and gas deposits in the world, so the development of those resources could affect the region in new ways which deserve careful study. And the way long-distance pipelines are becoming routine suggests that, at some point, fresh water pipelines may become economically viable in this region, as a way to convert desert areas to agricultural production. And what about the instabilities emerging from Syria, Iraq, and the growth of Islamic fundamentalism; will that affect the current fragile stability of Central Asia? In this situation China has been looking over its shoulder toward the vast regions to its West. An article by influential Professor Jisi Wang, former Dean of the School of Foreign Studies at prestigious Peking University, citing a quote from Mao, suggested that, rather than pushing and shoving with Koreans, Japanese and Americans to its crowded East, China should "March West." The phrase and the concept resonated. Statistics now show that the Chinese are, in fact, marching west in huge numbers. They are leaving the overcrowded Eastern coastal regions and re-locating in the relatively under-populated areas of Xinjiang, China's Central Asian far west.

Statistics on growth in the Central Asian region are not easy to find, partly because there are a number of different countries, and also because none of them has strong traditions in statistical disciplines. Some, in fact, are only now emerging, or have not yet emerged, from the status of developing countries. But regardless of the situation on the ground, a race is beginning, or has already begun. It is a race for access to resources and the rights to develop them, for new markets trading new goods such as super TV sets, computers, phones, and air conditioners, for the development of transit routes, and for the maintenance of the sort of stability which will make development of all this possible. The Foreign Devils are back, in force, and the competition is just as fierce for business now as it was for antiquities a hundred years ago.

SOVIET AND POST-SOVIET POLITICS AND SOCIETY

Edited by Dr. Andreas Umland

ISSN 1614-3515

1 Андреас Умланд (ред.)
   Воплощение Европейской
   конвенции по правам человека в
   России
   Философские, юридические и
   эмпирические исследования
   ISBN 3-89821-387-0

2 *Christian Wipperfürth*
   Russland – ein vertrauenswürdiger
   Partner?
   Grundlagen, Hintergründe und Praxis
   gegenwärtiger russischer Außenpolitik
   Mit einem Vorwort von Heinz Timmermann
   ISBN 3-89821-401-X

3 *Manja Hussner*
   Die Übernahme internationalen Rechts
   in die russische und deutsche
   Rechtsordnung
   Eine vergleichende Analyse zur
   Völkerrechtsfreundlichkeit der Verfassungen
   der Russländischen Föderation und der
   Bundesrepublik Deutschland
   Mit einem Vorwort von Rainer Arnold
   ISBN 3-89821-438-9

4 *Matthew Tejada*
   Bulgaria's Democratic Consolidation
   and the Kozloduy Nuclear Power Plant
   (KNPP)
   The Unattainability of Closure
   With a foreword by Richard J. Crampton
   ISBN 3-89821-439-7

5 Марк Григорьевич Меерович
   Квадратные метры, определяющие
   сознание
   Государственная жилищная политика в
   СССР. 1921 – 1941 гг
   ISBN 3-89821-474-5

6 *Andrei P. Tsygankov, Pavel
   A. Tsygankov (Eds.)*
   New Directions in Russian
   International Studies
   ISBN 3-89821-422-2

7 Марк Григорьевич Меерович
   Как власть народ к труду приучала
   Жилище в СССР – средство управления
   людьми. 1917 – 1941 гг.
   С предисловием Елены Осокиной
   ISBN 3-89821-495-8

8 *David J. Galbreath*
   Nation-Building and Minority Politics
   in Post-Socialist States
   Interests, Influence and Identities in Estonia
   and Latvia
   With a foreword by David J. Smith
   ISBN 3-89821-467-2

9 Алексей Юрьевич Безугольный
   Народы Кавказа в Вооруженных
   силах СССР в годы Великой
   Отечественной войны 1941-1945 гг.
   С предислозием Николая Бугая
   ISBN 3-89821-475-3

10 Вячеслав Лихачев и Владимир
   Прибыловский (ред.)
   Русское Национальное Единство,
   1990-2000. В 2-х томах
   ISBN 3-89821-523-7

11 Николай Бугай (ред.)
   Народы стран Балтии в условиях
   сталинизма (1940-е – 1950-е годы)
   Документированная история
   ISBN 3-89821-525-3

12 *Ingmar Bredies (Hrsg.)*
   Zur Anatomie der Orange Revolution
   in der Ukraine
   Wechsel des Elitenregimes oder Triumph des
   Parlamentarismus?
   ISBN 3-89821-524-5

13 *Anastasia V. Mitrofanova*
   The Politicization of Russian
   Orthodoxy
   Actors and Ideas
   With a foreword by William C. Gay
   ISBN 3-89821-481-8

14 Nathan D. Larson
Alexander Solzhenitsyn and the
Russo-Jewish Question
ISBN 3-89821-483-4

15 Guido Houben
Kulturpolitik und Ethnizität
Staatliche Kunstförderung im Russland der
neunziger Jahre
Mit einem Vorwort von Gert Weisskirchen
ISBN 3-89821-542-3

16 Leonid Luks
Der russische „Sonderweg"?
Aufsätze zur neuesten Geschichte Russlands
im europäischen Kontext
ISBN 3-89821-496-6

17 Евгений Мороз
История «Мёртвой воды» – от
страшной сказки к большой
политике
Политическое неоязычество в
постсоветской России
ISBN 3-89821-551-2

18 Александр Верховский и Галина
Кожевникова (ред.)
Этническая и религиозная
интолерантность в российских СМИ
Результаты мониторинга 2001-2004 гг.
ISBN 3-89821-569-5

19 Christian Ganzer
Sowjetisches Erbe und ukrainische
Nation
Das Museum der Geschichte des Zaporoger
Kosakentums auf der Insel Chortycja
Mit einem Vorwort von Frank Golczewski
ISBN 3-89821-504-0

20 Эльза-Баир Гучинова
Помнить нельзя забыть
Антропология депортационной травмы
калмыков
С предисловием Кэролайн Хамфри
ISBN 3-89821-506-7

21 Юлия Лидерман
Мотивы «проверки» и «испытания»
в постсоветской культуре
Советское прошлое в российском
кинематографе 1990-х годов
С предисловием Евгения Марголита
ISBN 3-89821-511-3

22 Tanya Lokshina, Ray Thomas, Mary
Mayer (Eds.)
The Imposition of a Fake Political
Settlement in the Northern Caucasus
The 2003 Chechen Presidential Election
ISBN 3-89821-436-2

23 Timothy McCajor Hall, Rosie Read
(Eds.)
Changes in the Heart of Europe
Recent Ethnographies of Czechs, Slovaks,
Roma, and Sorbs
With an afterword by Zdeněk Salzmann
ISBN 3-89821-606-3

24 Christian Autengruber
Die politischen Parteien in Bulgarien
und Rumänien
Eine vergleichende Analyse seit Beginn der
90er Jahre
Mit einem Vorwort von Dorothée de Nève
ISBN 3-89821-476-1

25 Annette Freyberg-Inan with Radu
Cristescu
The Ghosts in Our Classrooms, or:
John Dewey Meets Ceauşescu
The Promise and the Failures of Civic
Education in Romania
ISBN 3-89821-416-8

26 John B. Dunlop
The 2002 Dubrovka and 2004 Beslan
Hostage Crises
A Critique of Russian Counter-Terrorism
With a foreword by Donald N. Jensen
ISBN 3-89821-608-X

27 Peter Koller
Das touristische Potenzial von
Kam''janec'–Podil's'kyj
Eine fremdenverkehrsgeographische
Untersuchung der Zukunftsperspektiven und
Maßnahmenplanung zur
Destinationsentwicklung des „ukrainischen
Rothenburg"
Mit einem Vorwort von Kristiane Klemm
ISBN 3-89821-640-3

28 Françoise Daucé, Elisabeth Sieca-
Kozlowski (Eds.)
Dedovshchina in the Post-Soviet
Military
Hazing of Russian Army Conscripts in a
Comparative Perspective
With a foreword by Dale Herspring
ISBN 3-89821-616-0

29 Florian Strasser
    Zivilgesellschaftliche Einflüsse auf die Orange Revolution
    Die gewaltlose Massenbewegung und die ukrainische Wahlkrise 2004
    Mit einem Vorwort von Egbert Jahn
    ISBN 3-89821-648-9

30 Rebecca S. Katz
    The Georgian Regime Crisis of 2003-2004
    A Case Study in Post-Soviet Media Representation of Politics, Crime and Corruption
    ISBN 3-89821-413-3

31 Vladimir Kantor
    Willkür oder Freiheit
    Beiträge zur russischen Geschichtsphilosophie
    Ediert von Dagmar Herrmann sowie mit einem Vorwort versehen von Leonid Luks
    ISBN 3-89821-589-X

32 Laura A. Victoir
    The Russian Land Estate Today
    A Case Study of Cultural Politics in Post-Soviet Russia
    With a foreword by Priscilla Roosevelt
    ISBN 3-89821-426-5

33 Ivan Katchanovski
    Cleft Countries
    Regional Political Divisions and Cultures in Post-Soviet Ukraine and Moldova
    With a foreword by Francis Fukuyama
    ISBN 3-89821-558-X

34 Florian Mühlfried
    Postsowjetische Feiern
    Das Georgische Bankett im Wandel
    Mit einem Vorwort von Kevin Tuite
    ISBN 3-89821-601-2

35 Roger Griffin, Werner Loh, Andreas Umland (Eds.)
    Fascism Past and Present, West and East
    An International Debate on Concepts and Cases in the Comparative Study of the Extreme Right
    With an afterword by Walter Laqueur
    ISBN 3-89821-674-8

36 Sebastian Schlegel
    Der „Weiße Archipel"
    Sowjetische Atomstädte 1945-1991
    Mit einem Geleitwort von Thomas Bohn
    ISBN 3-89821-679-9

37 Vyacheslav Likhachev
    Political Anti-Semitism in Post-Soviet Russia
    Actors and Ideas in 1991-2003
    Edited and translated from Russian by Eugene Veklerov
    ISBN 3-89821-529-6

38 Josette Baer (Ed.)
    Preparing Liberty in Central Europe
    Political Texts from the Spring of Nations 1848 to the Spring of Prague 1968
    With a foreword by Zdeněk V. David
    ISBN 3-89821-546-6

39 Михаил Лукьянов
    Российский консерватизм и реформа, 1907-1914
    С предисловием Марка Д. Стейнберга
    ISBN 3-89821-503-2

40 Nicola Melloni
    Market Without Economy
    The 1998 Russian Financial Crisis
    With a foreword by Eiji Furukawa
    ISBN 3-89821-407-9

41 Dmitrij Chmelnizki
    Die Architektur Stalins
    Bd. 1: Studien zu Ideologie und Stil
    Bd. 2: Bilddokumentation
    Mit einem Vorwort von Bruno Flierl
    ISBN 3-89821-515-6

42 Katja Yafimava
    Post-Soviet Russian-Belarussian Relationships
    The Role of Gas Transit Pipelines
    With a foreword by Jonathan P. Stern
    ISBN 3-89821-655-1

43 Boris Chavkin
    Verflechtungen der deutschen und russischen Zeitgeschichte
    Aufsätze und Archivfunde zu den Beziehungen Deutschlands und der Sowjetunion von 1917 bis 1991
    Ediert von Markus Edlinger sowie mit einem Vorwort versehen von Leonid Luks
    ISBN 3-89821-756-6

44 *Anastasija Grynenko in Zusammenarbeit mit Claudia Dathe*
Die Terminologie des Gerichtswesens der Ukraine und Deutschlands im Vergleich
Eine übersetzungswissenschaftliche Analyse juristischer Fachbegriffe im Deutschen, Ukrainischen und Russischen
Mit einem Vorwort von Ulrich Hartmann
ISBN 3-89821-691-8

45 *Anton Burkov*
The Impact of the European Convention on Human Rights on Russian Law
Legislation and Application in 1996-2006
With a foreword by Françoise Hampson
ISBN 978-3-89821-639-5

46 *Stina Torjesen, Indra Overland (Eds.)*
International Election Observers in Post-Soviet Azerbaijan
Geopolitical Pawns or Agents of Change?
ISBN 978-3-89821-743-9

47 *Taras Kuzio*
Ukraine – Crimea – Russia
Triangle of Conflict
ISBN 978-3-89821-761-3

48 *Claudia Šabić*
"Ich erinnere mich nicht, aber L'viv!"
Zur Funktion kultureller Faktoren für die Institutionalisierung und Entwicklung einer ukrainischen Region
Mit einem Vorwort von Melanie Tatur
ISBN 978-3-89821-752-1

49 *Marlies Bilz*
Tatarstan in der Transformation
Nationaler Diskurs und Politische Praxis 1988-1994
Mit einem Vorwort von Frank Golczewski
ISBN 978-3-89821-722-4

50 *Марлен Ларюэль (ред.)*
Современные интерпретации русского национализма
ISBN 978-3-89821-795-8

51 *Sonja Schüler*
Die ethnische Dimension der Armut
Roma im postsozialistischen Rumänien
Mit einem Vorwort von Anton Sterbling
ISBN 978-3-89821-776-7

52 *Галина Кожевникова*
Радикальный национализм в России и противодействие ему
Сборник докладов Центра «Сова» за 2004-2007 гг.
С предисловием Александра Верховского
ISBN 978-3-89821-721-7

53 *Галина Кожевникова и Владимир Прибыловский*
Российская власть в биографиях I
Высшие должностные лица РФ в 2004 г.
ISBN 978-3-89821-796-5

54 *Галина Кожевникова и Владимир Прибыловский*
Российская власть в биографиях II
Члены Правительства РФ в 2004 г.
ISBN 978-3-89821-797-2

55 *Галина Кожевникова и Владимир Прибыловский*
Российская власть в биографиях III
Руководители федеральных служб и агентств РФ в 2004 г.
ISBN 978-3-89821-798-9

56 *Ileana Petroniu*
Privatisierung in Transformationsökonomien
Determinanten der Restrukturierungs-Bereitschaft am Beispiel Polens, Rumäniens und der Ukraine
Mit einem Vorwort von Rainer W. Schäfer
ISBN 978-3-89821-790-3

57 *Christian Wipperfürth*
Russland und seine GUS-Nachbarn
Hintergründe, aktuelle Entwicklungen und Konflikte in einer ressourcenreichen Region
ISBN 978-3-89821-801-6

58 *Togzhan Kassenova*
From Antagonism to Partnership
The Uneasy Path of the U.S.-Russian Cooperative Threat Reduction
With a foreword by Christoph Bluth
ISBN 978-3-89821-707-1

59 *Alexander Höllwerth*
Das sakrale eurasische Imperium des Aleksandr Dugin
Eine Diskursanalyse zum postsowjetischen russischen Rechtsextremismus
Mit einem Vorwort von Dirk Uffelmann
ISBN 978-3-89821-813-9

60 Олег Рябов
«Россия-Матушка»
Национализм, гендер и война в России XX века
С предисловием Елены Гощило
ISBN 978-3-89821-487-2

61 Ivan Maistrenko
Borot'bism
A Chapter in the History of the Ukrainian Revolution
With a new introduction by Chris Ford
Translated by George S. N. Luckyj with the assistance of Ivan L. Rudnytsky
ISBN 978-3-89821-697-5

62 Maryna Romanets
Anamorphosic Texts and Reconfigured Visions
Improvised Traditions in Contemporary Ukrainian and Irish Literature
ISBN 978-3-89821-576-3

63 Paul D'Anieri and Taras Kuzio (Eds.)
Aspects of the Orange Revolution I
Democratization and Elections in Post-Communist Ukraine
ISBN 978-3-89821-698-2

64 Bohdan Harasymiw in collaboration with Oleh S. Ilnytzkyj (Eds.)
Aspects of the Orange Revolution II
Information and Manipulation Strategies in the 2004 Ukrainian Presidential Elections
ISBN 978-3-89821-699-9

65 Ingmar Bredies, Andreas Umland and Valentin Yakushik (Eds.)
Aspects of the Orange Revolution III
The Context and Dynamics of the 2004 Ukrainian Presidential Elections
ISBN 978-3-89821-803-0

66 Ingmar Bredies, Andreas Umland and Valentin Yakushik (Eds.)
Aspects of the Orange Revolution IV
Foreign Assistance and Civic Action in the 2004 Ukrainian Presidential Elections
ISBN 978-3-89821-808-5

67 Ingmar Bredies, Andreas Umland and Valentin Yakushik (Eds.)
Aspects of the Orange Revolution V
Institutional Observation Reports on the 2004 Ukrainian Presidential Elections
ISBN 978-3-89821-809-2

68 Taras Kuzio (Ed.)
Aspects of the Orange Revolution VI
Post-Communist Democratic Revolutions in Comparative Perspective
ISBN 978-3-89821-820-7

69 Tim Bohse
Autoritarismus statt Selbstverwaltung
Die Transformation der kommunalen Politik in der Stadt Kaliningrad 1990-2005
Mit einem Geleitwort von Stefan Troebst
ISBN 978-3-89821-782-8

70 David Rupp
Die Rußländische Föderation und die russischsprachige Minderheit in Lettland
Eine Fallstudie zur Anwaltspolitik Moskaus gegenüber den russophonen Minderheiten im „Nahen Ausland" von 1991 bis 2002
Mit einem Vorwort von Helmut Wagner
ISBN 978-3-89821-778-1

71 Taras Kuzio
Theoretical and Comparative Perspectives on Nationalism
New Directions in Cross-Cultural and Post-Communist Studies
With a foreword by Paul Robert Magocsi
ISBN 978-3-89821-815-3

72 Christine Teichmann
Die Hochschultransformation im heutigen Osteuropa
Kontinuität und Wandel bei der Entwicklung des postkommunistischen Universitätswesens
Mit einem Vorwort von Oskar Anweiler
ISBN 978-3-89821-842-9

73 Julia Kusznir
Der politische Einfluss von Wirtschaftseliten in russischen Regionen
Eine Analyse am Beispiel der Erdöl- und Erdgasindustrie, 1992-2005
Mit einem Vorwort von Wolfgang Eichwede
ISBN 978-3-89821-821-4

74 Alena Vysotskaya
Russland, Belarus und die EU-Osterweiterung
Zur Minderheitenfrage und zum Problem der Freizügigkeit des Personenverkehrs
Mit einem Vorwort von Katlijn Malfliet
ISBN 978-3-89821-822-1

75 Heiko Pleines (Hrsg.)
Corporate Governance in post-sozialistischen Volkswirtschaften
ISBN 978-3-89821-766-8

76 Stefan Ihrig
Wer sind die Moldawier?
Rumänismus versus Moldowanismus in Historiographie und Schulbüchern der Republik Moldova, 1991-2006
Mit einem Vorwort von Holm Sundhaussen
ISBN 978-3-89821-466-7

77 *Galina Kozhevnikova in collaboration with Alexander Verkhovsky and Eugene Veklerov*
Ultra-Nationalism and Hate Crimes in Contemporary Russia
The 2004-2006 Annual Reports of Moscow's SOVA Center
With a foreword by Stephen D. Shenfield
ISBN 978-3-89821-868-9

78 *Florian Küchler*
The Role of the European Union in Moldova's Transnistria Conflict
With a foreword by Christopher Hill
ISBN 978-3-89821-850-4

79 *Bernd Rechel*
The Long Way Back to Europe
Minority Protection in Bulgaria
With a foreword by Richard Crampton
ISBN 978-3-89821-863-4

80 *Peter W. Rodgers*
Nation, Region and History in Post-Communist Transitions
Identity Politics in Ukraine, 1991-2006
With a foreword by Vera Tolz
ISBN 978-3-89821-903-7

81 *Stephanie Solywoda*
The Life and Work of Semen L. Frank
A Study of Russian Religious Philosophy
With a foreword by Philip Walters
ISBN 978-3-89821-457-5

82 *Vera Sokolova*
Cultural Politics of Ethnicity
Discourses on Roma in Communist Czechoslovakia
ISBN 978-3-89821-864-1

83 *Natalya Shevchik Ketenci*
Kazakhstani Enterprises in Transition
The Role of Historical Regional Development in Kazakhstan's Post-Soviet Economic Transformation
ISBN 978-3-89821-831-3

84 *Martin Malek, Anna Schor-Tschudnowskaja (Hrsg.)*
Europa im Tschetschenienkrieg
Zwischen politischer Ohnmacht und Gleichgültigkeit
Mit einem Vorwort von Lipchan Basajewa
ISBN 978-3-89821-676-0

85 *Stefan Meister*
Das postsowjetische Universitätswesen zwischen nationalem und internationalem Wandel
Die Entwicklung der regionalen Hochschule in Russland als Gradmesser der Systemtransformation
Mit einem Vorwort von Joan DeBardeleben
ISBN 978-3-89821-891-7

86 *Konstantin Sheiko in collaboration with Stephen Brown*
Nationalist Imaginings of the Russian Past
Anatolii Fomenko and the Rise of Alternative History in Post-Communist Russia
With a foreword by Donald Ostrowski
ISBN 978-3-89821-915-0

87 *Sabine Jenni*
Wie stark ist das „Einige Russland"?
Zur Parteibindung der Eliten und zum Wahlerfolg der Machtpartei im Dezember 2007
Mit einem Vorwort von Klaus Armingeon
ISBN 978-3-89821-961-7

88 *Thomas Borén*
Meeting-Places of Transformation
Urban Identity, Spatial Representations and Local Politics in Post-Soviet St Petersburg
ISBN 978-3-89821-739-2

89 *Aygul Ashirova*
Stalinismus und Stalin-Kult in Zentralasien
Turkmenistan 1924-1953
Mit einem Vorwort von Leonid Luks
ISBN 978-3-89821-987-7

90 Leonid Luks
    Freiheit oder imperiale Größe?
    Essays zu einem russischen Dilemma
    ISBN 978-3-8382-0011-8

91 Christopher Gilley
    The 'Change of Signposts' in the
    Ukrainian Emigration
    A Contribution to the History of
    Sovietophilism in the 1920s
    With a foreword by Frank Golczewski
    ISBN 978-3-89821-965-5

92 Philipp Casula, Jeronim Perovic
    (Eds.)
    Identities and Politics
    During the Putin Presidency
    The Discursive Foundations of Russia's
    Stability
    With a foreword by Heiko Haumann
    ISBN 978-3-8382-0015-6

93 Marcel Viëtor
    Europa und die Frage
    nach seinen Grenzen im Osten
    Zur Konstruktion ‚europäischer Identität' in
    Geschichte und Gegenwart
    Mit einem Vorwort von Albrecht Lehmann
    ISBN 978-3-8382-0045-3

94 Ben Hellman, Andrei Rogachevskii
    Filming the Unfilmable
    Casper Wrede's 'One Day in the Life
    of Ivan Denisovich'
    Second, Revised and Expanded Edition
    ISBN 978-3-8382-0044-6

95 Eva Fuchslocher
    Vaterland, Sprache, Glaube
    Orthodoxie und Nationenbildung
    am Beispiel Georgiens
    Mit einem Vorwort von Christina von Braun
    ISBN 978-3-89821-884-9

96 Vladimir Kantor
    Das Westlertum und der Weg
    Russlands
    Zur Entwicklung der russischen Literatur und
    Philosophie
    Ediert von Dagmar Herrmann
    Mit einem Beitrag von Nikolaus Lobkowicz
    ISBN 978-3-8382-0102-3

97 Kamran Musayev
    Die postsowjetische Transformation
    im Baltikum und Südkaukasus
    Eine vergleichende Untersuchung der
    politischen Entwicklung Lettlands und
    Aserbaidschans 1985-2009
    Mit einem Vorwort von Leonid Luks
    Ediert von Sandro Henschel
    ISBN 978-3-8382-0103-0

98 Tatiana Zhurzhenko
    Borderlands into Bordered Lands
    Geopolitics of Identity in Post-Soviet Ukraine
    With a foreword by Dieter Segert
    ISBN 978-3-8382-0042-2

99 Кирилл Галушко, Лидия Смола
    (ред.)
    Пределы падения – варианты
    украинского будущего
    Аналитико-прогностические исследования
    ISBN 978-3-8382-0148-1

100 Michael Minkenberg (ed.)
    Historical Legacies and the Radical
    Right in Post-Cold War Central and
    Eastern Europe
    With an afterword by Sabrina P. Ramet
    ISBN 978-3-8382-0124-5

101 David-Emil Wickström
    Rocking St. Petersburg
    Transcultural Flows and Identity Politics in
    the St. Petersburg Popular Music Scene
    With a foreword by Yngvar B. Steinholt
    Second, Revised and Expanded Edition
    ISBN 978-3-8382-0100-9

102 Eva Zabka
    Eine neue „Zeit der Wirren"?
    Der spät- und postsowjetische Systemwandel
    1985-2000 im Spiegel russischer
    gesellschaftspolitischer Diskurse
    Mit einem Vorwort von Margareta Mommsen
    ISBN 978-3-8382-0161-0

103 Ulrike Ziemer
    Ethnic Belonging, Gender and
    Cultural Practices
    Youth Identitites in Contemporary Russia
    With a foreword by Anoop Nayak
    ISBN 978-3-8332-0152-8

104 Ksenia Chepikova
‚Einiges Russland' - eine zweite KPdSU?
Aspekte der Identitätskonstruktion einer postsowjetischen „Partei der Macht"
Mit einem Vorwort von Torsten Oppelland
ISBN 978-3-8382-0311-9

105 Леонид Люкс
Западничество или евразийство?
Демократия или идеократия?
Сборник статей об исторических дилеммах России
С предисловием Владимира Кантора
ISBN 978-3-8382-0211-2

106 Anna Dost
Das russische Verfassungsrecht auf dem Weg zum Föderalismus und zurück
Zum Konflikt von Rechtsnormen und -wirklichkeit in der Russländischen Föderation von 1991 bis 2009
Mit einem Vorwort von Alexander Blankenagel
ISBN 978-3-8382-0292-1

107 Philipp Herzog
Sozialistische Völkerfreundschaft, nationaler Widerstand oder harmloser Zeitvertreib?
Zur politischen Funktion der Volkskunst im sowjetischen Estland
Mit einem Vorwort von Andreas Kappeler
ISBN 978-3-8382-0216-7

108 Marlène Laruelle (ed.)
Russian Nationalism, Foreign Policy, and Identity Debates in Putin's Russia
New Ideological Patterns after the Orange Revolution
ISBN 978-3-8382-0325-6

109 Michail Logvinov
Russlands Kampf gegen den internationalen Terrorismus
Eine kritische Bestandsaufnahme des Bekämpfungsansatzes
Mit einem Geleitwort von Hans-Henning Schröder
und einem Vorwort von Eckhard Jesse
ISBN 978-3-8382-0329-4

110 John B. Dunlop
The Moscow Bombings of September 1999
Examinations of Russian Terrorist Attacks at the Onset of Vladimir Putin's Rule
Second, Revised and Expanded Edition
ISBN 978-3-8382-0388-1

111 Андрей А. Ковалёв
Свидетельство из-за кулис российской политики I
Можно ли делать добро из зла?
(Воспоминания и размышления о последних советских и первых послесоветских годах)
With a foreword by Peter Reddaway
ISBN 978-3-8382-0302-7

112 Андрей А. Ковалёв
Свидетельство из-за кулис российской политики II
Угроза для себя и окружающих
(Наблюдения и предостережения относительно происходящего после 2000 г.)
ISBN 978-3-8382-0303-4

113 Bernd Kappenberg
Zeichen setzen für Europa
Der Gebrauch europäischer lateinischer Sonderzeichen in der deutschen Öffentlichkeit
Mit einem Vorwort von Peter Schlobinski
ISBN 978-3-89821-749-1

114 Ivo Mijnssen
The Quest for an Ideal Youth in Putin's Russia I
Back to Our Future! History, Modernity, and Patriotism according to *Nashi*, 2005-2013
With a foreword by Jeronim Perović
Second, Revised and Expanded Edition
ISBN 978-3-8382-0368-3

115 Jussi Lassila
The Quest for an Ideal Youth in Putin's Russia II
The Search for Distinctive Conformism in the Political Communication of *Nashi*, 2005-2009
With a foreword by Kirill Postoutenko
Second, Revised and Expanded Edition
ISBN 978-3-8382-0415-4

116 Valerio Trabandt
Neue Nachbarn, gute Nachbarschaft?
Die EU als internationaler Akteur am Beispiel ihrer Demokratieförderung in Belarus und der Ukraine 2004-2009
Mit einem Vorwort von Jutta Joachim
ISBN 978-3-8382-0437-6

117 Fabian Pfeiffer
   Estlands Außen- und Sicherheitspolitik I
   Der estnische Atlantizismus nach der
   wiedererlangten Unabhängigkeit 1991-2004
   Mit einem Vorwort von Helmut Hubel
   ISBN 978-3-8382-0127-6

118 Jana Podßuweit
   Estlands Außen- und Sicherheitspolitik II
   Handlungsoptionen eines Kleinstaates im
   Rahmen seiner EU-Mitgliedschaft (2004-2008)
   Mit einem Vorwort von Helmut Hubel
   ISBN 978-3-8382-0440-6

119 Karin Pointner
   Estlands Außen- und Sicherheitspolitik III
   Eine gedächtnispolitische Analyse estnischer
   Entwicklungskooperation 2006-2010
   Mit einem Vorwort von Karin Liebhart
   ISBN 978-3-8382-0435-2

120 Ruslana Vovk
   Die Offenheit der ukrainischen
   Verfassung für das Völkerrecht und
   die europäische Integration
   Mit einem Vorwort von Alexander
   Blankenagel
   ISBN 978-3-8382-0481-9

121 Mykhaylo Banakh
   Die Relevanz der Zivilgesellschaft
   bei den postkommunistischen
   Transformationsprozessen in mittel-
   und osteuropäischen Ländern
   Das Beispiel der spät- und postsowjetischen
   Ukraine 1986-2009
   Mit einem Vorwort von Gerhard Simon
   ISBN 978-3-8382-0499-4

122 Michael Moser
   Language Policy and the Discourse on
   Languages in Ukraine under President
   Viktor Yanukovych (25 February
   2010–28 October 2012)
   ISBN 978-3-8382-0497-0 (Paperback edition)
   ISBN 978-3-8382-0507-6 (Hardcover edition)

123 Nicole Krome
   Russischer Netzwerkkapitalismus
   Restrukturierungsprozesse in der
   Russischen Föderation am Beispiel des
   Luftfahrtunternehmens "Aviastar"
   Mit einem Vorwort von Petra Stykow
   ISBN 978-3-8382-0534-2

124 David R. Marples
   'Our Glorious Past'
   Lukashenka's Belarus and
   the Great Patriotic War
   ISBN 978-3-8382-0574-8 (Paperback edition)
   ISBN 978-3-8382-0675-2 (Hardcover edition)

125 Ulf Walther
   Russlands "neuer Adel"
   Die Macht des Geheimdienstes von
   Gorbatschow bis Putin
   Mit einem Vorwort von Hans-Georg Wieck
   ISBN 978-3-8382-0584-7

126 Simon Geissbühler (Hrsg.)
   Kiew – Revolution 3.0
   Der Euromaidan 2013/14 und die
   Zukunftsperspektiven der Ukraine
   ISBN 978-3-8382-0581-6 (Paperback edition)
   ISBN 978-3-8382-0681-3 (Hardcover edition)

127 Andrey Makarychev
   Russia and the EU
   in a Multipolar World
   Discourses, Identities, Norms
   With a foreword by Klaus Segbers
   ISBN 978-3-8382-0629-5

128 Roland Scharff
   Kasachstan als postsowjetischer
   Wohlfahrtsstaat
   Die Transformation des sozialen
   Schutzsystems
   Mit einem Vorwort von Joachim Ahrens
   ISBN 978-3-8382-0622-6

129 Katja Grupp
   Bild Lücke Deutschland
   Kaliningrader Studierende sprechen über
   Deutschland
   Mit einem Vorwort von Martin Schulz
   ISBN 978-3-8382-0552-6

130 Konstantin Sheiko, Stephen Brown
   History as Therapy
   Alternative History and Nationalist
   Imaginings in Russia, 1991-2014
   ISBN 978-3-8382-0665-3

131 Elisa Kriza
Alexander Solzhenitsyn: Cold War Icon, Gulag Author, Russian Nationalist?
A Study of the Western Reception of his Literary Writings, Historical Interpretations, and Political Ideas
With a foreword by Andrei Rogatchevski
ISBN 978-3-8382-0589-2 (Paperback edition)
ISBN 978-3-8382-0690-5 (Hardcover edition)

132 Serghei Golunov
The Elephant in the Room
Corruption and Cheating in Russian Universities
ISBN 978-3-8382-0570-0

133 Manja Hussner, Rainer Arnold (Hgg.)
Verfassungsgerichtsbarkeit in Zentralasien I
Sammlung von Verfassungstexten
ISBN 978-3-8382-0595-3

134 Nikolay Mitrokhin
Die "Russische Partei"
Die Bewegung der russischen Nationalisten in der UdSSR 1953-1985
Aus dem Russischen übertragen von einem Übersetzerteam unter der Leitung von Larisa Schippel
ISBN 978-3-8382-0024-8

135 Manja Hussner, Rainer Arnold (Hgg.)
Verfassungsgerichtsbarkeit in Zentralasien II
Sammlung von Verfassungstexten
ISBN 978-3-8382-0597-7

136 Manfred Zeller
Das sowjetische Fieber
Fußballfans im poststalinistischen Vielvölkerreich
Mit einem Vorwort von Nikolaus Katzer
ISBN 978-3-8382-0757-5

137 Kristin Schreiter
Stellung und Entwicklungspotential zivilgesellschaftlicher Gruppen in Russland
Menschenrechtsorganisationen im Vergleich
ISBN 978-3-8382-0673-8

138 David R. Marples, Frederick V. Mills (Eds.)
Ukraine's Euromaidan
Analyses of a Civil Revolution
ISBN 978-3-8382-0660-8

139 Bernd Kappenberg
Setting Signs for Europe
Why Diacritics Matter for European Integration
With a foreword by Peter Schlobinski
ISBN 978-3-8382-0663-9

140 René Lenz
Internationalisierung, Kooperation und Transfer
Externe bildungspolitische Akteure in der Russischen Föderation
Mit einem Vorwort von Frank Ettrich
ISBN 978-3-8382-0751-3

141 Juri Plusnin, Yana Zausaeva, Natalia Zhidkevich, Artemy Pozanenko
Wandering Workers
Mores, Behavior, Way of Life, and Political Status of Domestic Russian Labor Migrants
Translated by Julia Kazantseva
ISBN 978-3-8382-0653-0

142 Matthew Kott, David J. Smith (eds.)
Latvia – A Work in Progress?
100 Years of State- and Nation-building
ISBN 978-3-8382-0648-6

143 Инна Чувычкина (ред.)
Экспортные нефте- и газопроводы на постсоветском пространстве
Анализ трубопроводной политики в свете теории международных отношений
ISBN 978-3-8382-0822-0

144 Johann Zajaczkowski
Russland – eine pragmatische Großmacht?
Eine rollentheoretische Untersuchung russischer Außenpolitik am Beispiel der Zusammenarbeit mit den USA nach 9/11 und des Georgienkrieges von 2008
Mit einem Vorwort von Siegfried Schieder
ISBN 978-3-8382-0837-4

145 Boris Popivanov
Changing Images of the Left in Bulgaria
The Challenge of Post-Communism in the Early 21st Century
ISBN 978-3-8382-0667-7

146　*Lenka Krátká*
　　A History of the Czechoslovak Ocean
　　Shipping Company 1948-1989
　　How a Small, Landlocked Country Ran
　　Maritime Business During the Cold War
　　ISBN 978-3-8382-0666-0

147　*Alexander Sergunin*
　　Explaining Russian Foreign Policy
　　Behavior
　　Theory and Practice
　　ISBN 978-3-8382-0752-0

148　*Darya Malyutina*
　　Migrant Friendships in
　　a Super-Diverse City
　　Russian-Speakers and their Social
　　Relationships in London in the 21st Century
　　With a foreword by Claire Dwyer
　　ISBN 978-3-8382-0652-3

149　*Alexander Sergunin, Valery Konyshev*
　　Russia in the Arctic
　　Hard or Soft Power?
　　ISBN 978-3-8382-0753-7

150　*John J. Maresca*
　　Helsinki Revisited
　　A Key U.S. Negotiator's Memoirs
　　on the Development of the CSCE into the
　　OSCE
　　With a foreword by Hafiz Pashayev
　　ISBN 978-3-8382-0852-7

***ibidem*-Verlag /** *ibidem* **Press**
Melchiorstr. 15
70439 Stuttgart
Germany

ibidem@ibidem.eu
ibidem.eu